*Other books on animal behavior from
the American Museum of Natural History*

THE LIVES OF BIRDS
by Lester L. Short

FROM THE
AMERICAN MUSEUM OF NATURAL HISTORY

The Lives of WHALES and DOLPHINS

RICHARD C. CONNOR

and

DAWN MICKLETHWAITE PETERSON

HENRY HOLT AND COMPANY
NEW YORK

Henry Holt and Company, Inc.
Publishers since 1866
115 West 18th Street
New York, New York 10011

Henry Holt ® is a registered trademark
of Henry Holt and Company, Inc.

Library of Congress Cataloging-in-Publication Data
The lives of whales and dolphins / by Richard C. Connor and
Dawn Micklethwaite Peterson.—1st ed.
p.   cm.
At head of title: From the American Museum of Natural History.
Includes index.
1. Cetacea—Behavior.   I. Peterson, Dawn Micklethwaite.
II. American Museum of Natural History.   III. Title.
QL.737.C4C595 1994   93-46665
599.5'0451—dc20   CIP

ISBN 0-8050-1950-2
ISBN 0-8050-4565-1 (An Owl Book: pbk.)

Henry Holt books are available for special promotions and
premiums. For details contact: Director, Special Markets.

First published in hardcover in 1994 by
Henry Holt and Company, Inc.

First Owl Book Edition—1996

Designed by Richard Kraham Design Unit

Printed in the United States of America
All first editions are printed on acid-free paper.∞

10 9 8 7 6 5 4 3 2 1
10 9 8 7 6 5 4 3 2   (pbk.)

To my parents,
who sent me
off to California to rekindle a dream,
to Jim and Elizabeth
for putting up with me that summer,
and to my friend John Hession,
whose stroke and recovery
kept things in perspective.
R.C.C.

To Erica, Sabrina, and Gabrielle,
who sacrificed many months of bedtime stories
so that this book could be written.
D.M.P.

ACKNOWLEDGMENTS

Having been interested in dolphins for as long as I can remember, I pursued my dream to the University of California at Santa Cruz, whose educational philosophy and stunning beauty suited my rebellious nature perfectly. There, I was fortunate to have the noted cetologist Kenneth S. Norris as my undergraduate mentor. I owe Elizabeth Gawain a huge debt for introducing me to the research possibilities at Shark Bay, Western Australia, where my colleagues and I have been studying bottlenose dolphins since 1982. Since the early 1960s, several dolphins have been visiting a fishing camp called Monkey Mia in Shark Bay, where people feed and stroke them. The tame dolphins and clear protected waters of Shark Bay make it ideal for a researcher, and I am incredibly fortunate to be working there. I am also fortunate to be working with researchers Rachel Smolker, Andrew Richards, Janet Mann, Per Berggren, and Amy Samuels. At the University of Michigan, I found a thriving intellectual atmosphere that I have not seen equaled elsewhere and two outstanding graduate supervisors in Richard Alexander and Richard Wrangham.

I thank Hugh Howard and John Gallagher of Gallagher/Howard Associates for inviting me to join Dawn Micklethwaite Peterson in this collaboration. I can't imagine that many collaborations are as enjoyable as this one—or progress as smoothly. I also would like to thank Theresa Burns, senior editor at Henry Holt and Company. I thank, of course, the American Museum of Natural History and, in particular, Scarlett Lovell there. Bernd Würsig kindly helped me with literature on conservation problems. And thank you, too, to Sam Ridgway for his thorough review of this manuscript.

Contents

Preface xi

1
At Sea with Whales and Dolphins 1

2
How Whales and Dolphins Perceive Their World 21

3
The Endless Search for Food 49

4
Communication 75

5
The Social Lives of Whales and Dolphins 103

6
Courtship and Reproduction 137

7
Bringing Up Baby 161

8
Intelligence 181

9
Learning from Our Mistakes 199

Glossary 219

Index 221

Preface

From some of our earliest historical records we learn that humans were intrigued by the mammals that make their home in the sea. Their massive size alone would make them worthy of our attention, for many are counted among the largest beasts in the world. However, this book is devoted almost exclusively to the *behavior* of whales and dolphins because cetaceans, the taxonomic name for these creatures, are adapted to ocean life in many fascinating ways.

This book is the second of what will be a number of volumes devoted to animal behavior. The first was on the lives of birds, creatures most of us see everyday but that nonetheless continue to surprise us. To those inclined to pay attention to the fascinating and complex behavior of the other creatures that inhabit the planet, I recommend this series, which will explore the remarkable native abilities of many animals.

One of the marvels of nature is its astounding diversity with its millions of species. Unfortunately, we are currently in the midst of a mass extinction of species that may rival anything in the history of life on earth. Because of the grossly apparent evidence that it is we humans who are the cause of the current extinctions, we have been urged to more carefully consider the long-term consequences of our actions. We do not have to harpoon a whale to kill it. When we damage the ocean ecosystem with our pollution or by depleting the resources upon which whales and dolphins depend, we are indirectly contributing to their demise.

Although cetaceans of the same species are each other's strongest competitors for food and mates, they also cooperate with one another, especially when rearing their young, seeking safety from predators, or sharing food. One example of such cooperative behavior has been observed among sperm whale females which "babysit" a fellow whale's calf when the other is diving for food. Without such cooperative behavior, the vulnerable young might well succumb to the ocean's many perils. Or consider the way bottlenose dolphins in South African waters have been observed dividing their foraging labor. As the dolphins herded fish against the shoreline, some dolphins chased the fish, while others patrolled offshore, keeping the fish school from escaping out to sea.

Dolphins are responsible for some of the most remarkable examples of cooperation in the animal world. They even form symbiotic relationships with humans. One example of human-dolphin mutualism is found in a coastal Brazilian village. There, generations of bottlenose dolphins have been helping generations of fishermen catch the mullet upon whose sale the villagers depend. Armed with crude nets, the men stand at the shore, waiting for the dolphins in the bay to make a move. Then it comes! A dolphin dives, and is seen a moment later traveling at full speed toward the line of men. Just when it seems the dolphin will crash into the men, the animal comes to an abrupt halt and dives just out of range of the nets. The men quickly throw their nets, their efforts rewarded with a bulging catch. Simultaneously, the dolphin catches its reward: a belly full of fish, naturally.

Despite a widespread interest in these majestic creatures, most of us have yet to see one in the wild. Thus, it isn't difficult to understand why the average person tends to lump whales and dolphins into a single category, when there are, in fact, seventy-five species of mammals that belong to the taxonomic order Cetacea, many of them with markedly different habitats, social organization, and life-styles.

The purpose of this book is to better acquaint you with the creatures we call whales and dolphins because only by knowing them can we understand how remarkable their lives truly are.

My own entire professional life is centered upon the study of dolphins and whales in the wild. Since my days as an undergraduate at the University of California I have been fascinated by these creatures, especially dolphins. In 1982, I had my first opportunity to study them in detail at Shark Bay in Western Australia. One of the many remarkable features of this dolphin research site is the story of how it began.

In the 1960s, people who came to vacation near this remote old fishing camp reported that dolphins would approach the small boats returning to shore to beg for a portion of the day's catch. Eventually, the dolphins began accepting fish from people wading in the shallows. Elizabeth Gawain, a roving American teacher of yoga, was the first to realize the scientific potential of having wild but tame dolphins so near at hand. During her visits to Shark Bay, Elizabeth kept a detailed journal of her dolphin observations she later published as a book, *The Dolphin's Gift*. She also alerted scientists to the possibilities at Shark Bay, and it was during her presentation to a group of marine mammal biologists at the University of California at Santa Cruz that I met her. There were only two undergraduates listening to Elizabeth that day, myself and Rachel Smolker, and both of use knew immediately that we *had* to go to Shark bay.

Our first visit there, in 1982, lasted three months, and by the time our work was completed, we were planning how to return. Since then we have been back to Shark Bay frequently, and today, the Shark Bay dolphin research project is an international effort conducting half a dozen separate studies of the behavior and ecology of bottlenose dolphins. I have concentrated on the behavior of males, who form alliances that are as complex as any to be found in nonhuman animals.

Only a small portion of the dolphin research cited in this book comes from our work at Shark Bay, however. The study of whales and dolphins is an international collegial effort and without the hard work of numerous scientists a book such as *The Lives of Whales and Dolphins* would not be possible.

Our hope for this and the other books in the animal behavior series is that they will fascinate you, teach you something of the wonders of the natural world, and kindle or feed your interest in the animals that share this planet with us. If we are to begin to heal the many problems that threaten its well-being, that is the first and most important step.

The Lives of
WHALES
and
DOLPHINS

1

At Sea with Whales and Dolphins

The whale was born on a warm July day in the tropical Pacific waters off the Galapagos Islands. His tail was the first part to emerge from the underbelly of his mother.

As the mother struggled to free her body of the burdensome cargo it had carried for fifteen months, she was surrounded by other females, many of whom she had known all her life. They provided protection from opportunistic predators, perhaps even offering reassurance with gentle strokes of their flippers. But the mother needed little help. She forcefully expelled her newborn, breaking the cord, and then gently nudged him to the surface. There, he inhaled his first breath of life-sustaining oxygen in an action that separates his kind from the rest of the sea's inhabitants.

The young whale gasped great gulps of the warm air. After his first need was satisfied, he felt a need of a different sort, probably the same sort of urgent emptiness that newborns of all species feel. Understanding, the mother slowed her pace, allowing her calf to take her large nipple into his mouth and drink the fat-rich milk that soon would transform his body into a formidable presence.

He was a sperm whale, the largest of the toothed whales, the Odontoceti, a suborder that includes dolphins, porpoises, and beaked whales. At birth he was a mere twelve feet long and weighed only one ton, small indeed compared to the size that he would someday attain. In the kingdom of whales he was certainly not the most beautiful. Neither elegant nor streamlined, the whale's body appeared to be in possession of a head that was too large. By the time he reached adulthood, his massive, boxlike snout would account for 40 percent of his entire length.

What they lack in beauty, however, the sperm whales of the world once made up for in utility. In the past, they were among the creatures most prized by all whales' most dangerous predator, humans. Literature's best-known whale, Moby Dick, was a sperm whale, who took a terrible revenge upon the men who had come to kill him because of the treasure contained within his gigantic head. It is here that the sperm whale's spermaceti organ rests, a huge cone-shaped structure filled with a waxy oil used as a sound conduit that humans found useful for the production of items ranging from lamp oil to lubricants. A sexually mature male could yield as many as three thousand quarts of this liquid gold in the days when men were allowed to hunt freely for the whales. But because this little whale's ancestors had been destroyed in such large numbers, it is now illegal to kill sperm whales and most other species of whale, as well.

The baby whale's mother was almost sixteen years old, having borne one other calf, six years earlier. Had she had been aware of statistics, she would have known that the chances of her latest arrival surviving to adulthood were not good. But she did know what he didn't, that the watery world he had just entered was full of hazards.

Although there are anatomical differences between this male sperm whale now suckling his mother and a nearby female baby also engaged in nursing, it would be impossible for an onlooker to spot them because they don't become apparent for the first several years of life. Sperm males and females are, in fact, the most sexually differentiated of all whale species. The male is markedly larger (almost one and one-half times longer and more than three times heavier than the female, his head is proportionately bigger, and his spermaceti organ grows forward to project further beyond the tip of the skull. Another major difference is the age of sexual maturity. While the calf's mother had become sexually mature around the age of nine, he and other males of his species would be at least twenty-five years old before they sired off-spring.

When they leave their mothers' group, sexually imma-ture males form loosely organized groups with other similarly sized young males and gradually begin the movement away from the tropical breeding grounds into higher latitudes. As the males grow bigger and near sexual maturity, the groups fragment. Traveling alone or perhaps with one or two others, the huge bulls turn their course toward the equator in the di-rection of the females only as the breeding season nears. And, some speculate, it may well be that not every mature bull at-tempts to breed every year.

Few mammal communities are as stable and have members as helpful toward each other as the one into which this baby was born. It was a group of about twenty whales, fe-males mostly, but with some immature young males who had not yet left their mothers. Males with young mothers typically leave the group before age ten, but those lucky enough to have older mothers may enjoy maternal attention for much longer periods. As they grow older, females give birth at longer intervals and spend more time raising and suckling each infant. One thirteen-year-old male was discovered to have milk in his stomach!

The bonds between this baby's mother and the others appeared to be strong, and the arrival of her young one and that of the female calf stimulated a spirit of cooperation throughout the group. Perhaps it was because the females were all related or so dependent upon each other that their maternal instinct extended to each other's infants, but the newborns found a world full of babysitters who wanted to help protect them. Naturally, each preferred its mother, but when she wasn't nearby, there was usually another female or even an immature male to look after it.

It is possible that the sperm whales form such a coop-erative society, in part, because of the way in which they must search for food. The daily fare of the sperm whale in this part of the Pacific is the large squid that inhabit the ocean depths. Sperm whales are among the deepest divers, having been tracked by researchers to as low as six thousand feet beneath the ocean surface. Many of the squid that live in deep water harbor luminescent bacteria, and may appear as small beacons of light to the hunting whale.

It was into this dark, mysterious world of which we know little that the mother whale was forced by the demands of her enormous appetite to retreat. Her infant, whose body may not have been capable of such arduous feats, remained closer to the surface. Alone, he would be easy prey for a shark or a killer whale, so the "babysitting" system may be essential for infant survival.

The mother whale had been foraging for squid almost an hour, while her son swam under the watchful eye of a caretaker female. It was getting to be time for her to surface, as she was nearing the end of her oxygen supply. Suddenly, like an enormous cannonball, she broke through the still water, her explosive exhalation shooting up at a forty-five-degree angle, as is characteristic of her species.

During his mother's absence, the young whale had not been idle. Like the young of many mammal species, he was curious.

In his earliest days he spent most of his time at the surface watching a frenzy of activity around him. There were the dorados, believed by many to be the most beautifully colored fish in the sea, with their ever-changing rainbow hues, which the whale saw not as colors but as waves of shimmer. The dorados chased the flying fish, who used a mighty thrust of their tail blades to fling themselves into the air, their breast fins opening like wings to carry them along until their momentum was lost and they plunged downward into the sea, only to do it again and again. Tiny schools of fish swam to and fro, small bits of life that from a distance seemed to merge together as one. Dolphins frolicked.

The whale was busy during his early weeks and months. When he wasn't drinking from his mother's breasts, he delighted in leaping and slapping the water surface with his tail. He learned that if he started to dive, he could then reverse his motions, accelerate speed, and propel his body out of the water, flying through the air until the demands of gravity sent it crashing downward again. Called a breach, this display, however thrilling, required an awesome amount of energy. Another enjoyable way to pass the time was by "lobtailing," a maneuver in which the whale raised his tail flukes above the water's surface and brought them crashing down.

Scientists have long wondered about the significance of these aerial feats that whales perform. Is the purpose to remove the large sucking fish and whale lice that latch onto the animal's thick hide? Much breaching and lobtailing seems to be social, occurring at higher rates in the afternoon and when more than one group of sperms is together. We don't know its purpose, but we do know that females and young males like this one are much more likely to engage in such energetic behavior than mature males.

Although the whale observed the world to the extent his eyes and the murky blackness of the ocean would allow, by far his most important sense was that of hearing. Gliding through the darkness, he and the others in his group emitted steady streams of clicks, usually one every half second. Many other species of whales and dolphins also produce clicking sounds, packaged in a variety of ways. To the human ear, the rather monotonous cadence of the sperm whale seems simple compared to the variety of squawks, squeals, and other strange sounds that dolphins produce. But they are certainly loud, far louder than the sound of the hoofbeats of galloping horses or a carpenter's hammer meeting wood, because the sperms' clicks can be heard for miles beneath the sea. Nineteenth-century whalers were probably the first humans to be aware of sperm whale vocalizations. They reported hearing sperm whales' knocking and hammering sounds through the hulls of their ships.

The sperm whales' clicks are thought to originate from cartilaginous valvelike structures in the nasal passages toward the front of the head. The sound travels back through the spermaceti organ—he same organ that cost so many of their ancestor's lives—before being reflected off air sacs over the huge domed skull. The whole setup makes for a huge reverberation chamber for broadcasting their characteristically loud clicks into the watery void.

Many toothed whales use clicks to "echolocate." The clicks bounce off objects in the animal's path, producing echoes from which it is able to create a sort of acoustical picture of its surroundings. It is in this manner that the animals are able to locate food in a dark world where the eyes are of little use.

During feeding the group would often become separated. But the whales would rise to the surface clicking and break through the water within sight of each other. Although the individual whales were not usually inclined to linger on the surface for more than ten minutes between dives, usually once a day—often in the afternoon or early evening—the group of sperms would gather for a few hours at the surface, resting in tight clusters, still clicking, but in different patterns from before, patterns that suggest social communication.

Some sperm whale clicks occur in repetitive patterns called "codas," which may be the whale equivalent of a conversation, albeit a simple one. A coda is usually anywhere from three to thirty clicks and may be directed toward another whale. While gathering with her group, the whale's mother emitted a coda of eight regularly spaced clicks and then paused. Another whale responded with seven clicks. One can only guess at what the two were saying to each other, but researchers who have analyzed recorded codas from whales off the Galapagos have categorized twenty-three distinct types of codas, based on the number and spaces between clicks. A team from the Woods Hole Oceanographic Institute led by Bill Watkins has found that many conversations include the same five-click coda. They suspect the shared calls might be a not-so-friendly greeting meaning something like "Get lost." Because each whale appears to have a distinctive coda, it isn't unreasonable to suspect that one purpose of this form of communication may be, in fact, to identify individuals—useful information in a world with little light.

By the time the whale neared his first birthday, he had experienced many changes. He still frequently visited his mother's breasts and would continue to take some nourishment from her for several more years. But by now the whale also had begun to dive for solid food, although his body was not yet capable of the deep dives characteristic of more mature sperms. It is difficult to know whether any of his teeth had as yet erupted but it is believed that sperms' teeth have little influence on their feeding behavior; they may not need them to consume the squid that is their dietary staple. The prey the young whale had "selected" was undoubtedly smaller and less varied than his huge mother's diet and even less similar to the diet he would someday have as a sexually mature male. Some scientists have speculated that although young whales such as this one are physically capable of eating larger squid, they may prefer smaller prey because they are easier to catch.

In April a major change occurred in the composition of the group. The large bulls had returned, for it was the breeding season, the only time of the year when the huge males are known to associate with the female groups. The whale's mother was not ready to breed and would not mate for several years yet, but a few females in the group were at the right time in their reproductive cycle and it was for these cows that the bulls searched.

Our knowledge of exactly what takes place during breeding season in the world's community of sperm whales is rather sketchy becasue these deep-diving creatures spend most of their lives shrouded by the ocean's black curtain. On occasion, however, human observers in airplanes or boats have witnessed what might be interpreted as mating behavior among sperms.

In one such sighting a group of nine cows and a bull were observed, with the male underneath the group of females, only one tip of its pair of triangular tail flukes showing above the surface. Other observers have reported seeing sperm bulls and cows resting belly to belly, one on top of the other, for thirty seconds or longer.

The clicks were like nothing the yearling whale had ever heard, loud, widely spaced, and metallic. A dark shadow appeared in the direction of the booming clicks, as a huge bull, one of a handful of bulls roaming the area, joined the whales' group.

At fifty-two feet in length and weighing more than forty-three tons, the newcomer dwarfed the females, who until then had seemed so majestic; now, in the presence of the male, they were almost petite. Aside from his imposing size and the larger head that was a hallmark of his status as an important whale, the breeding male was further distinguished by wounds and scars, most of which were on his head, but a few even around the flipper.

The breeding system of the sperm whale has been compared to that of the African elephant. In a world in which there are relatively few ready females during any given year, it may be that the best way for the sperm bull to maximize his breeding opportunities is to travel from group to group, searching for any chance to spread his genetic heritage.

Such opportunities do not come easily. It stands to reason that in a society where a relatively small number of females are ready to mate in any given breeding season, the competition between males is intense and sperm males do not appear to be shy in expressing their hostility toward one another. Scientists who have examined the corpses of the large bulls have ruled out the possibility that a giant squid or other prey could have caused the scars that are often found on the males, for the wounds run in parallel lines, typically in pairs or in threes, damage that could not be inflicted by the hooks on the arms or tentacles of squid. As further evidence that breeding males can be each other's worst nightmare, researchers point to the spacing between the scars, which conforms with the dental pattern of the mature male sperm.

The bull's intent was clear. He stayed for several hours, possibly as long as a day, mating with any available female, and then left, presumably in search of another group within which to broaden his reproductive horizons.

After the bull left, the females, the two calves, and the immature males were once again back to their normal routine. For any whale or dolphin, a large part of everyday life—as much as three-quarters—involves searching the depths of the ocean for enough food to enable them to survive. The yearling's mother and the other mature females needed to eat approximately three hundred squid a day; the young whale's needs were undoubtedly less because of his smaller size and the additional nourishment he was still getting from his mother's milk, but he, too, spent most of the day foraging.

Typically, sperms dive for about forty minutes and then surface for ten minutes before diving again. Whalers have described them as "lined up almost like soldiers," and studies have confirmed that the sperms do indeed forage in ranks aligned perpendicular to the direction of travel, with a distance of about one hundred and thirty feet between each whale when feeding. Why this particular method? At the very least, it may keep the whales from getting in each other's way. Some people speculate that rank foraging may increase the chance that some whale in the group discovers food, because by spreading out they can search a larger area. The whale's mother, for example, may come across a source of squid. Through her clicks, she might communicate her discovery to other group members. Even if she makes no concerted effort to share her find, the fact that she stops and begins to feed may be all a nearby whale needs to redirect its movements.

In its undersea dominion the sperm whale had little to fear, now that the International Whaling Commission had banned man from stalking with his harpoons, a ban that most, although not all, nations have complied with. After all, none of the creatures that make their home within the ocean is larger than the sperm, except some other species of baleen whales, which have no teeth. The group of whales often came across fellow mammals in their forages. These the sperms eyed with mild curiosity, certainly no hostility. The various species played, swam, foraged in the same waters, separate but coexisting, and then went the ways dictated by the unwritten rules of their individual species, neither the worse for the experience.

Two species of fellow ocean dwellers, however, had a taste for blood and preyed upon the sperm whales: sharks and the pack-hunting killer whales.

It may be difficult to see how a large fish and a whale that is half as long and a fraction of the weight of the larger species could pose a serious threat to a mature sperm whale, so long as the sperm is healthy and traveling in a group. There may be an an occasional bite from a shark or killer whale, but it is unlikely that they pose a serious threat to life. The same cannot be said, however, for the calves and weakened older whales, both of which are prime targets for predation. One sperm calf stranded on a beach in South Africa was missing part of its left tail fluke and bore a host of other scars courtesy of killer whales. And oceanic white-tipped sharks have been observed following schools of sperm whales in the southwest Indian Ocean. Normally, the sharks are scavengers, dining on the ocean's garbage. (One shark was observed eating the after-birth of a sperm whale calf.) But stranded sperm calves bearing shark bites are evidence of this fearsome creature's potential menace.

One day the yearling whale was to learn firsthand what it is to be stalked by a formidable enemy.

The whale's group and a similar-sized neighboring group had split into smaller subgroups of one to three whales, each traveling in the same direction in a line several hundred yards long. The whales regularly lifted their flukes and dived more than twelve hundred feet beneath the surface, clicking continuously. All of a sudden, the clicking stopped. The ocean was filled with an eerie silence. The sperms at once coalesced again into two groups. A moment later, ten killer whales had surrounded one of them, the group in which the whale and his mother swam.

The sperms did not attempt to flee from the faster killer whales. Nor did they elude the attack by diving to depths to which the killer whales could not have followed them. This may have been because the whale calf was still incapable of making such a deep dive. Rather, the sperms under attack immediately formed a circle, with each member packed tightly against the next, and the young whale, the most vulnerable, in the center. Slowly, the sperms began to move toward the nearest group of killer whales.

As the killer whales attacked, the sperms turned, in an attempt to face their attackers. Apparently, both the sperms and the killer whales consider the front of the sperm whale to be its least vulnerable area to attack. This line of defense is in direct contrast to toothless whales such as the humpback, which rolls its belly toward attacking killer whales, presumably so that it can better use the flukes of its tail as weapons. Some sperms arched their tails so that they hung vertically with their flukes at the surface; others raised their heads out of the water; still others lobtailed. The ocean, moments before dead silent, literally pulsated during the attack with the abnormally intense clicking that emanated from the sperms.

The killer whales began their assault on the sperms. Between two and seven males skirted around the sperms, approaching their target from the rear. When they were about one hundred twenty feet from their prey, they dived and remained submerged for approximately three minutes, darting in and out between the whales. Clouds of feces filled the water. Bodies thrashed in unchoreographed chaos.

As quickly as they had arrived the killers were gone; moments later, they surfaced hundreds of feet away. It was immediately apparent that their attack had produced injuries. Three sperms surfaced, each bearing deep cuts around the forehead, testament to the skill with which the killer whale uses its most lethal weapon, its teeth. It was only when the killers had moved fifteen hundred feet away to the west that the sperms stopped circling. The blood in the water had attracted the attention of the ever-present sharks. It was time to move. Slowly, the young whale's group swam away, traveling northeastward and maintaining constant speed and direction for the remainder of the afternoon. They remained silent. The whale stayed very close to his mother.

Dolphins and Whales: The Mammals That Went to Sea

The world in which our dolphins and whales make their home is a dangerous place where fearsome predators are never far away. In the open ocean, there is no rock or bush to hide behind, no hole to escape down, no tree to climb. The creatures that live in this three-dimensional world have nothing to hide behind except each other.

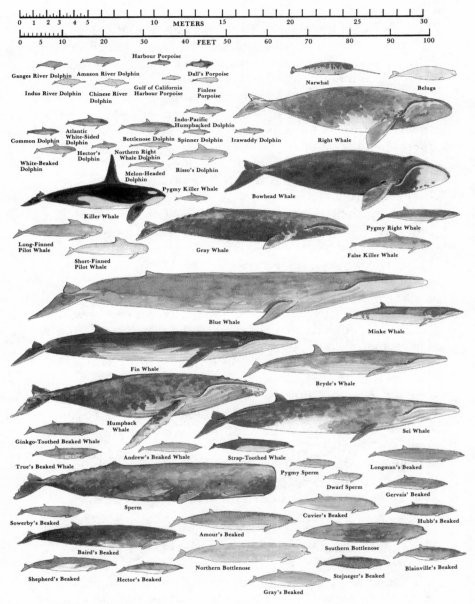

Harbour Porpoise

Ganges River Dolphin Amazon River Dolphin Dall's Porpoise

Gulf of California
Indus River Dolphin Chinese River Harbour Porpoise Finless
Dolphin Porpoise

Narwhal Beluga

Indo-Pacific
Humpbacked Dolphin

Atlantic
White-Sided
Common Dolphin Dolphin Bottlenose Dolphin Spinner Dolphin Irawaddy Dolphin Right Whale

Hector's Northern Right
White-Beaked Dolphin Whale Dolphin
Dolphin Risso's Dolphin

Melon-Headed
Dolphin
Pygmy Killer Whale Bowhead Whale

Killer Whale Pygmy Right Whale

Long-Finned Gray Whale False Killer Whale
Pilot Whale

Short-Finned
Pilot Whale

Blue Whale Minke Whale

Fin Whale Bryde's Whale

Humpback
Whale Sei Whale
Ginkgo-Toothed Beaked Whale

Andrew's Beaked Whale Strap-Toothed Whale
True's Beaked Whale Longman's Beaked
Pygmy Sperm

Dwarf Sperm
Gervais' Beaked

Sperm Cuvier's Beaked
Sowerby's Beaked Hubb's Beaked

Amour's Beaked Southern Bottlenose
Baird's Beaked
Northern Bottlenose Blainville's Beaked

Shepherd's Beaked Hector's Beaked Stejneger's Beaked

Gray's Beaked

Comparative sizes of whales and dolphins

If the task of survival seems hard, consider that dolphins and whales must reproduce and rear young in this perilous environment. Being mammals, they, unlike fish, can't simply fling a million eggs into the water and hope that a few survive. Instead, whales and dolphins put all their reproductive energy into the creation of one being, an infant that they nurse and protect, in some cases for several years, before attempting to produce another.

Early civilizations believed that dolphins and whales were simply fish, albeit extraordinarily large ones. Aristotle, the Greek philosopher who lived almost four hundred years before Christ, was the first to record observations to the contrary. In his *Historia Animalium*, Aristotle wrote, "All creatures that have a blowhole respire and inspire, for they are provided with lungs. The dolphin has been seen asleep with his nose above water and when asleep he snores." The philosopher went on to tell about how, like humans, whales did not lay eggs but gave birth to their young.

Folklore from virtually every corner of the world is replete with tales about whales and dolphins. Anyone who has read the Bible knows the story of Jonah, who survived being thrown into the sea by sailors who thought that sacrificing him would appease the raging storm, only to be swallowed by a giant fish (a whale?) and then later vomited unharmed onto dry land.

Writers in thirteenth century Scandinavia described "bad" whales. They were branded with names such as horse whale and pig whale, although well-known species including sperm and narwhals were also regarded in this light. These evil whales were said to roam the ocean, searching for any vessel to sink. Some, it was said, had an insatiable hunger for the flesh and blood of humans. In some parts of Iceland sailors so dreaded these mighty villains that the mere mention of one was cause for punishment, usually the withholding of food rations.

This is not to say that all whales were considered bad. Fin whales, in particular, were thought to be friends of mankind. In one often-told tale, a fin whale defended a ship all day against the evil whales. As the ship was sailing back to shore, one ungrateful sailor threw a stone at the whale, hitting its blowhole and causing the whale to burst. The man was banned from the sea for twenty years as his punishment. In his nineteenth year of exile, he could stand it no longer and went fishing. A whale killed him.

While the average person today probably knows little about whales and dolphins, he or she undoubtedly does understand that they are mammals. Like us they are warm-blooded. They breathe air with lungs. They give birth to live young. The mother whales have milk-filled glands with which they suckle their young. And some of them—particularly some toothed whales—have unusually large brains for their body size, evidence that these may be among the most intelligent of all animals.

Because they and their world are so far removed from our lives, we may have a tendency to oversimplify, to lump them together as though they were one entity rather than many with markedly different habitats, social organization, and life-styles. There are, in fact, just over seventy-five species of mammals that belong to the taxonomic order Cetacea. Within this one classification are the ninety-foot blue whale, the largest creature on earth, and, at the other extreme, Hector's dolphin, a diminutive animal just under five feet long. Cetaceans are further divided into two suborders: the mysticetes or baleen whales and the odontocetes, the toothed whales and dolphins.

The baleen whales are generally much larger than the toothed whales and dolphins, with the females slightly longer and heavier than the males. Instead of sharp teeth, these whales have thin, long plates called baleen, made of a horny material similar to fingernails, that hang from their upper jaws and are used to strain out and capture their small prey from huge mouthfuls of seawater. There are three families of baleen whale species whose members are fairly similar to each other and share a more recent common ancestor than they do with the other whales.

The bowhead and northern and southern right whales belong to one family, characterized by a robust body, big head, and long baleen. The pygmy right whale, a mere twenty feet long, is in its own family. The rorquals have shorter baleen plates and are slender, compared to the right whale family. There are six rorquals ranging from the diminutive (by whale standards anyway) thirty-foot minke whale to the ninety-foot blue whale. The "singing" humpback whale, with its long knobby flippers, is the oddball of this group. The forty-five-foot gray whale, whose yearly migration up and down the west coast of North America has made it a whale-watchers' favorite, is in a family by itself.

Baleen whales feed on a variety of small food sources, including krill (shrimplike crustaceans), other zooplankton, and schooling fishes. The food preference of a particular baleen species is reflected in the structure of the baleen plates, the size and flexibility of the individual bristles, and their density.

The odontocetes include the dolphins and porpoises, the unusual river dolphins, sperm whales, and the mysterious beaked whales. The dolphin family contains more than thirty species, ranging from the pudgy five-foot Hector's dolphin of New Zealand to the majestic killer whale, a whale that is really a dolphin. Some scientists believe the tusked narwhal and white whale or beluga are closely related to the dolphins but in a family of their own. The six members of the porpoise family have spade-shaped teeth rather than the conical teeth typical of other odontocetes. In rivers as far afield as the Orinoco in South America, the Indus in Pakistan, and the Yangtze in China dwell the long-snouted river dolphins. Their exotic names—susu, boto, and baiji—reflect their diverse homes. Although they are similar in some ways, each of the river dolphins is as different from each other as they are from other dolphins and porpoises.

The sperm whale has two little siblings in its "super-family," the dwarf and pygmy sperm whales, bizarre, needle-toothed caricatures of their large relative.

But the most mysterious cetaceans of all are the nineteen (at least we think there are nineteen; a new one was discovered in 1991 and there may be others awaiting discov-

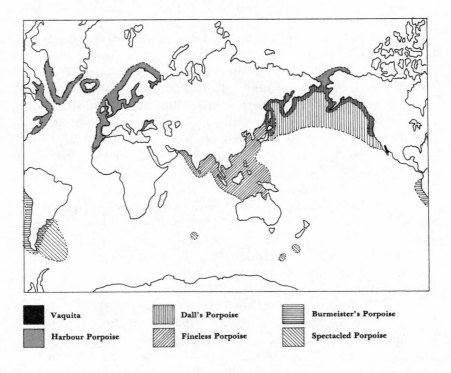

| ■ | Vaquita | ▥ | Dall's Porpoise | ▤ | Burmeister's Porpoise |
| ▨ | Harbour Porpoise | ▧ | Fineless Porpoise | ▨ | Spectacled Porpoise |

There are only six species of porpoises. The tiny vaquita, one of the most endangered cetaceans, is found only in the Gulf of California.

ery) species of medium-sized beaked whales. They make their living diving deep into the open ocean void, far from the eye of watchful scientists. Among these are the strap-toothed, Cuvier's and the Tasman beaked whales.

In general, the odontocetes are fish and squid eaters, although shrimp and other marine invertebrates show up in the diet of some. Killer whales were thought to be the only whale species that eat fellow cetaceans, but the closely related false and pygmy killer whales have also been observed to nosh on a dolphin or two.

The neat and tidy division between toothed and baleen whales was turned on its head recently when scientists compared the DNA of different whales. The sperm whale, it turns out, is more closely related to baleen whales than it is to the other toothed whales. Of course, as so often happens in science, what seems surprising upon discovery is found, upon further reflection, to fit with other findings. For example, the discovery in Oregon of a fossil baleen whale with teeth has made it clear that baleen whales had a toothed whale for an ancestor. When the first baleen whales were making their appearance, there were a number of lineages of toothed whales. But suppose that members of the toothed whale lineage that produced baleen whales also gave rise to modern sperm whales, which would mean that sperm and baleen whales would be more closely related to each other than to the descendants of other toothed whales that were around at the time.

The baleen whales tend to travel alone or in small groups. For many of these creatures, daily food intake is measured not in pounds but in tons, so the small group size may reflect the fact that a given area would not be able to adequately sustain a large group of hungry whales.

Odontocetes, on the other hand, are often very gregarious, living in larger groups, the size of which presumably depends on factors such as food supply and the threat from predators. The stability of these groups vary. Pelagic (open-sea) dolphins, for example, may form temporary groups of hundreds or even thousands. However, these groupings generally are exclusively for feeding or migrating, after which clusters of anywhere from five to one hundred dolphins emerge. Then there are the killer and pilot whales, whose group stability has no rival in the mammal world. If you were born a resident killer whale off the coast of Vancouver Island in British Columbia, you would stay with your mother throughout her life. You—no matter what your sex—would live in a pod or community containing three and possibly four generations of your ancestors.

Perhaps you are one of the lucky people who has witnessed firsthand the easy grace with which a dolphin or whale cuts a swath through the water? Most of us are not so fortunate. Coming within nodding distance of a whale or dolphin in the wild is no easy task. Unlike the bird life profiled in the first book in this series, these massive creatures are not easily accessible to the vast majority of the world's human beings. A person who wants to watch birds need do nothing more than sit back in an easy chair in front of a window to behold an amazingly diverse population of avian life. But even if you live right by the sea, chances are you have yet to see a live whale or dolphin. And, if you have, it probably wasn't more than a fleeting glimpse.

But let's pretend it was possible for you to take your curiosity about dolphins and whales beneath the ocean's surface. What kind of world would await you? Certainly, it would not be uniform nor would it be boring, for the sea, like the land is a world of ecological niches, peaks, and valleys bursting with life in a myriad forms.

Traveling in the icy waters of southeast Alaska, you might encounter a humpback whale casting a net of its own bubbles around a patch of krill and then devouring them all in one gigantic gulp. Off Vancouver Island, you might see a gray whale vacuuming the ocean's muddy bottom with its mouth and then practically disappearing in a cloud of the expelled dirt that pours from its cavernous maw. If you were adventurous enough to venture toward the Arctic Circle you might hear a beluga whale singing. Sailors call them "sea canaries," and with their varied repertoire of mews, screams, yaps, chirps, croaks, and burps, they are the vocal virtuosos of the whale world.

During the rainy season in the Amazon, you might encounter the pink river dolphin or boto winding its way among trees in the flooded tropical rain forest. Off the coast of western Australia in Shark Bay, you would witness a community of bottlenose dolphins, creatures that possess one of the highest ratios of brain size to body mass in the animal world. Theirs is a machiavellian world of social gamesmanship where two alliances of males may be on friendly terms one day and enemies the next.

And, if you were as intrepid as an undersea photographer who, off the coast of Argentina, couldn't resist the urge to pat a young right whale, you, too, might know what it is like to be nuzzled by an animal the size of a bus.

Throughout this book, we will explore the remarkable world of whales and dolphins that has given rise to some extraordinary sensory, behavioral, and social adaptations. Every day of research teaches us more about these mysterious and unique creatures, large and small, of river and ocean, that dwell beneath the water, yet rise above it to breathe.

EVOLUTION: FROM THE LAND TO THE SEA

Although it may be difficult to detect a family resemblance, probably some of the closest relatives to a whale or dolphin can be found in your local barnyard. Deer, sheep, bison, pigs, camels, and cattle, the so-called artiodactyls or even-toed ungulates, all share a tie to the sea mammals whose evolutionary predecessors lived on land.

The extinct mesonychids—the most likely ancestors of today's cetaceans—lived in the tropics along lagoons and estuaries. Unlike the artiodactyls, however, the mesonychid ancestors of cetaceans were carnivorous. The warm shallow seas presented new opportunities, new sources of food. The earliest cetaceans began making their appearance at least 5 0 million years ago. They fed on fish, but probably spent some time on land as well. As they became increasingly adapted to living in the water, they diversified. Some were medium-sized animals, others up to sixty feet long.

Among the adaptations to an aquatic existence were a backward shift of the nostrils and structures designed to seal them and prevent water from entering. The body became more streamlined as the long neck was reduced, the hair and external hind limbs lost. A paddlelike tail evolved as a means of locomotion. A new form of insulation evolved—a thick cushion of tissue called blubber that enabled the creature to survive in frigid waters and to house massive energy stores that permitted some species to fast for months. Extensive modification of senses allowed the early cetaceans to hear and see underwater. Smell was of little use and was gradually lost.

In attempting to unravel the mystery of origin, paleontologists must piece together the clues they find concealed within, in this case, sediments deposited in seabeds. The bits and pieces of fossil history that emerge from these ancient graves tantalize with new information, yet without revealing the entire truth, for there are too many gaps in time and too many geographic areas in which no remains have been found for the complete story to be known.

A remote desert valley in Egypt, however, is filling in some of the gaps. Philip Gingerich, a University of Michigan paleontologist, was mining a treasure trove of fossilized whale skeletons in the valley when he made an astounding discovery: whale feet. Forty million years ago and more than ten million years after the first whales appeared, fifty-foot-long Leviathans still had legs and feet. But these hind limbs were tiny, clearly of no use in helping the whale move around on land or under the sea. Gingerich suspects the legs were used to help guide the whales into the right position for mating.

So while there are still many unanswered questions and it is difficult to know for certain when modern-day baleen and toothed whales evolved, it appears that creatures closely resembling present-day cetaceans were alive twenty-two to thirty-seven million years ago. By the late Pliocene era—a mere four to five million years ago—modern forms of cetaceans were traveling the world's oceans and seas.

How Whales and Dolphins Perceive Their World

The land mammals that moved to the sea millions of years ago could not have done so without a host of physical changes that enabled them to survive in the very different world from which their ancestors had come.

These physical changes included the thick cushion of blubber that insulated them against frigid waters, the stream-lined shape so right for gliding through the sea, the addition of flukes instead of legs for propulsion, and hairless skin. A complete restructuring of the respiratory system produced, among other things, blowholes in place of nostrils.

But these physical adaptations are only part of the story, for without an equally radical overhaul of their sensory systems, cetaceans would not have been able to adapt to an aquatic environment.

Think about your own sensory world and what it requires of you. Your vision is probably your most important sense, the one you would most miss if it were one day taken from you. A pair of working eyes allows you to see the beauty in the world, the faces of those you love, your spring garden in bloom, and a hillside on fire with the colors of fall. Your eyes enable you to read the classics and the daily newspaper, marvel at the deft brushstrokes of a Renoir painting, or watch a movie. Aside from its aesthetic benefits, vision makes it possible for you to navigate your day-to-day world with relative ease. Using your eyes, you can safely cross the street, drive to work, volley in a tennis game, move from room to room, place to place. Your eyes can act as a barometer, reading malice on an

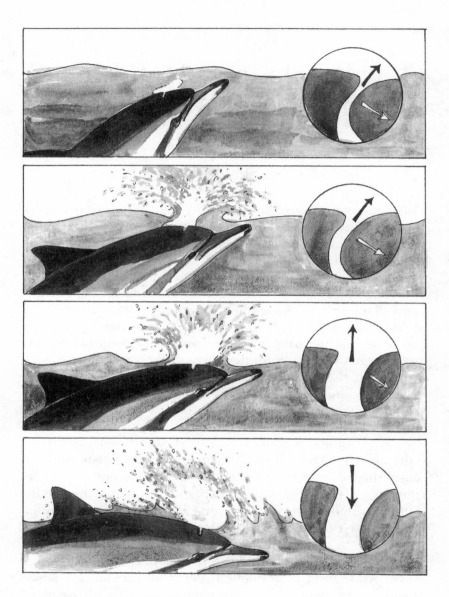

A dolphin exhales explosively as it surfaces and then rapidly in-hales before diving again. The inset shows how air leaves and enters the blowhole during breathing.

approaching stranger's face or recognizing through subtle body language the feelings of someone you care about.

In our world the sense of hearing is also invaluable. Someone asks you a question and you answer. Your child cries and you rush to comfort her. The phone rings and you pick it up. As you're about to cross the street, a honking horn blares and you retreat back to the safety of the curb.

The other senses—taste, touch, and smell—offer additional insight into the way we perceive things. A bite of a favorite food, a lover's touch, the fresh smell of the air after a spring shower, are all pleasures that these senses enable us to enjoy. Your taste buds can often detect if something is wrong with a food, which may prevent you from eating it and subsequently getting sick. And the same nose that enjoys a whiff of French perfume or the aroma of brewing coffee can also recognize the acrid smell of smoke in time to save lives.

Our sensory system exists to serve our behavior, and in our land environment it serves us well. But how well would it work if we were somehow transported hundreds of feet beneath the ocean's surface? In a murky world with little light, would perfect vision count for anything? Without the ability to see clearly, could we successfully maneuver around obstacles, find enormous quantities of food, care for our young, and steer clear of predators?

We couldn't. Yet dolphins and whales can because their senses have developed in a way that enables them to cope with their primarily underwater existence.

Hearing One's Way to Dinner

One morning off the coast of Baja California, the crashing waves brought the usual undersea refuse to rest on the sun-drenched beach. A small group of beachcombers strolled the beach, toeing the fiddler crabs, picking up an interesting shell here and there. Had this been your typical assortment of beach wanderers, the skeleton that lay half buried in the sand might not have elicited more than a passing glance.

As luck would have it, though, Ken Norris, a dolphin expert and the author of many scientific articles and books on the subject, was with the group that day back in the early 1960s. Like a treasure-hunter spotting evidence of a long-buried chest of gold doubloons, Norris sank to his knees and began digging feverishly with his hands to uncover what turned out to be the perfectly preserved skeleton of a large bottlenose dolphin. The dolphin had died from an unknown cause, been washed ashore, and then partially buried within the sand. A prize such as this would never escape the attention of opportunistic beach predators; along with time, they had robbed the dolphin of everything but its bones. The sun had bleached the skeleton white.

Holding the skull in his hands as though it were the most prized of possessions, Norris marveled both at the perfection of the specimen and at the shape and delicacy of the bones. Digging further down, he unearthed the dolphin's lower jaws, the pointed teeth still attached. As he studied the skeleton, Norris was struck by how strange its jaws were. Most land mammals have stout jaws, just right for chewing or tearing. This dolphin jaw, however, was thin toward its rear, as translucent as the finest china. Another oddity was that the mandibular canal, a tube that carries blood vessels and nerves to the teeth and jaw tissues in land mammals, monopolized the entire rear end of the jaw in the dolphin skull. The dense, ivorylike ear bones, normally missing in a beach-buried skeleton, were intact.

When Norris fitted the jaw to the skull, meshing the upper and lower teeth, he observed that the mandibular canal pointed directly at the ear bone.

Norris had been one of the first scientists to confirm with experiments that dolphins do, in fact, use echolocation. The mammal is able to produce intense, short, broad-band pulses of ultrasonic sound which then bounce off objects in the animal's path, producing echoes that it hears and from which it is able to create an acoustical picture of its surroundings.

In experiments with a captive bottlenose dolphin named Kathy, Norris and his team had shown that even when Kathy's vision was blinded by suction cups placed over her

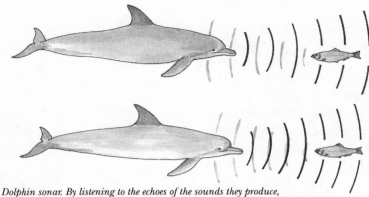

Dolphin sonar. By listening to the echoes of the sounds they produce, dolphins can locate fish. These echolocation clicks span frequencies well beyond the range of human hearing. The portion we do hear is reminiscent of a creaking door.

eyes, she was able to make her way to a target and press it with the tip of her snout, thus setting off a bell, the signal that she had done her job well and would be handsomely rewarded with a mouth-watering fish. While Kathy echolocated her way around the tank, a Navy sound expert listened to her underwater clicks, amplified with the use of underwater hydrophones. The noise he heard was a series of squeaking sounds like a rusty hinge. The dolphins' sophisticated echolocation is, even today, the envy of designers of the military's sonar system.

Making her clicks, Kathy could zero in on a dropped fish. First, at the sound of the initial splash, she would wheel around in the water, setting her course for the splash. Norris speculated that she could probably localize the position of the splash simply by using her excellent hearing. Then, when she was moving underwater toward the target, she would pick up the echoes of her clicks as they bounced off the sinking fish. The closer to the object of her pursuit, the faster the clicks, until, at the moment her mouth touched the fish, humans eavesdropping on her clicks could detect more than four hundred per second.

The big question was how did Kathy do this? It was obvious that her hearing was excellent. Yet if you've ever seen a dolphin up close, you know that you have to look closely to see any evidence of the animal's ear. The dolphin's external ear, in fact, consists of nothing more than two minuscule holes, located a couple of inches behind and below the eyes. Throughout the experiments with Kathy, the scientist had puzzled over how, with these reduced ear canals, she had been able to hear so well.

Months later, examining the sun-bleached skull bones of the bottlenose dolphin, an idea struck Norris. Could the strange canal in the dolphin's jaw be the path through which sound traveled?

Even today, many years later, scientists still ponder that question. Some believe that the dolphin's acoustic window is indeed through its lower jaw. Others maintain that the ear canals, reduced as they are, are still the major conduit to the inner ear. Like many aspects of the cetacean world, this question is still under debate.

Taking a page from Norris's use of blindfolds to confirm the echolocation hypothesis, one experimenter found that a bottlenose dolphin had a much more difficult time hearing its own echolocation clicks with a soundproof hood placed over its lower jaw. But critics answer that the ways in which a soundproof hood would reflect sound might even interfere with hearing through the ear canal. Russian researchers Vladimir Popov and Alexander Supin performed a clever experiment in which they recorded how long it took the brain to respond to artificial click sounds produced at different locations around a dolphin's head. By their calculations, sound entered the dolphin through the ear canal, but they agreed that there may be other routes by which sound travels to the inner ear.

What we do know is this: The dolphin nose is located on top of its head and houses a complex chamber in which the sound is produced. The sound is then conducted out of the melon, a waxy, lens-shaped body in the forehead. The melon focuses the sounds so that they are emitted in a narrow beam.

Returning sound waves may take multiple routes to the inner ear, among them traveling through the fat tissues in the lower jaw and through the ear canals. The inner ear itself is adapted for hearing ultrasonic frequencies far beyond the range of human hearing. In our youth, when our hearing is at its best, we are lucky if we can hear 20 kHz sounds; dolphins hear sounds well over 100 kHz. Baleen whales, on the other hand, have an inner ear adapted for hearing the subsonic moans of their fellows.

Thus far we know that about a dozen species of toothed whales and dolphins echolocate. Baleen whales possess nothing similar to the sophisticated echolocation of dolphins, but the jury is still out on whether they use echoes from low-frequency sounds that they produce in a kind of crude echonavigation.

By sending out its clicks, an echolocating cetacean is able to learn much about its surroundings simply by how long the echo takes to come back. In experiments dolphins have been taught to differentiate between balls made of copper and nickel, metals that have a different density. Similarly, they can readily tell the difference between species of fish by the sound that bounces off the prey.

Echolocating dolphins and whales appear to use this valuable tool primarily in the detection and tracking of prey. The intensity of sound as a dolphin zeroes in on its prey is so great that some researchers have speculated that an echolocating cetacean may actually stun the fish with its beam of sound. More research is needed, however, before this hypothesis becomes widely accepted.

If an echolocating whale or dolphin can, in fact, create an acoustical picture of its environment, why isn't life in the water always smooth sailing for these marvelous animals? Why, for instance, do thousands of harbor porpoises die in gill nets?

Perhaps cetaceans behave somewhat like bats, another animal that echolocates. Experiments in which bats were put into a blackened unfamiliar space showed that at first the creatures would use their echolocation powers to learn their way around. After they'd gotten the lay of the land, however, they stopped echolocating and were still able to navigate successfully through the area, presumably from a sort of mental map. Then the experimenter moved around the objects in the room, and, within seconds, bats were crashing into things.

It may be that cetaceans, like bats, initially use echolocation to acquaint themselves with their environment's terrain, memorize the nooks and crannies of their world, and then turn off the clicks. This would explain why so many dolphins and porpoises die in nets whose presence they are quite capable of detecting.

While echolocation is undoubtedly important for the species that use it, it is not the only way in which cetaceans use sound. The physical properties of water allow sound to be carried much more effectively than through the air. As one might expect, the underwater world is filled with noises, a veritable cacophony of squeals, clicks, groans, grunts, and squeaks, the sounds of countless creatures going about their day. Undoubtedly, a cetacean is able to learn much about its world simply by listening. Blindfolded dolphins have been observed chasing and catching fish, presumably by listening to the sounds that the fish made while moving through the water.

Imagine you are a dolphin, floating at the surface in warm, soothing tropical water. The sun-illuminated world of crimson coral and Day-Glo fish gives way to night. The world becomes black and your echolocation beam tells you only what is directly ahead. A large shark is looming up slowly, steadily from the depths, approaching from behind, unseen and unseeable in the dark. Let us hope, for your sake, that your hearing is good.

Sound is also used in communication, an important feature of any animal community and one that will be explored in a later chapter.

Taste and Smell

Can dolphins and whales taste and smell?

Scientists once believed that they could not. The brain of an adult toothed whale (odontocete) does not have an olfactory bulb and those in the baleen whales (mysticetes) are greatly reduced. Researchers looking for taste buds in various odontocetes reported mixed results, with some studies on the same species contradicting each other.

Studies have shown, however, that dolphins have some ability to taste. Thus far we know little about the baleen whales' sense of taste and smell. Scientists working with bottlenose dolphins in the Black Sea demonstrated that the animals were indeed capable of distinguishing between seawater and seawater solutions containing various chemicals. In another series of experiments in Hawaii, bottlenose dolphins were able to detect the four basic taste stimuli—sweet, sour, bitter, and salt.

The great taste-bud debate turns out to have a simple solution. One study found that young striped dolphins had rather conventional-looking taste buds, but that the taste buds of youth are modified or replaced in adult animals by pitlike structures on the back and roots of the tongue. Russian scientists have suggested that the taste buds function while a young animal is nursing, but that the pits sense a different set of chemicals, which reflect the different concerns of adults. Taste buds that enable a young one to enjoy the delights of mother's milk yield to receptors that screen for constituents of their fellows' urine and feces.

What use can this chemoreception system possibly be to dolphins and perhaps other cetaceans that possess the same or a similar sensitivity? Experts in the field speculate that chemoreception may be used in the following ways:

Locating Other Dolphins. Although many species of dolphin have brain-to-body-size ratios that are among the largest in the animal world, the same cannot be said for their bladders. The bottlenose dolphin, for example, urinates as often as every ten minutes. For dolphins traveling in large schools, one can imagine the amount of urine contained in the water through which they pass.

Dolphins are especially sensitive to substances found in mammalian urine and feces. So it may be that they use information from this chemical trail to guide their behavior. A small group, for example, might be able to link up with the full dolphin school by following its chemical scent. Conversely, the same sense might enable the dolphin to avoid another dolphin or even a predator.

Finding Food. Fish, a primary food source, often travel in schools containing thousands of individuals. After a school of fish moves through an area, a chemical trace lingers for hours. Dolphins may be capable of detecting this trail, and it is possible that they use it to help them locate food.

Orientation. Many of the ocean's currents have distinct chemical traces, whether they be of a particular inhabitant, seaweeds or sea grasses, or whatever. The dolphin's sense of taste may enable it to locate and remain within a particular current.

Reproduction. In Shark Bay, in Western Australia, we often see male dolphins swimming under females and pressing their beaks up to their genital areas. A female dolphin that is ready to breed (in estrus) does not appear any different physically from any other female, nor are there any apparent changes in her behavior. Yet male dolphins are drawn to her like moths to a light bulb.

We suspect this magnetlike attraction may be due to the release of some potent chemical stimuli, perhaps in the female's urine. Male dogs are often seen sniffing females; these Shark Bay male dolphins may be demonstrating the dolphin equivalent of a dog's sniffs.

Stress Sensitivity. When swimming through waters in which belugas had been killed, beluga whales have been observed showing alarm, apparently having sensed the blood through chemoreception. Similarly, other bodily products, especially urine, are thought to contain chemical indicators of physiological stress, which may alert others to the physical condition of a cetacean that has passed through the waters.

The Importance of Touch

Anyone who believes there is no such thing as a free ride has never observed bottlenose dolphins as they ride the waves generated by moving ships, small boats, and yes, even some of their larger whale relatives.

Why do dolphins have such a penchant for travel in the waves? In Hawaii, naval researcher Terrie Williams demonstrated that wave riding allows dolphins to conserve energy. Two bottlenose dolphins fitted with harnesses that monitored their heart rates were trained to swim alongside a moving boat. When the dolphins were traveling at a speed of about 6.5 feet per second their hearts beat about 76 times a minute, making them 10 times more energy-efficient than swimming humans. When the boat increased its speed to 9.8 feet per second, the dolphins seemed to have to exert more effort but continued to swim to the side of the boat as trained. However, when the boat's speed increased to 13 feet per second, the dolphins moved out of position and, despite repeated efforts by the experimenters to force them to swim at the boat's side, gravitated to a spot in the boat's wake. Here, the pressure of the water made swimming practically effortless and the dolphins, swimming a foot or two beneath the surface, rarely had to exert the energy to as much as flick their tails.

That wave riding is energetically prudent for dolphins does not mean that they don't play in waves and ride them for fun. A feeling of pleasure is as much a product of evolution as the dolphin's streamlined form. Behaviors will not evolve to be pleasurable unless they improve an animal's chances of survival and reproduction. So if going with the flow is good for dolphins, then it is not surprising that they find wave riding pleasurable and seek waves during times of play.

Positioning is just one way in which cetaceans use their tactile sensitivity or mechanoreception. Like a surfer trying to ride a wave, an aquatic animal must be able to judge the water's movement and flow, as well as to position itself in relation to other animals or to a hard surface such as the bow of a moving ship.

Many species of whales and dolphins have been observed swimming in echelon formation, one benefit of which presumably is greater swimming efficiency. And scientists have long marveled over the way in which dolphin calves are able to position themselves beside the mother's flank, coasting within the pressure wave created by her forward thrust. Small vibrissae (hairs) on the infant's snout, absent in adults, may help them maintain their station next to their mothers.

31

The position in which a whale or dolphin swims may also be an important indicator of its relationship with other dolphins in the group. Our observations of bottlenose dolphins in Shark Bay lead us to suspect that dominant animals position themselves behind subordinate individuals. Short distances between animals (less than a body width) may indicate a close or long-term association and are often observed among females and their young, juveniles, and sometimes adult males. Considering that whales and dolphins spend most of the time underwater, often at depths that never see the sun's light, being able to sense the water pressure and movement within that water may be essential in keeping each individual in its rightful place.

How a cetacean is able to "sense" the water's movement and then use it to its own advantage is unknown. However, we do know that many of the toothed whales including pilot whales, killer whales, beluga whales, and several species of dolphins, have ridges on their skin, the size and distribution of which is fairly consistent among members of the same species. The ridges in some ways resemble the fingerprint ridges on the human palm and may aid in detecting variations in water pressure on the dolphin's skin.

Trainers at Sea World, the aquarium/entertainment complex in San Diego, California, where they ride killer whales, have noticed that the ridges on the whales' skin become more pronounced as the animals travel faster, and have suggested that hydrodynamic drag may influence the whales' skin characteristics. The question of function still eludes us, though some researchers speculate that the ridges may help create a smoother flow of water over swimming whales and dolphins.

Aside from the animals' tactile sensitivity to water flow and space, cetaceans, like all mammals, use the sense of touch in both social and sexual situations. Adult cetaceans have no hair on their bodies but some species sprout a few scraggly chin tufts like those of a prepubescent boy. The function of these few hairs, called vibrissae, may be to glean information about the environment. The boto, a dolphin that inhabits the murky Amazon and Orinoco rivers, where even the visually gifted would have difficulty seeing beyond the end of their noses, certainly uses other senses to navigate through its environment, one of which may be the whiskers around its sensitive snout.

Although limbs were sacrificed in the interest of greater streamlining, cetacean skin is highly sensitive to touch. It feels good to be touched, and captive dolphins have been trained using touch alone as the positive reinforcement. Areas of the dolphin skin around the eye and blowhole are as sensitive to touch as our own lips and fingers. Human swimmers have given amazing accounts of massive baleen whales rubbing up against them, like a cat wanting its chin stroked.

Within dolphin communities, touch is as much a part of the day as foraging for fish. The dolphins stroke or pat one another with their pectoral fins or flukes, rub bodies together, and press their genitals against a neighbor, who doesn't necessarily have to be a member of the opposite sex. Commerson's dolphins have flippers (usually only the left flipper) with a serrated leading edge, possibly for grooming each other.

At the other end of the spectrum from pleasurable touching is aggression. Many cetacean species use tooth-raking as a sign of displeasure. One animal will draw its open jaws across another's body, leaving marks and on occasion even drawing blood. Anybody with much firsthand experience with dolphins is familiar with their repertoire of physical rebukes: a smack with the tail, a hit with the snout, even a karate chop with the flipper. Male humpbacks in pursuit of the same female will lash each other with their tails, while narwhals will use their formidable tusks in a jousting ritual that has been known to produce scars.

Dolphins may even use sound to titillate and irritate. While swimming with captive dolphins, animal psychologist Christine Johnson not only heard the dolphins echolocating, she felt it as a vibrating sensation on her skin. If I feel it, she wondered, perhaps they can as well. Later, watching wild spinner dolphins in Hawaii, she often saw dolphins buzz each other with echolocation at close range. Digging through the scientific literature on dolphin neuroanatomy and physiology, she found that not only do dolphins appear to have specialized structures in their skin for responding to sound, but that the sounds they produce are easily intense enough for a dolphin to feel. She suspects that dolphins may use the touch of sound in friendly, sexual, and even aggressive ways, since the loud clicks that might stun a fish probably wouldn't feel too good to a dolphin either.

Do Whales Have a Magnetic Sense?

Like birds, some baleen whales migrate thousands of miles over featureless terrain, yet always manage to return to their home waters. How these animals perform this feat has wrinkled more than one scientific brow over the years.

Not long ago one of the most controversial theories in the field of animal behavior was that the earth's magnetic field may play a role in many animals' uncanny navigational powers. The initial skepticism that greeted the theory was rooted in the lack of a similar ability in humans and the fact that there was no obvious way in which energy from the geomagnetic field was being transferred to an animal's nervous system. The discovery that bacteria possessed a magnetic sensitivity made the theory more palatable to scientists working on bees, birds, and whales.

Then scientists discovered particles of magnetite in the brains of several animals, among them common dolphins, humpback whales, Cuvier's beaked whales, and Dall's porpoises. This discovery made more credible the idea that some animals may, in fact, use the earth's magnetic field to navigate.

Although evidence is preliminary, many scientists believe that cetaceans follow features in the geomagnetic field for long-distance navigation. Like any sensory system, biomagnetism—if it does, in fact, exist—is not foolproof. A puzzling phenomenon is a live stranding, which occurs when one or more whales run into the beach and are unable, without help, to return to the water. Strandings often occur at coastal sites with magnetic anomalies. These anomalies in the geomagnetic field may somehow confuse the whales and lead to what are often tragic navigational mistakes.

Much more work in this area is needed before we understand this complicated sense.

Seeing in a Watery World

It was once held that vision was relatively unimportant to whales and dolphins, and that as a result cetaceans' visual senses were minimal. But as scientists have delved deeper into the many mysteries of the cetacean world, they have discovered that this simply isn't true.

If anything, a dolphin's or whale's vision in air or water is more acute than that of most land-dwelling mammals. For the vast majority of species, the ability to see is an important tool, crucial in everything from finding food to avoiding a predator to determining whether the approaching animal is friend or foe. Sight is probably important even to the "blind" river dolphin or susu of Pakistan, so called because its eye has no lens. A bare minimum of light passes into their muddy, tur-

The Platanista dolphin or susu, which dwells in the rivers of India and Pakistan, is the only cetacean that normally swims on its side. Here, a susu rights itself to breathe before rolling back on its side to cruise near the bottom in its search for fish.

bid world; even so, they are probably capable of some light detection through their pinhole-sized eye.

The underwater visual world of dolphins and whales is not the same as ours. The ancestors of today's cetaceans were equipped with visual systems allowing them to view a wide range of light intensities, with a predominance of yellow-green wavelength light like that of our world on terra firma. But once this former land mammal moved beneath the sea, the eye that had served it well on the surface was no longer so useful. Except near the surface, the underwater world is nearly monochromatic, with a bluish-green light. As the animals swim they must glean information from a world with little light, low temperatures, and radically fluctuating pressure conditions. Moreover, the eye itself is bombarded by a host of water borne invaders—dissolved ions, particles of matter, and microorganisms.

Evolution adapted the cetacean eye to its new environment. The retina evolved to provide vision in the dark monochromatic sea. The pink dolphin or boto of the Amazon basin even has a yellow lens that may filter out glare from back-scattered light in its murky habitat. Secretions constantly bathe the eyes with a layer of fluid, flushing away irritants and possibly reducing water distortion of the cornea. A thickened eye wall helps protect the eye from high underwater pressures and a special network of blood vessels keeps it warm.

The bottlenose dolphin's eye is capable of rapidly detecting moving objects. This species' eyes are not spherical in shape as are those of most land vertebrates but horizontally elliptical, so that objects moving in the animal's peripheral visual field cross a broader area of the retina than they otherwise would. The result is the faster projection of a larger image—a definite advantage when it comes to detecting food, avoiding enemies, and coordinating movements with the rest of the group. Large nerve fibers built for speed flash the information to the brain.

Many cetaceans have overlapping visual fields, so they may be capable of binocular vision over at least part of their visual field, although that field varies between species. A number of dolphins have overlapping visual fields looking both forward and down. The false killer whale can look upward behind its head with both eyes, while the pygmy killer whale has overlapping vision directly backward. One trainer who was swimming with a very angry pygmy killer whale moved directly behind the animal, only to watch in amazement as the pygmy poked its eyes out of its head and stared directly back into the face of what had to be a somewhat nervous trainer.

The bottlenose dolphin has a 180-degree visual range forward, to the side, and back, but cannot see upward. This

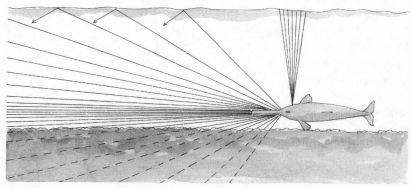

While feeling its way along the bottom of muddy rivers in India and Pakistan, the side-swimming susu uses echolocation to scan ahead; it is believed to be able to detect light and darkness although its eyes are almost nonexistent.

may be why bottlenose dolphins have frequently been seen chasing jumping fish at the surface, the dolphins bellyside up, a position that would enable them to see better.

One particularly remarkable adaptation found in bottlenose dolphins is the apparent independence of the two eyes. Evidence suggests that one eye can be looking at a bright light while the other is adjusting to a dim light. This makes sense because a dolphin often must swim on its side, with one eye exposed to the sun and the other to the underwater darkness. Dolphins can also move their eyes independently, looking at something forward and above them with one eye, while the other is scrutinizing an object to the rear and below on the other side.

Many species of cetaceans spend a considerable amount of time at or near the surface. There is much useful information a whale or dolphin can acquire by poking its head up into our world. While dolphins see better at a range of three feet or less underwater, their aerial vision improves with distance. The dolphin eye is able to change according to whether it is under the water or in bright light. When the dolphin surfaces, its pupil narrows to a double slit, an adaptation to allow it to see well both underwater and in the air.

What are whales and dolphins looking at?

Foraging. If survival in the sea could be reduced to a single rule it would undoubtedly be to find as much food as is possible (without, of course, serving as another creature's dinner). While other senses are also used in the capture of food and avoidance of becoming prey, vision certainly has a part to play.

Whether underwater vision is useful in foraging depends upon several factors including the clarity of the water, the depth and time of day in which the prey are taken, the conspicuousness of the prey, and how elusive they are. It might seem obvious that the pelagic dolphins benefit most from underwater vision because they feed in the clear upper regions of the sea. However, most of the squid pursued by sperm whales are bioluminescent, so even in the black depths vision may be important for locating prey.

Scientists speculate that, when foraging, dolphins and whales may use their vision to locate areas rich in prey and to gauge distances accurately while pursuing food. Although many odontocetes use echolocation to track prey, this is not without limitations. Echolocation beams are narrow and directed forward. Thus, the cetacean's vision may pick up where its echolocating abilities leave off. The ability to see underwater is probably most useful in tracking prey that is close by.

Aerial vision is often important in foraging. Observers have frequently noted schools of dolphins looking around above the surface when they breathe. They may, in fact, be surveying the lay of the land to get a feel for where they are and what, if any, feeding opportunities are in the vicinity. Seabirds circling at a distance are a cue that fishermen who seek out shoals of fish have long appreciated. If people have learned to heed this sign, perhaps dolphins and whales have too. During his studies in Argentina, Bernd Würsig, of Texas A&M University, noticed that dusky dolphins leap more when they have spotted prey. The dolphins, he suspects, may be attempting to communicate to others that food is nearby.

In Shark Bay we often see fish leap and skitter across the surface in front of a pursuing dolphin, out of the reach of echolocation clicks. That dolphins are visually tracking their quarry is revealed by impressive midair catches. Similarly, in the tidal creeks of Georgia and South Carolina, bottlenose dolphins have been seen herding fish toward steep banks. When the fish leap up on the bank the dolphins follow, grabbing the fish off the mud, then sliding back into the water. And killer whales have been known to pursue young sea lions and elephant seals onto beaches. It is believed that all these feeding feats were aided by the animals' ability to see.

Many species perform a sort of aerial surveillance at the surface. One form of such covert activity is known as spy-hopping, which has been observed in both mysticetes and odontocetes. The whale or dolphin rises vertically out of the water, head first. Often with just its eye above the surface, sometimes its entire head, the animal will rotate, scanning a 360-degree field. Killer whales inspect ice floes for resting seals in this way. When a seal is located, the orcas attempt to bump the hapless animal into the water.

Looking Out for Danger. Vision may enable a dolphin to spot a shark or killer whale rising from below it or approaching from the side, or in the case of pygmy killer whales, sneaking up from behind. Such a monitoring system is essential for an environment that, judging from the large scars on some individuals, is not for the timid.

Of course, for this visual warning system to work, a dolphin has to be paying attention. During his study of female bottlenose dolphins in Shark Bay, Andrew Richards, of the University of Michigan, watched as a large shark swam up from behind a group of snoozing mothers and infants. Andrew felt a rush of fear that the apparently oblivious dolphins would also have felt had they had seen the shark coming. Fortunately, in this case, the shark did not attack and merely turned away and swam off.

Spy-hopping may help cetaceans avoid becoming food as well as finding it. One gray whale was seen spy-hopping after a recording of killer whale screams had driven it to flee into a bed of kelp. It seems as if the whale was searching for signs of the killers before it dared leave the protection of the kelp bed.

Determining Who's Who. Nature has designed the cetacean face to be relatively immobile and, as such, devoid of expression. Yet dolphins and whales give off many visual clues that provide information about species, sex, age, dominance, and in some cases, even individual identity.

Whales and dolphins don't come in a variety of colors; most are some combination of black, brown, white, and various shades of gray. This limited range of color is combined into a variety of patterns, some dull, some beautiful. Dull coloration may make a whale or dolphin less visible to predators. In some cases, color may afford the animal better feeding success by disorienting, attracting, or making it less conspicuous to prey.

Often it appears, however, that an important function of color is in a social context. While sound probably plays an important role in species recognition, whales and dolphins can also recognize members of their own species by the way they look. Contrasting coloring such as the black and white found on Dall's porpoise may enable a porpoise to locate another in murky water or in the open sea.

Patches of color or pigmentation may actually be movement and orientation signals. Many cetacean species have contrasting color around the pectoral flipper. The sudden appearance of such a color may be an indication that the animal is changing direction and could serve to coordinate the movement of individuals in a school. Such coordination may be critical for individuals that are trying to escape predators.

Scientists are often able to identify specific individuals by their distinctive markings. The size and shape of the diagonal band of white on the pectoral fins of the minke whale varies between individuals, as do the patterns on the flukes of humpback whales and the patterns on the heads of southern right whales. The size and shape of the white "saddle" behind the dorsal fin of the killer whale makes it possible to pick an individual out of a crowd. If humans can use these cues, perhaps cetaceans can also.

Color conveys the age and social status of the Pacific spotted dolphin. As the dolphin ages, its color pattern changes. The male lion grows a mane as a testament to his authority. An older male spotted dolphin at the peak of his prowess possesses white jaw tips that can be seen in tropical waters for more than one hundred and fifty feet, a status symbol that no dolphin is apt to miss. In what may be a re-markable adaptation that advertises status, the skin of adult Risso's dolphins seems to highlight tooth-rakes from encounters with other Risso's dolphins. Perhaps battle-scarred veterans are regarded with respect and fear in this species as they are in our own.

The appearance of a whale or dolphin may provide clues to the age and sex of the individual because in many species the animals' looks undergo radical changes as they mature. While a large adult male dolphin might be interested in advertising his status, an infant needs to be difficult for predators to see. Spotted dolphin parents produce unspotted calves, which gradually develop spots as they grow. Gray whale and narwhal young are born with unmottled skin, unlike the adults. As narwhals and white whales age, they become lighter in color; the reverse is true with humpback whales, which are born with light coloration that darkens over the years.

Color, while important, is not the only characteristic that differentiates young from old. Proportions also change. A young common dolphin's skull comprises one-fourth of its total body length; in the adult the head accounts for a third of the dolphin's length. Young killer whales' pectoral fins make up one-ninth of their body length, compared to one-fifth in adults.

How does a cetacean tell a male from a female? Visual clues probably provide information in many cases. In some species males look strikingly different from females; in others, the sexes are virtually indistinguishable. In Shark Bay male and female bottlenose dolphins are about the same size and look alike. We are fortunate that they enjoy riding the bows of our boats upside down, enabling us to peek at their genitals.

But nobody would have a difficult time telling a male and female narwhal apart. The huge spiral tusk found only on the male narwhal is one of the most striking secondary sexual characteristics in mammals. Male strapped-toothed whales, members of the enigmatic beaked whale family, have two large teeth that grow up over either side of the jaw so that they can barely open their mouths.

Even in species where males are not endowed with such bizarre dental weaponry, size may still reveal sex. Females belonging to the baleen species generally are slightly larger than males but the differences are subtle. The species in which males and females differ most radically in size is the sperm whale. A mature male sperm may be 1 1/2 times longer and more than three times heavier than an adult female. In some species, the appearance or size of the head, flippers, and teeth differ among the sexes. The beak of the female spinner dolphin is longer than that of a male, while the dorsal fin of the male common dolphin is more curved and its flukes proportionately broader than those of a female.

Sometimes the visual aspects of an animal's behavior may offer a clue to identification. A spinner dolphin can be readily identified from a distance by human observers because of its twisting leap; other cetaceans may use the same information to establish identity. In some species, the young perform movements differently from older animals—again, useful information in determining identity. A newborn bottlenose dolphin, for instance, will lift its entire snout out of the water when it surfaces to breathe; adults expose only the blowhole.

And the leaps (breaches) of humpback whale calves cannot compare in grace or vigor with those of their elders.

Expressing Anger and Affection. Cetaceans use their visual sense to read the gestures and displays—body language—of their fellow creatures. Several dolphin species and humpback whales have been seen bent into an **S**-shaped posture, in which the animal arches its back, possibly making it seem larger than it actually is. It appears that this may be used in situations where two individuals are competing for the same mate. The slightest gape of the jaws, the spreading of the pectoral fins, and nodding or shaking the head with open jaws are threat displays commonly used by many species of dolphins. A bottlenose dolphin that wishes to issue a threat may face the other animal, open its mouth, and bare numerous sharp teeth, often with the back arched and the head down. The recipient of such information need not ponder the implication of these gestures. The animal *knows* there is a problem.

Keeping One's Proper Distance. A humpback whale sometimes emits streams of densely packed bubbles from its blowhole that trail well behind it as it swims. Scientists in an aircraft often are able to follow this trail of bubbles right to the humpback. Although it is unclear exactly how the humpback uses its bubble-making ability, one function may be to signal its location, especially if the bubbles are as visible to other humpbacks as they are to humans. That question has not yet been answered, although scientists suspect that like its fin whale cousin, the humpback's vision is well developed. Researchers observing humpbacks around Hawaii have reported seeing the whales' eyes moving in their sockets and even staring at underwater divers. Imagine how one diver felt when a massive humpback gently raised its outstretched fin over his head and then lowered it after the obstacle was cleared.

It is quite possible that many cetaceans use their visual sense to coordinate their movements in large groups. Many dolphins and smaller whales leap while traveling, a display that can be seen from a distance. By leaping, the animal may be able to determine the location of the other members of its group, as well as estimate the direction and speed of the group's movement.

Even underwater, vision may have a role in maintaining proper spacing between school members. A killer whale's tail flukes are white, flashing a conspicuous road sign for those trailing behind in dark waters. The contrasts of color on the humpback whale also may be useful in alerting others to its whereabouts. The whale's long mobile pectoral fins are a brilliant white, which can still be seen by a human diver long after the rest of the whale's dark body is no longer visible.

Orientation and Navigation. Cetaceans no doubt use many senses for orientation and navigation, one of which is vision.

For those of us who have spent time watching whales and dolphins, a relatively common sight is a cetacean leaping or breaching into the air. Humpback whales have frequently been seen breaching when a boat or aircraft is nearby, the animals' eyes turned in the direction of the offending piece of machinery.

Spy-hopping may also be a method used for orientation. Gray whales reportedly scan the area when they are close to land, suggesting they may use this information to determine their position. And even the boto, the Amazon River dolphin, appears to spy-hop, interesting because this species' vision does not seem to be well developed. Nevertheless, in one study done in an area where three small lakes were joined to the main river by a narrow channel, the botos repeatedly raised their heads out of the water—possibly to locate any logs or other dangerous floating debris—before swimming as far as they could through the channel.

In the underwater world where the vast majority of their lives are played out, cetaceans also appear to use their eyes. When the water is relatively clear, the sea's topography may steer cetaceans to areas where prey is plentiful or orient them in space. One researcher noted that common dolphins in the coastal waters of southern California and Mexico skirted the steep cliffs that rise from the ocean's floor. The cliffs are home to a host of sea creatures. The researcher surmised that the dolphins might be drawn by the sounds of this bursting-with-life marine community. Even so, the dolphins probably rely on some visual cues; during dives they may see the prey directly or changes in the clarity of the water caused by an abundance of tiny particles may alert them to feeding opportunities.

Off the coast of Hawaii and in other tropical locations, humpback whales congregate in waters less than five hundred and fifty feet deep. Although tongues of deeper water cut through these more shallow sections, the whales usually turn back when they come upon such areas. We don't know why they prefer the shallow waters, but whatever their motivation, vision certainly contributes to the whales' orientation.

Asleep or Awake?

Our senses, for the most part, go on leave while we sleep. During sleep we are blind. If someone tries to awaken a sleeping human, chances are that it will take awhile before the sleeper can respond coherently.

Although we are fair game for any lurking predator every time we close our eyes for the night, most humans can lock their doors on the world, relatively secure in their beds. But the ocean offers the sleeping dolphin no such luxury. If a dolphin were to shut off its senses to the extent that we do during sleep, it would be shark bait.

Again, natural selection has come to the rescue with an ingenious solution to the dolphin's dual need to sleep and yet remain alert to predators: dolphins sleep with only half their brain at a time.

Russian scientists recorded brain waves from slumbering bottlenose dolphins, harbor porpoises, and the boto and found that, like us, dolphins have several stages of sleep. It is during the deepest sleep, stage three, that one side of the dolphin's brain is asleep, the other half is awake. Even the sleeping side of the dolphin brain, though somewhat numbed to the sense of touch, is alert to the sights and sounds it receives. Dolphins continue to swim, watch, and listen during sleep.

They can't afford not to.

Why Cetaceans Don't Get the Bends

Anyone who has been scuba diving has been warned about the bends, a painful and potentially fatal condition that may occur during deep dives when a diver surfaces too quickly.

Yet the champions of all divers—dolphins and whales—can dive to astonishing depths; pilot and beluga whales travel at a depth of more than 2,150 feet under the sea and sperm whales have been recorded diving to more than 6,000 feet. And yet they never get the bends.

It was long held that dolphins and whales did not get the bends because, unlike scuba divers who breathe compressed air from tanks, they hold their breath under water. But more recent studies have shown that breath-holding human divers who make repeated dives with no air equipment still develop aching joints, blurred vision, breathing difficulties, and abdominal pain—classic symptoms of the bends.

Obviously, our respiratory system was designed by evolution to meet the demands of air breathing. When we do have a yen to explore the world underwater beyond our breath-holding capabilities, we need to take along a supply of air to ensure that the air pressure within our lungs is equal to or slightly exceeds the pressure of the surrounding water. Even in shallow water our feeble muscles can't expand our lungs to take a breath and at greater depths our chest would be crushed.

The problem is that when we breathe compressed air, the nitrogen within it dissolves into the bloodstream and can invade the body's tissues. As the diver moves toward the surface, the decrease in pressure causes this dissolved nitrogen to form bubbles, which may accumulate anywhere in the body. When the bubbles move into the muscles, the diver gets the bends.

The cetacean respiratory system evolved in response to the demands of deep diving and the need to take in fresh air and expel the old at the surface. Many scientists once believed that the reason cetaceans don't get the bends is because they dive with very little air in their lungs, nearly emptying the system before they descend. But that isn't the case; researchers noted that dolphins actually inhale before diving. As they plunge into the depths below three hundred feet, and the pressure becomes crushing, their unusually flexible chest area and relatively small, elastic lungs collapse. The numerous tiny pockets in the lung called alveoli, where gas is exchanged with the bloodstream, are forced shut and the nitrogen-containing air is driven into the resilient bronchial passages and windpipe. Once the alveoli have collapsed, no more nitrogen can get into the bloodstream. Sound drastic? It would be for us. But dolphins and whales do it every time they dive into deep water and yet they always seem to surface again, good as new.

And what of the shallower dives that do not exceed three hundred feet below the surface? Many dolphins make numerous dives to shallower depths that would not trigger alveolar collapse but would still give humans the bends. Even then, with high levels of nitrogen in their tissues, dolphins somehow manage to elude this condition. Just how they do it, though, remains a mystery.

It used to be thought that only dolphins used the S-posture in courtship displays but the same display has been seen in humpback whales. The top figure shows the typical posture of a surfacing humpback, while in the bottom drawing the S-posture is observed in a male who is competing with others to escort a female.

3

The Endless Search for Food

Yan was a loner, somewhat of an odd duck in a community of social butterflies. A female bottlenose dolphin in Shark Bay, Australia, Yan spent most of her time alone, having failed to form the close ties with other females that are typical of one of the most gregarious societies in the animal kingdom. Perhaps she simply didn't have any close kin in the area.

A short time after the birth of her calf, we noticed that Yan's flanks seemed to be shrinking, instead of full and slightly rounded as they should have been. Over the next few months, Yan grew more emaciated, her flanks now noticeably sunken. Shortly thereafter, Yan's calf died.

We can only speculate on the cause of the small dolphin's death. Many dolphin calves succumb to sharks in their infancy. Disease probably claims a fair share. But then so does starvation.

It was obvious that Yan herself was not getting enough to eat, despite the fact that the other females appeared to be eating well, judging from their rounded figures. Perhaps it had something to do with feeding territory and this solitary, rather antisocial dolphin had been left with the dregs. Or Yan may not have been as skilled a hunter as the others. Whatever the reason, we do know from many such observations that life under the sea is not one endless feeding opportunity. Prey is not always plentiful nor easy to catch. Moreover, cetaceans must compete for food. When food is abundant, group size may reflect that; schools of common dolphins in the Black Sea contain as many as three thousand individuals when food is plentiful.

Although many species have a preferred food, most cetaceans cannot afford to rely on one or a few species of prey. Some species consume a bewildering variety of fish and squid,

A gray whale dines on fare found on the ocean's floor. The whale rolls on its side to skim the sea's muddy bottom vacuuming up bottom-dwelling amphipods.

but even then there is not always enough to go around. There is a huge variety of fish on the bottlenose dolphin menu in Shark Bay, but that didn't help Yan and her infant.

That some whales and dolphins do undoubtedly die of starvation is not surprising. As with any animal species, the search for food (along with reproduction and avoiding predators) dominates the lives of dolphins and whales. Considering the demands of the gargantuan cetacean appetite, it isn't difficult to see why. The blue whale, the world's largest creature, needs several tons of food a day. This whale species, which spends approximately one hundred and twenty days a year at its feeding grounds and then migrates thousands of miles to warmer waters for breeding, must consume half a million tons to endure the months when its food source is not available.

How Cetaceans Feed

The diet of a particular species depends largely upon whether it has baleen plates or teeth. Nature endowed the mysticetes or baleen whales with a series of horny plates that grow down from the sides of the upper jaw and through which enormous quantities of water are strained, while the prey collects on the baleen. The size and shape of a baleen whale's skull and the consistency of the baleen itself reflects both what the whale will eat and how it captures that prey.

Baleen whales have been described as 1) swallowers, 2) skimmers, or 3) swallowers and skimmers.

"Swallowers" (most of the rorquals: blue, pygmy blue, fin, Bryde's, humpback, and minke whales) tend to search for large concentrations of plankton. The whale then opens its mouth, which expands like a bullfrog's, allowing huge quantities of water to flow in. The mouth closes, and the water is forced out through the fine baleen, while the food is trapped on coarser baleen plates.

Right whales are skimmers (as are bowhead and pygmy right whales) and are equipped with the finest baleen fringes. These whales swim near the surface to feed, straining plankton through the sieve created by the mat of baleen. The whale then uses its tongue to move the prey from the baleen into the back of its mouth for swallowing. This very large-headed whale has a long narrow upper jaw that arches upward to accommodate what may be as many as two hundred to four hundred baleen plates on each side of the jaw, each lined with fine bristles.

Sei whales incorporate both methods of feeding to some degree. A sei whale will speed through swarms of copepods, a preferred prey, with its mouth half open and its head slightly above the water. A constant flow of water passes into the mouth and out the baleen, while the food particles collect on the inner baleen bristles. After awhile the sei closes its mouth, dives, and swallows the food.

Somewhat of an anomaly in the world of the great baleen whales is the gray, the only large whale that feeds primarily on the organisms that live on the ocean's floor. As you can imagine, there are cleaner places to eat. It isn't uncommon to see gray whales surface from foraging expeditions covered with mud and ocean sediment, spraying a great plume of mud as they leave their underwater sanctum.

The way in which gray whales feed is not completely understood, although scientists suspect that this whale, whose baleen plates are thicker, coarser, and fewer in number than any other mysticete species, probably is able to suck or vacuum in its prey, separating the food to some degree from the surrounding sediments.

A hat of barnacles typically covers the head of the gray whale, but researchers have found that the barnacles are absent from the lips and jaws on one side of the head and that the baleen on that side is also shorter. They speculate that when the gray whale feeds, it turns on one side, which either abrades the barnacles from that area or prevents the larvae from becoming attached in the first place.

This is how a captive young gray whale named Gigi II captured the squid her keepers had strewn around the floor of her small cement pool. As she approached the squid, Gigi first rolled one hundred and twenty degrees onto her left side so that her cheek was parallel to the bottom, slightly above it. As she passed over the squid, she seemed to create a pulsating suction with her mouth, leaving a clear swath where a moment before there had been food. The food apparently was sucked through the side of her mouth. She then expelled the water between the baleen plates and swallowed her meal. Similarly, a gray filmed feeding in the Straits of Juan de Fuca, off the coast of Washington State, rolled onto its side, swept near the bottom, righted itself, and disappeared in a cloud of sand, leaving a definite impression of its head in the ocean floor.

Gray whales are not limited to groveling in the mud for a meal; they are also known to feed on plankton and schools of small fish. Gray whales may also be the only whale

It may seem strange that the world's largest creatures eat some of the smallest inhabitants. For most baleen whales, the tastiest morsels are found among the many minute varieties of sea life we know as plankton.

to consume vegetable matter. Large amounts of plant material have been found in the stomachs of a few grey whales and there is some indication that microbes present in the stomach may aid in the breakdown of plant material, in a process similar to what goes on in the stomach of a cow.

To look at them, one would think that these enormous baleen whales would be capable of partaking of the largest prey the ocean has to offer. On the contrary, the diet of the largest baleen whales is made up of tiny zooplankton—albeit tons of them—and some small fish. The mighty blue, whose diet is among the most selective of all whales', consumes only certain species of krill, a type of zooplankton. At the other extreme are the fin and sei whales, apparently willing to eat anything suitable they can find. Bryde's whales will eat shoaling fishes the size of herring and even small sharks up to a couple of feet in length. Amphipod crustaceans, none larger than an inch, are the mainstay of the gray whale's diet. And humpback whales eat krill, small fish, and even squid.

Unlike their larger toothless counterparts, most odontocetes have a long row of even, conical teeth (which are actually spade-shaped in the porpoise family), that enable them to grasp rapidly moving prey. The boto of the Amazon and Orinoco river basins has modified teeth in the rear of its mouth that resemble molars, good for crushing the armored catfish that rank high on its menu. Most toothed whales and dolphins feed upon fish and squid, although killer whales also eat birds and warm-blooded mammals. Killer whales were once thought to be the only cetacean who would eat another, but recent observations indicate that their close relatives, the false and pygmy killer whales, may also occasionally dine on dolphins.

As with the baleen whales, the shape of the odontocete skull and jaws is related to the way in which it captures its prey. At one extreme, the long, pincerlike jaws and needle-sharp teeth of the susu river dolphins of Pakistan give them a long reach to impale prey in front of them. More typical are the fairly long narrow jaws, large number of teeth (anywhere between twenty and sixty-five pairs in both jaws), and powerful

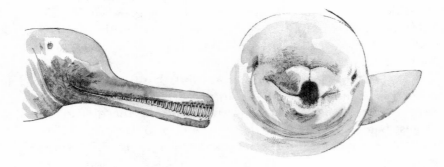

Dolphins are adapted for capturing fish in different ways. The river-dwelling susu impales fish with its pincerlike jaws, while the beluga uses suction feeding. The beluga has the remarkable ability to mold the shape of its mouth to achieve the most efficient suction.

rear jaw muscles found in several dolphin species, which help the animals grasp the small fish that are the staple of these species' diets.

At the other extreme are short, wide-jawed species such as the pilot whales and belugas, which have a different way of capturing prey in front of them. Specialized muscles allow them to suddenly retract their tongue deep into their mouth like a piston, rapidly sucking in water and any hapless fish or squid that are nearby. Belugas can even mold their lips to form a circle as though pronouncing the letter "O." This kind of suction feeding can explain why strange objects such as stones and sand dollars are sometimes found in the stomachs of pilot whales. Two short-jawed suction feeders, the narwhals and white whales, have extremely flexible necks, which aid the whales in scanning a broader area of sea bottom.

The sperm whale, a squid eater, has no functional teeth in its upper jaw, while the beaked whales, which also have a taste for squid, typically have only a single pair of teeth protruding from the lower jaw. Teeth apparently aren't useful for capturing and holding the slippery bodies of squid. Instead, beaked whales have a ribbed palate, which may help them hold onto a squid they have captured. In species where teeth are more prominent or numerous in males (sperm whales and most beaked whales), they are used more as weapons against competitors for females than to assist in subduing prey.

There is much variation in the diet of some species, depending upon the waters they inhabit and, of course, the prey within those waters. Off the coast of southwestern Nova Scotia, fin whales have been seen eating krill, while further south near Massachusetts they feed on schooling fish. White whales hunting in the Saint Lawrence estuary in Canada feed mainly upon capelin and sand eel, two small fishes, yet elsewhere eat white fish such as cod, haddock, and herring.

Probably the most fascinating example of one species eating a radically different diet has nothing to do with geographic location. Off the coast of central British Columbia two different communities of killer whales inhabit the same waters, yet apparently never mix. One group known as the resident killers primarily consumes a diet of salmon, while the so-called transients prey upon sea lions, seals, otters, marine birds, and have also been known to kill the small porpoises that live in those waters.

Going Where the Food Is

Although there were historical records of bottlenose dolphin sightings in Monterey Bay in the nineteenth century, it wasn't until 1982 and 1983 that humans again saw these southern California cetaceans in the cooler waters of central California.

The movements of the world's population of bottlenose dolphins varies from seasonal migrations of several hundred miles to those "resident" groups that spend their lives within their own well-defined home range. Until 1982, California bottlenose dolphins were established residents in the southern part of the state. That year things changed, however, when between 5 and 10 percent of the population migrated hundreds of miles to the north.

The northern movement came in the wake of the El Niño warm-water incursion, which made the waters off the central California coast much warmer than usual, although not quite as warm as the southern waters the dolphins were accustomed to. Rather than reacting to the warmth of the water itself, the dolphins' movement northward probably can be attributed to the secondary effects of the change in water temperature—namely, a change in the distribution of prey. Not coincidentally, many of the fish species that the southern California dolphins feed on also set their sights northward during the El Niño years.

Even within a permanent resident population of bottlenose dolphins, there may be substantial differences in where individuals look for food. As a high school student in the early 1970s, Randy Wells began watching bottlenose dolphins in Sarasota Bay, Florida. He is still at it today. Wells and his team found that the Sarasota dolphins' home range extends slightly more than fifty square miles. Based on countless boat tours of the bay in which they documented who was where and with whom, the Sarasota researchers concluded that the dolphins were year-round residents of the area. Within the bay, many dolphins have favored "core" areas where they spend most of their time. Dolphins that have different favorite areas may also have different tastes in fish.

Ace, a loner, had the smallest area of them all, a deepwater hole a few hundred feet across. Whenever Wells happened by, there was Ace in the hole by himself; evidently the hole supplied enough fish for his needs. Perhaps Ace was particularly good at fishing in the hole or simply wasn't welcome elsewhere, but we are learning from Ace and others like him that we can't assume that a species or group of dolphins are all cut from the same behavioral mold. Dolphins and whales are individuals, and their individuality often shows up in distinctive traveling and foraging habits.

In a perfect world where all a dolphin's or whale's food requirements could be met in a small space, perhaps many animals, like Ace, would remain in a relatively small home range. Such is not the case under the vast expanse of our world's oceans. What is plentiful one day may be gone the next. Supplies are not endless and what is taken needs time to be replenished. Thus cetaceans must move around to find,

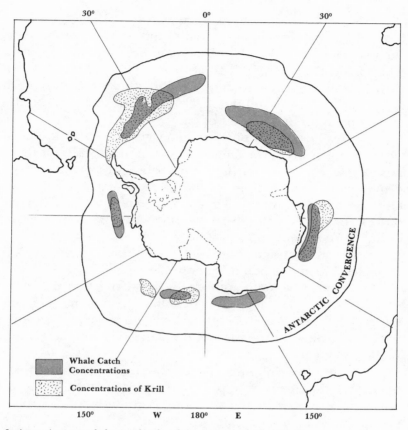

In Antarctic waters whales are often found among concentrations of krill.

among other things, adequate amounts of food.

The best place for feeding may not be the best place for breeding. Many of the baleen whales undertake long migrations; the gray whale's annual migration is more than twelve thousand miles from its feeding to its breeding grounds. A baleen whale may spend the summer in a confined area, feeding. When the food runs low, it leaves, only to return the following year. Like birds who amaze us by returning year after year to the same area, some whale species have a strong attachment to both their feeding and breeding grounds and continually manage to find their way back to each.

Hunting Techniques

Side by side, the bottlenose dolphins moved in a line beneath the warm waters of the Black Sea. Soon the dolphins surfaced, rearranged their row, and then dived again simultaneously, this time in another direction. Within thirty seconds there again was the row of dolphin backs and fins, as straight as the creases on a just-pressed pair of pants.

This herd of dolphins was engaged in one of the most necessary pursuits in the animal kingdom: the search for food. How a cetacean looks for food is probably governed to a large degree by the type of food it eats and its availability. Food can be large or small, found in huge aggregations or solitary. At one extreme, tiny krill can feed a blue whale because they are found in enormous concentrated swarms. At the other end of the spectrum, that same blue whale might be a single, though huge, food item to a pod of killer whales.

Dolphins sometimes hunt for fish that live a solitary existence. One of the more unusual solitary prey items in Shark Bay is called a snake eel. Dolphins make quite a show of eating snake eels, flinging them around several times before finally swallowing their prey.

Groups of dolphins, like many animals, probably form because of the threat from predators. Many eyes searching the ocean for sharks are better than two. But in areas rich in prey, groups may form to enhance foraging efficiency. Feeding groups of bowhead whales may line up in a V-formation like flocks of migrating birds. They may be using their neighbors as barriers to prevent their prey from escaping to the side.

Many dolphins and whales feed upon prey that travels in schools. Oftentimes, particularly in dolphin species, that prey is present in such quantities that one animal couldn't begin to eat it all. In one report, ten thousand belugas gathered to pursue migrating schools of fish up Straits of Novaya Zemlya in the high Arctic. Individuals can actually save energy by searching in a large group if such a group can find food more quickly than a lone animal and if everyone in it has enough to eat.

On the other hand, there may not always be enough to eat. The school of fish might be too small to feed the whole group or the dolphins might be hunting solitary fish that could only feed one individual. Sometimes when the members of our scientific research team at Shark Bay are following a group of dolphins, the animals will spread out into a line and begin foraging by lifting their tails high and diving toward the bottom. They may be spreading out to increase the chance they will encounter a school of fish they can all share. Or the purpose in putting space between themselves may be to avoid fighting over the same solitary fish. Until we find out what they are after, we can't be sure.

Biologist Robin Baird had a better handle on what his killer whales were eating. Baird was studying the feeding habits of the transient killer whales in British Columbia, which are particularly fond of seals and sea lions, unlike the resident pods of killer whales, which prefer salmon. Because the salmon they feed on are found in large schools, resident killers can afford the luxury of traveling in fairly large groups. Transients, on the other hand, average only three to a group. It turns out that three is the perfect number; Baird found that three killers had more success hunting than did larger or smaller groups. If transients formed larger groups, they wouldn't eat as well. Interestingly, the transient killer whales release their blows more quietly than the residents, an adaptation, Baird suspects, that allows them to sneak up on seals.

The larger baleen whales may also compete for food. These house-sized creatures' food requirements are so large that an average-sized plankton concentration set before several would be tantamount to offering a ravenous team of college athletes a tray of crustless cucumber sandwiches for lunch. That may be, in fact, why baleen whales often forage alone or with only one companion.

In the search for food many dolphins and whales may use the ocean's topography as a guide. One documented example of this is off southern California where schools of dolphins were observed gathering over prey-rich escarpments and seamounts that may be as deep as six thousand feet below the surface. The researchers speculated that the dolphins may be able to "hear" such landmarks simply by listening since there is an increase in sea noise around these areas.

Echolocation certainly plays a part in food foraging for the species capable of such acoustical feats. A susu dolphin living in the muddy Indus River in West Pakistan swims on its side, the only cetacean that normally does so, head angled down, scanning the bottom with a never-ending spray of clicks. In clear waters, dolphins often swim without uttering a sound. Silence may be necessary in instances where a sneak attack is more productive, and it may also allow dolphins to listen for movements of prey.

Vision, too, is a critical foraging tool for most species, whether it be watching the movements of other searching cetaceans, scanning the water for signs of prey, or zooming into the air after a leaping fish for a midair catch.

The search for food in the cetacean world runs the gamut from the single whale who roams the icy waters of the North Atlantic in search of krill to thousands of dolphins scrutinizing a broad swath of ocean for large fish schools. Common dolphins, spinner dolphins, and spotted dolphins often gather in broad hunting schools that extend for miles.

Dolphins use a variety of methods to catch prey. Here, fish are trapped between two lines of hunting dolphins

The ways in which the schools travel vary. Pilot whales move in slow broad ranks of generally fewer than one hundred animals, each one abreast of the next. Spinner and spotted dolphins move quickly, leaping into the air as they search the water. And killer whales seeking fish will often travel abreast in flank formations, oriented at right angles to the shoreline, slapping tails and fins on the water and breaching. The killers then will circle the area, continuously milling, often for more than an hour.

In Shark Bay, dolphins often leap when pursuing a school of fish in water fifteen to twenty feet deep. The dolphins are trying to get up to the surface for a breath and back down to the fish as quickly as possible and their momentum carries them flying into the air. Surfacing in a more casual manner could only be accomplished by moving more slowly—not a good idea if you want to fill your stomach.

The old wagon trains of the American West had scouts, so why not dolphin herds? Scientists watching bottlenose dolphins in the Black Sea observed instances when two to four dolphins (not always the same ones) would leave the herd to explore the coastline. While the rest of the herd swam on a parallel route farther out to sea, the scouting party searched for fish, driving them into the shallows or against the beach. Once fish were detected, the rest of the group joined them in feeding. Of course, being a scout may have its advantages; the first to arrive will be the first to feed.

From watching bottlenose dolphins in Shark Bay, however, we suspect that "scouting" is too generous a word here. More likely, the scouts were simply hungrier than the rest, who couldn't be bothered unless fish actually were found.

Another way in which some cetacean species as well as other sea creatures maximize their foraging efforts is to let a better hunter do the hardest part. Bottlenose dolphins often follow northeastern Pacific pilot whale schools. Groups of fewer than twenty dolphins will swim at the ends of pilot whale foraging ranks and scientists do not believe this is a coincidence. The dolphins appear to travel above the deeper-diving whales, changing course as they do. The dolphins, because of their lesser oxygen capacity, cannot stay underwater as long as the whales, so they break the surface first; minutes later, the whales rise to rest on the water, on the same spots where their dolphin followers were resting moments earlier.

A somewhat similar association can be found between yellowfin tuna, which follow spotted and spinner dolphins, two animals with superior hunting powers, that feed largely on fish and squid. We don't know how dolphins are affected by having tuna swim with them but this association certainly took a devastating toll on the dolphins once tuna fishermen learned that they could reliably locate tuna under dolphin schools. Hundreds of thousands of dolphins have died in tuna nets during over the past three decades.

Never let it be said that dolphins are not opportunists, especially when it comes to getting enough to eat. Consider the bottlenose dolphins that follow shrimp boats in the northern Gulf of Mexico and off Florida's Atlantic coast, dining on the prey stirred up by boats' trawls. Typically, the dolphins follow the working boats—they have learned to differentiate between cruising shrimp boats and those that are dragging full nets. Splitting into subgroups, the herd swims back and forth through the boat's wake, in an erratic choreographed zigzag, diving, and occasionally surfacing with fish. Dolphins also have learned to take advantage of the "trash" fish the shrimpers typically dump back into the sea after they have separated the commercially valuable fish out of the catch. Even an idle shrimp boat is the potential source of a meal. A combination of net debris and bilge discharge seems to attract many fish, even sharks, to anchored boats and these areas are frequently patrolled by watchful dolphins.

Australian biologist Peter Corkeron took advantage of dolphins' fondness for shrimp boats to learn more about their feeding preferences. On a shrimp boat in Moreton Bay, Queensland, Corkeron did his own trawling and then tossed the catch to the expectant dolphins to see which species of fish they would eat. Some fish were highly prized by the dolphins, some were never touched, and some were eaten only by a few.

Hunting dolphins encircle their prey.

Whiting were almost always rejected but on one occasion a female ate fifty!

Individual differences in food preferences may be based on different needs. Spotted dolphins who are lactating eat a higher proportion of fish than other females in the group. Fish are more consistently available and may be preferred because lactating females are hunting to feed two stomachs. It may also be too risky to dive to the greater depths where squid are found because the mother must leave her vulnerable offspring near the surface.

A favorite bottlenose dolphin at Shark Bay was a sweet old male we named Steps. He had lost his buddy Kodoff the year before, spent most of his time alone, and his flanks were sunken in. Clearly, Steps had seen better days. One day we found Steps holding a small shark in his mouth. He carried the shark for about a half hour, rubbing it against the bottom as if he were trying to break it up as dolphins often do with large fish and rays. None of the research team at Shark Bay had ever seen a dolphin trying to eat a shark before. With their rough hide, sharks don't exactly look appetizing. Later in the afternoon Steps had caught another small shark. We suspect that shark meat wasn't high on Steps' list of favorite fish, but he was no longer able to catch enough of what he preferred. Old and slow, he was simply doing the best he could under the circumstances.

FISHING COOPERATIVES: MAN AND DOLPHIN WORKING TOGETHER

In obscure coastal villages throughout the world, generations of fishermen have relied on the help of dolphins to earn their livelihood.

This is the story of one such cooperative in the town of Laguna near the southern tip of Brazil.

Weather permitting, every day except during the winter months of July and August, fishermen gather at the beaches in much the same way that their ancestors did, casting nets for the mullet whose sale supports about one hundred families in the town.

Each fisherman is armed with a circular nylon throw net rimmed with weights. In a single line parallel to the shore, the men stand, a net's diameter apart, and wait. One or two bottlenose dolphins inside the line of men face toward the sea, floating or moving slowly at the surface. Then a dolphin dives and the men dig their heels into the ground. A few seconds later, the dolphin surfaces, traveling full speed at the line of men. Like a speeding car whose brakes have been pushed to the floor, the dolphin comes to an abrupt halt and dives just out of range of the nets, performing a surging roll, a movement that has not been seen in this context before.

The men throw their nets, which are empty one moment and the next are bulging with fish. Then those who have made their catch leave the line and other men seeking fish take their place and repeat the process.

The dolphins' payment, of course, is fish. Apparently the nets cause mass panic within fish schools, which may make it easier for the dolphins to catch more than they normally would. Scientists observing the fishing at Laguna noted that in one half hour a lone dolphin brought fish six times to the line of fishermen. Each man typically caught at least ten large mullet, weighing up to 4 1/2 pounds each. About twenty-five pounds of fish would be an ample daily ration for an average-sized adult bottlenose. So it isn't difficult to see that the rewards of the fishing cooperative for the dolphins are great, offering more food for a modicum of effort.

When it comes to the fishing cooperative, the dolphins seem to be in the driver's seat. The water is murky, and the men cannot see the fish. Their only inkling that there are indeed fish in the water is the dolphins' behavior. The men never cast their nets before the dolphin has performed its entire ritual; refolding the net takes time and no one wants to be caught with his net out of the water when a school of mullet is approaching.

At times witnesses have seen a dolphin leave a line of men and head for another section of beach. When this occurred, some of the men immediately reformed a line at the new site and waited for the dolphin to commence fishing.

An estimated two hundred bottlenose dolphins live in the waters off Laguna, although only about twenty-five to thirty participate in the fishing. These the fishermen refer to as "good" dolphins; the others are "bad" dolphins or *ruim* in Portuguese. Fishermen say the *ruim* interfere with their fishing, occasionally damaging nets or dispersing fish. The fishermen claim the so-called good dolphins defend the commercial fishing effort by behaving aggressively toward the *ruim*.

The good dolphins, most of whom have been named and are readily recognized by the fishermen, comprise as many as three generations in some families. They are mainly a cohesive group of females, their calves, and some older offspring, and a mixed-age group of males.

Some of the dolphins who are helping this generation of Laguna fishermen once fished with their fathers and even their grandfathers, continuing a tradition that, if local legend is to be believed, goes back to 1847.

Catching the Prey

One winter day off the coast of the Dominican Republic's Samana Bay, a female humpback whale was making her way along under the watchful eye of researchers who were filming her every move. To an untrained observer, one whale undoubtedly looks like any other of the same species but analysis of the film proved this one to be an individual who had first been observed off Cape Cod. Scientists years before had named her Manta.

As the researchers watched, Manta dived. Moments later, a huge cloud of bubbles broke the water. Thirty feet in diameter, the bubble cloud was still for one moment; the next, Manta broke the calm, surfacing in the midst of the mass of bubbles, an action she was to repeat several times.

Although we don't know precisely the function of the humpback's bubble cloud, it has something to do with assisting the animal in its detection or capture of prey. It may be that the bubbles somehow immobilize or confuse schools of small prey, causing them to clump together, an action that may make them more visible to the searching whale. Studies on krill concentrations in Alaska found that within humpback bubble nets the krill population ranged between 850 and 1,100, whereas outside the nets in adjacent surface tows, the concentration was between 0 and 4 krill. Another possible explanation is that the curtain of bubbles may make it impossible for the prey to see its formidable predator. Whatever its precise function, it is clear that humpbacks typically use this method during foraging.

The bubble cloud is one of several ways in which humpbacks catch their prey. One method that developed among North Atlantic humpbacks during the 1980s was lob-tail feeding. A lobtailing whale dives, lifting its tail into the air, then smashing it against the water as it plunges beneath the surface. Then the animal emits a bubble cloud and lunges through it, eating its way to the other side. Again, it isn't known how the slap of the whale's tail affects its prey, in this case usually a small fish such as the sand lance. We do know, however, that schooling fish respond to a disturbance by con-gregating. This may give the whale a denser concentration on which to use its bubble cloud. Or the slap may produce mass confusion among the fish, causing them to slow down. Either way, the humpback probably feeds better.

Most of the baleen whales capture prey in less dramatic but equally effective ways. Fin whales may herd swarms of krill and schools of fish toward the surface. Just before the whale breaks the surface, it rolls to the side with its cavernous maw open. Then it turns abruptly, as though to drive the prey across its path, where it then lunges, gulping the entire mass. Bowhead and right whales, skimmers by profession, swim open-mouthed through clouds of plankton, stopping often to flick weeds and other debris off their baleen with their tongues.

Then there are the odontocetes, the toothed whales and dolphins. Many—particularly some dolphin species—have been extensively studied, far more so than the elusive baleen whales. Nevertheless, although we are able to provide more details on the ways in which many of these creatures catch their prey, their lives are still lived beyond the realm of human scrutiny. Often the most we can do is speculate, based on shreds of observational evidence.

For example, do they use their intense echolocation clicks to debilitate prey? Some scientists believe that many odontocetes can produce sound of such high intensity that it is capable of stunning a fish into complacency. Dolphins are thought to be capable of producing sound within a range that could debilitate a fish and at no apparent harm to the dol-phin. During her study on dolphin vocalizations, Shannon Brownlee got firsthand experience about how painful dolphin sounds can be when she was listening through headphones to spinner dolphin vocalizations and someone tapped on the glass window of the dolphins' tank with a metal object. An obviously irate spinner dolphin sent a blast through the hydrophone that left Brownlee's ears ringing long after the dolphin had gone about its business.

Experiments on captive dolphins to test the validity of the stun theory have neither proven nor disproved the hypothesis. In one test conducted at the Oceanic Institute in Hawaii, three spinner dolphins were placed in a tank with small fish. First one dolphin and then another began to make clicking runs shortly after the fish were introduced. The dolphins always approached the school of fish from the side, racing toward it while clicking furiously. For the first hour the fish behaved normally. But after two hours there was a change. The fish were no longer pointed in the same direction; some began to wander away from the school. Seeing a wandering fish, a dolphin would chase it down, clicking relentlessly, although never eating the fish. The toll of this acoustical harassment was apparent on one unlucky wanderer whose color changed from silver to a lemon yellow.

Clearly, much more work is needed before we can say that odontocetes can stun their prey with sound. Although that issue is far from being resolved, we do know something about the way in which toothed whales and dolphins hunt for their food.

Once dolphins spot food they use a variety of methods to chase it down. In South African waters bottlenose dolphins have been seen herding fish against the shoreline. There was a division of labor in the attack: some dolphins chased the fish toward shore while others patrolled offshore to keep the school from escaping. Out of this order may appear chaos, as Black Sea observers report both dolphins and mullet catapulting out of the water so that the mullet appeared to rain down on the dolphins.

In the absence of a shoreline onto which to drive fish, dolphins may use their own bodies as the wall. One group of dolphins will chase the fish toward a barrier of other dolphins.

The effect is to slow down and trap the fish school, which is then attacked from both sides by the dolphins. Off Bahia Kino, Mexico, Bernd Würsig and Lisa Ballance watched as five dolphins approached a fish school and split into two groups which attacked the fish school from either side at precisely the same moment.

In a remarkable example of coordinated hunting, a pod of seven killer whales happened upon a lone crabeater seal on a small ice floe. One of the whales approached the floe and spy-hopped near its edge to get a better look. The whales then retreated up to 300 feet from the floe, turned, and swam directly toward it in rank formation, diving just as they reached the ice floe. The wave created by their charge was all it took to wash the unfortunate seal off the ice.

When threatened by predators, fish schools will sometimes clump themselves into a ball. To be successful, a predator usually has to zero in on a particular fish, and that becomes especially difficult when a school tightens into a co-ordinated mass, each fish moving synchronously with its neighbors. This clumping strategy, however, backfires when dolphins are involved in the hunt. Dolphins, it appears, find fish easier to catch when they are clumped together. One common technique they use to achieve this is to get the fish moving as though they were on a merry-go-round, the so-called carousel method. The dolphins surround the fish school, forcing the fish to travel in a sphrerical mass that is gradually tightened by the dolphins, which continue to swim around the fish. The dolphins then begin to dive, either under the mass or into the school of fish, often surfacing with a fish in the mouth. The size of the circle is determined by the initial size of the fish school. Some observers have noted carousels 450 feet in diameter.

Dusky dolphins were seen waiting their turn for a chance at a moving ball of anchovies. The dolphins herded the fish to the surface, using that as their wall through which the fish could not escape. Then the group swam under and around the school. One at a time, each dolphin broke rank and shot into the swirling mass of fish, coming out the other side with a full mouth. Some anchovies strayed from the ball, but usually a dolphin was there to diligently chase it back. Usually a fish school cannot be held hostage by a small number of dolphins for more than a few minutes, so each dolphin has to eat as much as it can while it can. Often, however, neighboring groups of dolphins will join in. Then the fish ball may become even larger as new schools are herded to join it, and feeding may go on for hours.

Another strategy for feeding on schooling fish is to confuse them so that they lose the ability to synchronize their movements with each other. With fish going this way and that, it becomes easy to zero in on an individual. The conspicuous black-and-white coloration of some dolphins may have just this effect. Experiments have shown that a broken black-and-white color pattern, with areas of white on black and vice versa, tends to confuse fish, making them less able to school together. Thus the white spot behind the eye of the killer whale and the alternating black-and-white pattern of the beautiful Commerson's dolphin may have evolved because they helped the animals feed better.

A killer whale need not participate in the kill to have a taste of the food. A sea lion pup was captured by a killer whale, which held the pup by one of its appendages, swinging it back and forth so that it struck both sides of the whale's head. The prey was then taken to an area where the rest of the pod was milling and passed back and forth, each whale having a chance to beat it or flip the body up to thirty feet into the air using its flukes. In a series of observations of killer whales in Argentine waters, researchers noted that various killers handled their prey differently. One pod usually dismembered its prey immediately after capture while other pods were more likely to release it and preface a kill by striking the sea lion and flipping it into the air.

Killer whales like to play with their food like a cat plays with a mouse. A pod of four to six killer whales will surround a seal, each one taking its turn to swim at the creature, hitting it with the killer's body, flukes, and fins. Usually within eighteen to twenty-four minutes, seals observed undergoing such a battering have disappeared, while the pod mills around the area, probably sharing in the meal. In one observation, a few minutes after the seal disappeared, one killer surfaced with entrails draped around its fin. Typically, the sky is filled with birds after such an attack, a possible indication that the killers leave some of their kill behind.

Not every member of a group uses the same method of prey capture. Minke whales appear to adopt one of two feeding techniques. Some minkes take advantage of the large number of fish to be found swimming below flocks of feeding gulls and auks. The minke approaches the feeding birds from under the water, causing a cloud of startled birds to shoot back to the skies. The whale then opens its mouth and eats. Other whales use lunge feeding, a technique in which the whale herds the prey up to the surface and lunges open-mouthed into the school. Interestingly, individual minkes consistently use the same technique.

Although dolphins often hunt in a group, solitary hunting is a method also used. Single dolphins have often been seen attacking fish against the shore. Suddenly, the dolphin rushes toward the shore, close to the surface, with its dorsal fin peeking out of the water. Near the shore, the dolphin usually turns upside down, grabs a fish, rights itself, and then swims back out to sea. Why upside down? Scientists believe that vision may be important for hunting in shallow clear water. The fish are swimming near the surface but the dolphin's best field of vision points downward. Thus, simply by turning on its back, the dolphin is better able to see its prey.

One quite dramatic type of solitary feeding was seen at Sanibel Island, Florida, where bottlenose dolphins were hunting for fish. Using its tail flukes, a dolphin would kick a fish into the air as deftly as a football player kicks a field goal. Bleeding and obviously hurt, the fish would catapult through the air, landing with a splash. Usually, the dolphin who did the kicking soon arrived to finish off the fish, although once another member of the dolphin group ate a fish it had not kicked. Killer whales sometimes punt seals and sea lions around in a similar fashion.

To what lengths will a hungry cetacean go for a satisfying meal? Dolphins and killer whales have been known to beach themselves to capture prey. Two bottlenose dolphins were seen on a marsh near Doboy Sound, Georgia, by an astonished witness. During low tide the dolphins swam up the tidal creek to an area where muddy spots were exposed through the grass. The dolphins moved toward each other and then abruptly rushed up the bank, moving onto their right sides and pushing a large wave ahead of them. The wave broke to reveal several small stranded fish, which the dolphins immediately ate, first biting off the heads. Because of the slick mud, the dolphins could readily slide back into the water and then were off like a shot out to sea.

Death by Killer Whale

They are the most feared of all sea creatures and with good reason. Killer whales are fierce, intelligent predators whose cooperative hunting behavior easily rivals those of the most cunning land-mammal hunters.

Greg Silber, Michael Newcomer, and Hector Perez-Cortez were conducting aerial surveys of porpoises off the northern Gulf of California, Mexico, when they happened upon a drama they will never forget.

From their single-engine Cessna, the scientists spotted an unfortunate Bryde's whale being pursued by a group of fifteen killer whales. When first seen, some of the killer whales were as close as 900 feet, while others lagged behind more than a mile. A few minutes later one killer had caught up to the flukes of the Bryde's whale. Within moments, four killers surrounded the baleen whale's head. Shortly afterward, the larger whale's speed slowed considerably. Then two killers bit the Bryde's whale on its right flank, while one swam on its back. Every time the Bryde's whale surfaced, the killers appeared abreast of its head, swimming directly in front of the whale. The killers stayed clear of the Bryde's whale's tail, a potentially dangerous weapon. Like wolves and lions, species that also display cooperative hunting, the killers' attack was coordinated, and left little doubt about what the outcome would be.

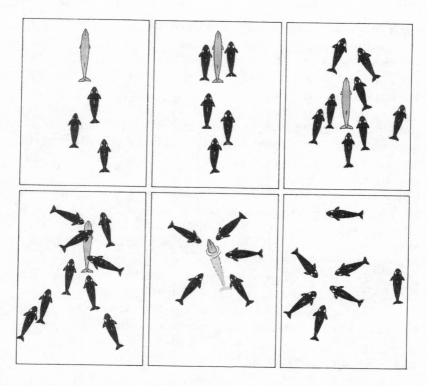

Schematic representation of the attack by a pod of killer whales on a Bryde's whale in the Gulf of California, as described in the text. At one point, fifteen killer whales converged on the lone baleen whale. Ninety-four minutes after the attack began, the Bryde's whale was dead.

The killers continued to swim on the larger whale's head and back, which seemed to impair the Bryde's whale's breathing. From the airplane, the observers watched as the killers began to rip at the whale's flanks with their sharp teeth, tearing off large chunks of skin and white blubber. About an hour after the attack began, the Bryde's whale was having difficulty swimming. It moved forward slowly, making shallow, short dives. Eight killers now surrounded it and, as the Bryde's whale blew after surfacing, the scientists saw red in the spray. The water began to fill with blood.

The Bryde's whale dived again, this time surfacing with three killer whales on its head and one draped across its back like a shawl. The large whale didn't dive but instead seemed to sink, without any evidence of drawing a breath. The killer whales surfaced and one raised its tail out of the water. For the last time, the Bryde's whale surfaced, head only, its jaw slack. Then it slid back into its ocean coffin.

As for the victors, they dived repeatedly for awhile, presumably eating. When attacking large whales, killers, unlike most terrestrial carnivores, are very selective about what they'll eat. They can afford to be picky with such a mountain of food, and typically end up leaving most of the kill. Sometimes they will simply strip away flesh and blubber and part of the fins, leaving the whale while it is still alive. Some scientists have witnessed them removing the tongue and lower jaw of gray whales, and the flippers and tail flukes of minke and bottlenose whales.

Two days later the remains of the Bryde's whale surfaced, the carcass just one of the sea's many casualties.

As for the killer whales, they milled around the death site for awhile, spending long periods at the surface, then swam away. It would not be too long before they began to search for their next meal.

4

Communication

In the early spring of 1984, an intrepid team of scientists arrived at Point Barrow, Alaska, to be greeted by temperatures that pushed the mercury to $-40°$ F. The team's mission was to locate, track, and count vocalizing bowhead whales.

In some waters this task might not have been so formidable, but the bowhead whale spends most of its life in a world of dark water and thick ice, not exactly conducive to whale watching. In late winter the whales start from the Bering Sea and migrate eighteen hundred miles before passing Point Barrow and entering the Beaufort Sea, where they spend the summer feeding in an underwater world sculpted from constantly changing ice formations. It is a world whose foundations meld the old and new; old ice that has built up over many years combines with new ice that begins to form in thin sheets, growing up to two inches a day until it reaches a thickness of eight feet. These sheets of ice grind against one another, colliding, each encroaching upon the next until massive ridges up to thirty-three feet high are formed.

Eavesdropping on cetacean conversation is never easy. Whales and dolphins spend most of their lives underwater and naturally that is where most of their communication takes place, way beyond the listening capability of the human ear. Scientists have to some degree broken through this barrier by using hydrophones, sophisticated microphonelike instruments that enable the sounds under the sea to be heard by those of us who dwell on the land.

Two Arctic-dwelling species, bowhead and beluga whales. Unlike most baleen whales, the bowhead does not migrate to warm waters. The beautiful white beluga is a close relative of the narwhal.

On the ice off Point Barrow, even the installation of a hydrophone proved no easy task. In order to set up the devices, members of the team had to cut trails through miles of ice ridges. Then holes had to be drilled through pan ice that in some sections measured eight feet thick, so that each hydrophone could be suspended at least twenty-five feet below the frozen surface. Hard, tedious work but not without an occasional unexpected reward, as Christopher Clark, a member of the team, was to find out. As he rappelled down from an ice ridge through a small spot of open water, he was startled by a forty-five-foot-long bowhead surfacing three feet beneath him. Within seconds, the whale was joined by another bowhead and four beluga whales, all apparently taking advantage of the break in the ice. The whales stayed on the surface breathing for several minutes before disappearing under the ice.

Once the hydrophones were set up, the team spent more than six hundred hours listening to the sounds of bowhead whales, whose vocal repertoire is among the most complex of any of the baleen species. They heard the bowheads singing in ranges that skipped up and down seven octaves as nimbly as well-practiced fingers traverse the keys of a piano. The whales' diverse vocalizations seemed to mimic the sounds of their world, the whining groan of slipping ice, the shrill scream of a beluga whale.

A bowhead, hidden by layers of ice but acoustically visible to the scientists because of the hydrophones, called out—a loud, low sound that told its human listeners its location. Thirty seconds later another voice, this one more distant and to the north, answered the call.

The scientific team found bowheads, unlike many humans, to be extremely polite in their conversation with one another. The whales rarely interrupted, each one apparently waiting patiently for the speaker to finish before it said its own piece. The researchers concluded that these whales listen carefully to what the others have to say; survival may depend on it.

Many years ago the renowned undersea explorer Jacques Cousteau described the sea as "the silent world" but to the creatures whose bodies have been designed to live in this aquatic environment, the sea offers an acoustical banquet, a rich array of utterances spoken by the living and, yes, even that which does not live.

It stands to reason that sound would be an important part of a cetacean's life, given the fact that the physical properties of water allow sound to travel longer distances beneath the sea than it does on land. The low-frequency sounds that many of the baleen whales use for communication can sometimes be detected hundreds of miles away.

What does a whale (or a human equipped with a hydrophone) hear when it listens? Depending upon the water in which the whale is listening, it may hear the fantastic sound repertoire of the belugas, the whales that sailors have dubbed sea canaries. These whales, as white as the snow, emit chirps, burps, grunts, squeaks, screams, and yaps. In these same Arctic waters the listening whale may hear the groans and squeals of one ice pan slamming into another, two nonliving entities whose sound, nevertheless, is said to remind one of the howl of a lone wolf or two cats trying to scratch each other's eyes out. In warmer waters a shrimp snaps. A dolphin whistles. A certain fish has been named after the grunting sound it makes. A loud crack made with the jerk of a dolphin's head signals its displeasure. Tails, flippers, and even entire bodies slap the water with such force that the noise is heard both above and below the surface. A whale eats and its stomach rumbles. One sperm whale sends a series of clicks to another. A humpback croons the latest version of a song that tomorrow may be slightly different. So many sounds—and yet, sadly, most of us never will hear them.

Because researchers have observed changes in behavior following such sounds, we assume that dolphins and whales use these methods, and others, to communicate. This isn't to imply that they talk to one another as humans do, a subject that we will address later in the chapter. There is substantial evidence, however, that some of these grunts, groans, whistles, clicks, gurglings, slaps, or whatever noise a particular species makes probably are used to communicate general information to others, as well as to convey general states of emotion. Moreover, the evidence suggests that some individuals recognize each other by the sounds they make.

Cetaceans also communicate in other ways. The sense of touch is an important communication tool, as is the animals' ability to detect in the water certain chemicals emitted from fellow cetaceans. And vision—once thought to be relatively unimportant—also figures quite heavily in the communication of many species.

But in the undersea habitat of dolphins and whales the ability to create and detect sound is undoubtedly the primary communication system.

The Many Voices of Dolphins and Whales

The voices that belong to the cetacean world are no more uniform than the species themselves. Broadly speaking, the sounds that emanate from odontocetes can be divided into two categories: the so-called pure-tone whistles and the pulsed sounds. The second group is sometimes broken down into regular echolocation clicks used to explore the environment and sounds emitted in an emotional context, so-called burst-pulsed sounds that have been described as barks, squeaks, squawks, grunts, mews, moans, and yelps.

The descriptions given to burst-pulsed sounds simply reflect how they sound to our ears, which is not necessarily the way a dolphin hears them. A dolphin squeal or mew is really a packet of clicks fired off so rapidly that our ears often don't perceive the individual clicks, but instead hear the entire utterance as one mew or squeal. Dolphins, whose brains process sound with tremendous speed, may well hear the individual clicks in a mew. The clicks of echolocation sound to us like a creaky door whose creaks increase as a dolphin zooms in to inspect an object closely. Again, we do not hear what a dolphin hears because most of the energy in a typical click is far above our hearing range. Some scientists have suggested that the division between burst-pulsed signals and echolocation clicks is an artifact of our common scientific desire to put things in mutually exclusive categories, and that what sounds like echolocation may often, in fact, be communication. Indeed, when we listen to bottlenose dolphins in Shark Bay, the echolocation-type click sounds seem to grade right into the burst-pulsed sounds used for communication.

Most of the toothed whales and dolphins probably produce pulsed sounds, some of which are used in echolocation, others probably in a social context. Species such as the bottlenose dolphin and beluga also have in their verbal repertoire pure-tone whistles, which scientists believe function solely in communication.

As for the mysticete or baleen whales, their vocalizations are very different from those of the odontocetes and more difficult to classify. In general, the sounds a baleen whale makes are of lower frequency and longer duration. Some sounds are simple and repetitive, such as the one-second tonal pulses made by fin whales. Others are more complex; the noises that migrating gray whales make have been described as moans, bubble-type sounds, and knocks; minke whales emit pings, clicks, and ratchetlike noises; and feeding humpback whales are said to grunt, yelp, and snort. Most complex are the elaborate songs of the humpback whales.

How do dolphins and whales make these curious sounds? We don't know precisely, although we have zeroed in on the source of dolphin sounds more closely than on that of the mysticetes. Unlike humans, cetaceans do not have vocal cords. Nor is there any movement around the mouth when a cetacean vocalizes, making it difficult for an observer to identify the source of the sound when there is more than one animal present.

The clicks and whistles of odontocetes are produced in a series of air sacs in the soft tissue below the blowhole in the animal's head. Pressurized air is forced up past a muscular tonguelike plug into a sac below the blowhole. The higher-frequency sounds are directed forward and out of the head through the dolphin's melon, a waxy lens-shaped body in the forehead. Lower-frequency sounds are less focused.

A single click of a sperm whale is actually a series of pulses of decreasing loudness. As we saw earlier, sperm whale sounds are generated by structures in the front of the enormously elongated head and reverberate off air sacs in front of the towering throne-like skull. It was initially thought that the sound blast was directed right out into the water. However, Bertl Mohl and Mats Amundin, both acoustics experts, made recordings of the sounds of a large sperm whale that suggest the initial pulse is actually directed in toward the skull.

In mysticete whales there is a constriction between the back of the larynx and the trachea that could be the source of their moans. All baleen whales (except the gray whale) have a laryngeal sac extending off the lower side of the laryngeal cavity, and this sac may be involved in sound production.

When a baleen whale "talks," it does not expel air from its mouth or nostrils (blowholes) as land mammals do, an indication that the air used to make the sound is contained within a closed system. Sometimes a tiny stream of bubbles emerges when a dolphin whistles, but not consistently.

What would we see if we could watch a humpback whale singing? We cannot be sure just where the sound emerges from this or any other cetacean but if you could have a front-row seat for this song virtuoso's performance, you would see the whale's head appear to be radiating, pulsating with energy as it crooned the messages of its kind.

Regardless of where the sound comes from, as anyone who has had the good fortune to hear their undersea utterances will tell you, many cetaceans are capable of an astonishing array of vocalizations. What sounds do these creatures make? Are they, in fact, communicating information about the world or their mood? And even when they are silent, cetaceans may well be communicating important information in other ways. Let's look at some of the varied sounds they make and what we think may be the functions of those sounds.

Odontocete Whistles. Many species of odontocetes, although by no means all, emit unpulsed or continuous signals known as whistles. In most cases, the whistles are in the mid- to upper-sonic range of frequency and last anywhere from 0.5 to two seconds.

Some have speculated that whistles may be the primary form of acoustic communication among odontocetes, but many species of the toothed whales and dolphins do not seem to whistle, so that hypothesis obviously does not tell the whole story.

Along those lines, scientists have sought to understand why some odontocetes whistle and others do not. Porpoises don't whistle. Neither does the sperm whale or Hector's dolphins, and whistles are rarely reported from killer whales. It was thought that none of the river dolphins whistled until Ding Wang recorded simple whistles from China's *baiji*. And simple whistles were also recorded from two young beaked whales that had stranded. A characteristic of many of the non-whistling species is that they tend to be less gregarious than many of the whistling odontocetes, traveling in small groups rather than large herds. Though there are exceptions such as the nonwhistling killer and sperm whales, both of which live in very stable social groups, in general it appears that whistling odontocetes travel in large groups and cooperate with one another in foraging.

Whistling may have evolved, in fact, because it improved the members of a foraging group's ability to maintain contact. Because of their low frequency, whistles can travel greater distances than pulsed sounds. Moreover, whistles do not overlap much in frequency with echolocation clicks, so there is little chance of one masking the other. A dolphin is capable of producing echolocation clicks *and* whistles simultaneously, so it would make sense that while the animals use echolocation to search for food, they use whistles to communicate other information while foraging. If broadcasting a lower-frequency call is the key, then sperm and killer whales might not need to whistle. Because they are so big, both species can broadcast loud pulsed sounds over large distances, and killer whales do produce some pulsed squeals that are similar to whistles.

Odontocetes have been observed whistling in response to a number of stimuli. Sometimes the stimulus need be nothing more than the sound of another animal's whistle. Both excitement and stress also appear to induce or increase whistling.

Scientists have noted that dolphins whistle more when arriving at a familiar place; indeed, observations of Hawaiian spinner dolphins showed that whistling rates were highest when the dolphins first entered the shallow bays that were their late morning and afternoon resting place. After the group had settled down, the whistling stopped, resuming later when the rest period was over.

Judging by the amount of whistles, riding the bow wave of a large boat or even a baleen whale appears to be an exciting experience for spinner and common dolphins. And few things (with the exception of sex) excite an animal as much as its next meal. In one experiment with a captive bottlenose dolphin, researchers noticed how her whistling peaked during the morning feeding. When the feeding schedule was changed to the evening, the whistles, too, became nocturnal.

Whistling also appears to accompany stress. Introduce a captive bottlenose dolphin into a tank and the animal may whistle nonstop. Obviously, few things are as stressful as when a mother and her calf become separated, an event that rarely fails to elicit a steady stream of whistles. And a stranded, captured, or harpooned dolphin or pilot whale will whistle its distress.

Yet a whistle in the dolphin world means more than simply an expression of distress or excitement. Why should evolution favor an animal making a constant racket just because it is aroused? That would simply be a waste of energy and perhaps worse, if predators were lurking about. A mother whose infant has strayed certainly is distressed, but her whistles probably have a practical effect in that they may enable the infant to find her.

There is evidence that in some dolphin species an individual's whistle may serve as its vocal signature, identifying it to other dolphins. Studies have shown that each dolphin's whistle, which accounts for a large percentage of an individual's vocalizations, is distinctive, unmatched by any others. Although the dolphin may vary certain aspects of its whistle such as rapidity, loudness, and frequency, the basic contour for most animals remains the same. In Shark Bay we actually named a dolphin "Waverly" after her peculiar wavering whistle.

Studying the behavior of a particular animal offers the fascinating possibility of being able to draw parallels between creatures who, on the surface at least, have little in common. In testing whether or not dolphins have signature whistles, scientists looked to the territorial songbirds, which will ignore the familiar melodies of neighbors yet rise to the offensive in response to the song of an encroaching stranger.

A large male pantropical spotted dolphin who was apparently a member of a herd in waters off Oahu, Hawaii, was captured and his nearly continuous whistles recorded. A week later the recording was played back to the animal's herd. When they heard the male in distress, the herd became alarmed and began to flee. The reaction was quite different, however, when the tape was played to a different audience, this time a herd of the same species that inhabited the waters off another island. This herd's response was one of curiosity. The dolphins approached the source of the sound; some even touched the underwater speaker.

These findings suggest that dolphins may respond in different ways to the calls of a neighbor as distinct from a stranger, which would help to support the idea of a signature whistle. Perhaps the captured dolphin's alarm was conveyed by a variation in its whistle. This same variation would fall on deaf ears when played to the other herds since they were strangers to the captured animal. Alternatively, the dolphins may simply have been more interested in finding out who this stranger was than in listening to its problems. To determine how a dolphin's signature whistle develops, Laela Sayigh, a researcher at Woods Hole Oceanographic Institute, studied bottlenose dolphin mothers and calves off the coast of Sarasota, Florida. Captive bottlenose dolphins have been known to produce whistles during the first year of life. If the signature whistle is learned, she reasoned, the youngster's whistle couldn't help but be shaped by its association with its mother.

Prior to the Sarasota study, several researchers had noticed that some mother-calf whistles were strikingly similar. This led to the idea that the young calves may initially mimic their mother's whistle—not an unlikely prospect, given the fact that captive bottlenose dolphins have shown a remarkable ability to mimic sounds in general.

What Sayigh found, however, was that male and female calves differed in their tendency to copy Mom. Male infants were more likely than females to produce a whistle like their mothers. Does this finding have something to do with the fact that Sarasota female dolphins associate primarily with members of their matrilineal group, while males tend to leave the extended family and form other relationships within the community? We don't know, but we do know that an exchange of whistles does appear to be crucial in maintaining contact between a mother and its calf.

In Shark Bay, bottlenose dolphin infants spend almost 20 percent of their time at a distance of more than 60 feet from their mothers. Predators pose a very real threat to calves, so it is imperative that a mother-calf pair be in contact when they are separated. Rachel Smolker and Janet Mann, biopsychologists from the University of Michigan, noted that when infants strayed from their mothers, the infants would whistle just before they began heading back. Mothers probably whistle sometimes, too, during these separations. Imagine how difficult that would be if several females in the area had similar whistles. On the other hand, since males do not maintain close ties with their mothers after they leave home, one whistle is as good as another.

The whistle itself is not the only difference between the sexes. Females do not appear to produce as wide a variety of whistles as their male counterparts. Again, this may reflect the different demands upon the sexes. If one of the most important functions of a female's signature whistle is to maintain close contact with her infant, a large repertoire of whistles might work against this purpose. The social world of the male may not be so constraining.

The question of whether a signature whistle does more than simply identify an individual has been debated in scientific circles. Does a specific whistle correlate with a particular event or social context? German biologist Vincent Janik found that signature whistles vary in consistent ways in different behavioral contexts.

Odontocete Clicks and Other Pulsed Sounds. If all the world's species of cetaceans were to have the equivalent of a cocktail party, the adult sperm whales' repartee might be found lacking. No squeals, whistles, chirps, moans, grunts, or squawks emanate from these large deep-diving whales. The sperm's vocal repertoire consists of only one sound, a click, a little dull perhaps when compared to others' vocalizations but no less effective.

Like many of the toothed whales and dolphins, sperms probably rely on echolocation clicks in their search for food. The sperms' clicking is reminiscent of the hoofbeats of galloping horses and can be heard several miles from its point of origin, as a result of the ease in which sound travels through water.

But this does not mean that a sperm is mute in its interactions with its fellow whales. On the contrary, scientists have discovered that the sperm uses clicks—this time in patterns resembling Morse code—when socializing with fellow whales. These repetitive click patterns, called codas, usually consist of between three and thirty clicks, often in a series that lasts up to about 1.5 seconds and that may be repeated several times.

Those who have spent time listening to the clicks of sperms can easily identify one individual's clicks from the next whale's. If we can do it, sperms probably can, too. At the same time, the function of these codas may be more than simply a means of identification because research indicates that the animals do share certain codas. Researchers in the southeast Caribbean recorded codas and discovered that two patterns comprised more than half of the sampling. Codas with characteristics similar to the main Caribbean sperm groups were found in whales in the northwestern Atlantic, while the codas of the Galapagos Islands sperms were markedly different. These shared codas apparently do not aid in the identification of an individual, which may indicate that they are used in the communication of other kinds of information.

In one study of sperms near the Galapagos, scientists listened to the whales in the act of what was assumed to be communication. One sperm might emit a coda of eight clicks, after which another might counter with seven clicks. The research team categorized the codas into twenty-three distinct types, according to the number and spacing of the clicks. They found that certain codas were more likely to follow others, and that each appeared to generate different responses.

While it is impossible to begin to speculate about what the sperms were saying to each other, it does appear likely that they were communicating in some way. Oftentimes a conversation would begin with a coda of five evenly spaced clicks, possibly the sperm version of our "Hi." On the other hand, the Caribbean team suspects that one of the shared codas may be an aggressive message such as "Go away!"

New Zealand biologist Steve Dawson undertook the daunting task of studying communication in Hector's dolphins. Daunting because Hector's dolphins not only do not whistle, but they have a vocal repertoire consisting almost entirely of ultrasonic clicks. Most tape recorders are built for the human hearing range, which only goes up to 20 kHz, or twenty thousand cycles per second. The Hector's dolphins' favorite frequencies are up around 125 kHz, necessitating special equipment.

Dawson found that although these dolphins did not seem to prefer one type of click signal when echolocating, they relied primarily on one click type when feeding. Clicks emitted in quick succession sound like a high-pitched cry. Hector's dolphins used cries more frequently when they were excited, jumping in the air, or under some kind of physical threat.

A variety of click or pulsed sounds in other odontocetes are used in communication. Prior to and during mating, male bottlenose dolphins have been known to yelp, while in a similar situation the harbor porpoise, a species that doesn't whistle, may let loose with a squeak, grind, or a sound reminiscent of an explosion. A bottlenose dolphin snaps its jaws shut with a resounding crack. Often called a jaw-clap, the crack sound is not the result of teeth impacting teeth but is produced inside the head like other sounds. In Shark Bay we observed male dolphins making low frequency "pop" sounds when herding females. The pop sound attracts the female to the male, yet is associated with threats and aggression. The pop is evidently a vocal threat that signals not just "come hither" but *"Come Hither!"*

A number of pulsed sounds emitted by the Shark Bay dolphins seem unfriendly, including one that sounds like a donkey's bray. Dolphins also scream and growl at each other. When the tame old male Snubby grew tired of being patted on the blowhole by well-meaning but naive tourists, he threw what can only be described as a temper tantrum, floating perfectly still at the surface while making burst-pulsed screams of increasing intensity until he turned and unleashed his anger on another dolphin.

A theory on the role of pulsed sounds in a more passive kind of communication has to do with one animal's ability to glean information from the signals made by another. This idea suggests that by "eavesdropping" on the echolocation clicks made by other cetaceans, a dolphin or whale may be led to a source of food, for instance.

Dolphins also may be able to interpret the echoes resulting from another dolphin's echolocation clicks, enabling them to decipher not only the sender's precise location but the object on which it is bouncing off its sound waves. It would certainly be useful to know what your neighbor is chasing for lunch.

The Sounds of the Mysticetes. The plaintive moans of a gray whale broadcast its location across the depths of the ocean. The bowhead whale whoops, purrs, and groans its message to another whale more than ten miles away. A blue whale sings its four-note song, a mere jingle compared to the ballads of humpback whales. Such is the vocal diversity of baleen whales.

Even clicklike sounds have been reported for some mysticetes, although this is highly controversial because there is little evidence that baleen whales echolocate and in some cases the sounds may have been merely an electrical click in the recording apparatus.

Again, the logical question is, What do the sounds mean? As with most whale and dolphin sounds, it is difficult to associate a specific vocalization with a particular behavior or event. Given the physical constraints of studying these enormous animals, it isn't hard to understand why we have known so little about their lives. Not only are baleen whales hard to see and follow, it was always largely guesswork to determine whether the individual seen yesterday was the same one in sight today. Nor could scientists always ascertain which animal in a group was making the sound.

Fortunately, relatively recent techniques have allowed us to more accurately identify individual cetaceans by using photographs of their natural markings, in concert with more accurate tracking methods and acoustical equipment. These improvements have made it easier for scientists to decipher something of the mysterious world of this world's largest creatures. Now, armed with the proper techniques and insights, they are attempting to determine vocal repertoires of various baleen species and to establish a correlation between these sounds and specific behavior. Singing humpback whales, for instance, make a ratcheting sound before surfacing in the tropical waters of the Atlantic, and a sound similar to a scream when charging a boat. The closer the whale gets to the vessel, the more intense its screams, until the moment just before it would be on top of the boat—when it becomes silent and dives. This, apparently, is the humpback's threat display.

Southern right whales on their calving grounds off the coast of Argentina were found to vary their calls in different contexts. When males were gathered together, they growled, presumably out of competition for a nearby female. After one of two competing males left the area, the growls were transformed into high-pitched melodic sounds that rose in frequency as the excitement level increased.

In a two-year study of these whales, Christopher Clark, the same scientist who found himself hanging a few feet above a gathering of bowheads and belugas, learned that calls were not random but related to the social context and activity of the animals. A lone swimming whale in search of companions produced a sound that Clark dubbed an "up" call, while a resting whale was mostly silent, occasionally emitting a long moan in the act of exhaling from its blowhole. A mother would growl through her blowholes when her calf left her, but when the offspring was nearby, she was silent. A swimming or resting whale, if joined by porpoises, sea lions, or even an intruding fellow southern right whale, would begin making loud, harsh blow sounds. When the sea lions or porpoises ignored this signal, the whale became slightly active. An encroaching whale, on the other hand, didn't hang around after the first whale produced several loud blow sounds.

Clark theorized that these blow sounds are threats that, in essence, serve notice to an intruder that it had better clear out. The intensity and harshness of the particular sound may be related to the whale's disturbance level. As for the long moan-blow sounds heard from resting whales, they may be the equivalent of hanging the Do Not Disturb sign on the door of your hotel room. Another possibility is that the creature, like so many in the human world, simply snores.

One way in which the bowhead whales at the beginning of this chapter may use communication is to coordinate movement through their ice-encrusted world so that each individual is able to maintain contact with the rest of the herd. The Point Barrow researchers found that there were probably between ten and fifteen bowheads in a group that was spread out over a four- to eight-square-mile area. The animals, few within sight of another, used a wide variety of calls during their travels. Whales traveling miles apart exchange individually distinctive calls for several hours, then one whale makes the call of another. Although maintaining contact with the herd was probably one function, Clark believes there is more to it than that. After years of listening to the ice, Clark and others have learned to associate certain sounds with particular ice conditions. If humans can do that, these expert ice travelers must also be capable of this discrimination.

We know that whales can listen to echoes of their own calls and the calls of others bouncing off the ice. But do these echoes sound different in different environmental conditions? Scientists used a computer model to project a bowhead call through a setup of conditions similar, first, to young thin ice and then to ice layered ten to twenty-five feet thick. The test showed that the sounds the whale hears in such situations are markedly different. A call through thin ice is without echo, so that the whale hears an undistorted sound similar to the call it can hear in open water. But when a bowhead calls out in thick ice, a cacophony of echoes is reflected, bouncing off the frozen terrain.

Do whales then use these sounds to probe their underwater environment? Evidence suggests that they may. Consider a sighting in 1985 of a group of more than one hundred bowheads changing course to avoid a large ice floe. The whales were traveling over a six-by-fifteen-mile area, with individuals separated by at least six hundred feet. As the first whales approached within a half mile of the ice floe, they began calling more and more frequently, in the same way that echolocating dolphins intensify their clicking as they approach their target, and long before the whales could see the edge of the floe, they diverted course. While the natural sounds from the ice may have signaled "no through route," the increase in frequency of calls suggests a kind of crude echolocation—which would be a first for baleen whales. Interestingly, the whales traveling behind the leaders also shifted course, but without increasing their calls. Obviously, the followers were listening. Whether they heard the changing location of the leaders' voices or the echoes of the leaders' calls off the ice, we don't know.

Nonvocal Communication

A cetacean need not whistle, click, moan, or sing to send out a message. A dolphin or whale is capable of creating many nonvocal sounds that undoubtedly have meaning to other creatures within earshot. The hard slap of a tail, flippers, head, or even entire body against the surface often occurs when an animal seems disturbed or angered. Some scientists think that an explosive loud exhalation through its blowhole typically indicates that a bottlenose dolphin is disturbed about something, while the underwater emission of a large air bubble (without sound) suggests inquisitiveness or surprise. And even the lowly stomach rumble is not without communicative power. Nearby cetaceans hearing such a sound are likely to recognize that here lies a whale who has just eaten, an indicator that there may be food nearby.

Even dead silence may pack a powerful punch. When a strange creature enters the environment, the sea may suddenly sound as though no one is home. Beluga, gray, and southern right whales all are apt to fall silent at the approach of killer whales (or even in response to a recording of killer whale sounds).

In addition to sound, cetaceans also rely on the communicative powers of the visual, tactile, and chemoreceptive senses. (See also Chapter 2, "How Whales and Dolphins Perceive Their World," page 21.)

The Song of the Humpback

How many humans, let alone wild creatures, have had their

croons immortalized on a hit record? Not many. One cetacean whose musical ability is his tour de force is the humpback whale, whose eerie moans, snores, and groans became an instant best-seller in stores around the country a few years back.

The humpback is by no means the only cetacean singer. Beluga whales produce an impressive array of birdlike trills, toots, and whistles and have by far the richest acoustical repertoire of any of the toothed whales. And bowhead whales sing complex songs, often producing two different sounds simultaneously.

But it is the humpback with his evolving song that has captured the attention of so many who seek to understand the message and motives behind the tune. Humpbacks have been known to serenade the sea for as long as twenty-two hours straight.

Before discussing the specifics of the song, we need to know a little about this large creature's yearly cycle. Like many whales, the humpback spends its summers in cold waters feeding on the small crustaceans and fish that are its nutritional mainstay. Come winter, the animals migrate to warmer waters where they probably eat little, if at all. Although no one has actually seen humpbacks mating, scientists have deduced that it is here that the whales breed.

It is also within these warmer waters that most humpback singing has been heard, typically a lone individual belting out its song for all who care to listen. While it is difficult to identify a singer's sex since males and females look alike, some determined scientists have actually dived beneath the singers to photograph their genital slits. In other instances, chromosomes have been examined from small tissue samples obtained from singers. Most of the singers examined by such methods have been male. This has led to speculation that this whale, like many species of birds, frogs, and even some mammals, sings in order to attract a mate.

The humpback song itself is a complicated series of sounds usually lasting anywhere from five minutes to a half hour; at first, that feat alone has one marveling at these animals' incredible memorization prowess. Upon analysis, however, the song requires a less agile memory than it initially appears. The humpback's song is composed of phrases, each a sequence of sounds lasting about fifteen seconds. The whale sings a phrase and then repeats it several times before moving on to a second phrase, repeating it, and so forth. Each sequence of repeated phrases is a theme. On average, a song contains between five and eight themes, and each time the whale sings the song, these themes are repeated in the same order. Thus, a whale need only memorize a limited number of notes, the way to structure the notes into phrases, and the order of each theme.

Perhaps one of the most fascinating aspects of the humpback's song is the way it is constantly changing. Even so, like teenagers attuned to the Top Forty, humpbacks always seem to keep up with the latest "hit" version of their song.

Although there is some individual variation, the basic song sung by most of a population of humpbacks is the same, although one study found that a few rebel whales don't conform to the group song but sing their own variations. Of course, one humpback population's song is often radically different from the next: those who breed near Hawaii sing one song; humpbacks in Bermuda another. Regardless of where the whale lives, though, the song's one constant is change.

Over the course of one singing season, slight changes are noticeable in almost every aspect of the song. Some themes may die out, replaced by new ones. The number of sequences may change. The length of the song may double. In one study that examined humpback songs recorded off Bermuda over a twenty-year period, researchers were hard-pressed to find any similarity between the twenty-year-old song and its latest version. In fact, these songs were as different from each other as they were from the songs of another population of humpbacks an entire continent away!

How does a humpback remember the ever-changing song of its group? It may be that whales use rhymes to help recall the notes, many of which contain rhymelike material with themes ending in similar sounds.

Explaining the evolving humpback melody is more difficult than documenting it. It was once proposed that the whales might somehow forget their song during their summer feeding. The problem with this explanation is that humpbacks at the onset of their winter singing season sing basically the same song they did six months before. The change occurs *during* the singing season. Moreover, recent evidence suggests that the old notion that feeding whales aren't singing ones may not be true. Scientists have recorded humpbacks singing in summer feeding grounds off Alaska, songs that are similar to but shorter than the ones they sing while wintering in Hawaii.

While scientists suspect that the humpback's song has something to do with breeding, its precise function is still a matter of conjecture. One theory is that, like some birds, insects, fish, amphibians, and mammals, humpbacks use a lek system for attracting mates. In such a system, the males gather together on the mating ground to display their wares—in the case of the humpback, their vocal abilities. The females come to look and choose a partner with whom to copulate, a strong, healthy male whose genes will serve her offspring well.

If humpback whales do, in fact, have a lek system, it may be that the quality of an individual's voice or the location from which he sings, is a deciding factor in whether a female allows him to mate with her. Perhaps only a healthy male can sing a long, complex song. The humpback's song, much like the male peacock's feathers, could be a secondary sexual characteristic to display male health and vigor. Female humpbacks over the centuries may have consistently chosen the males who sang the most elaborate songs. This, in turn, would create enormous incentive for all humpback males to produce their most complex and enticing songs. It would also create incentive for a male to copy his neigbor's song if he observed his neighbor doing a better job of attracting females. Imitation of successful males might explain why individuals tend to converge on the same song.

Dolphin Dialects
Even humans with tin ears can probably discriminate between

a Southern accent come north for the first time and the nasal twang of someone who has spent his or her life in Brooklyn, New York. The Bostonian asking for a frappe in an ice cream parlor away from home will undoubtedly end up having to explain that what he really wants is a milkshake. And in the bird world there are species whose trills and tweets differ from those of similar species who live across the world or even from relatives across town.

Human language is constantly evolving. As one language is on its way to becoming two or more languages, words are pronounced and used differently, and new words come into existence. But the same cannot be said for most mammals, whose vocalizations are generally the same for genetically similar populations, whether they live in the east or the west or somewhere in between.

Killer whales break the mold. These animals, the largest of all the dolphins, have their own dialects or distinct calls that are unique to each group. Even a group that lives "next door" to another will have its own accent, although many of the calls in the whales' repertoire will be similar.

In 1978, John K. B. Ford, research director of the Vancouver Aquarium, began what was intended to be a two-year study of the underwater communication of killer whales off the coasts of British Columbia and Washington State. What he found so amazed him that sixteen years later he is still listening in rapt attention, attempting to decipher a remarkable system of vocalizations in one of the most stable cetacean communities in the world.

Approximately 325 killer whales in this study area have been identified, 75 percent of whom are so-called residents, with the remainder referred to as transients. The focus of most studies has been on the former group.

The smallest social unit of killer whale society is the matrilineal group, which is made up of individuals, both male and female, related to a single living female and may contain up to four generations of a family. Then there is the subpod, comprising one or more matrilineal groups that always travel together. Finally comes the pod, which contains one or more subpods. Although they usually stay together, a subpod may separate from the pod for days or even months at a time. Sometimes a subpod will form a new pod as it gradually spends more time away from the pod, a process that usually evolves over years.

Resident pods often forage or travel with other pods in the same community. Along the British Columbia coast, there are two such communities. The northern one contains sixteen pods of whales and ranges from central Vancouver Island to southeast Alaska. The southern community has three pods and its domain includes the waters off southern Vancouver Island and Puget Sound in the state of Washington. Pods from the different communities don't interact.

Ford conducted his initial research from an island off northeastern Vancouver Island, following the northern pods in a small boat, collecting dozens of tapes, a vocal chronicle of killer whales going about their day-to-day activities. Then he moved to the waters off southern Vancouver Island to listen to the vocalizations of the southern pods.

The moment his hydrophone, lowered into the midst of a group of eighty whales, recorded the first note, Ford was struck by how different these whales sounded from their northern counterparts. Later, closely analyzing the tapes, he discovered that the discrepancies went beyond geography. Not only were the northern and southern groups vastly dissimilar but there were also noticeable differences within each community. Thus began the task of recording each separate pod to determine if, as Ford suspected, killer whale pods have their own dialects. Five years later, he could say with certainty that they do.

On average, killer whale pods, Ford found, emit about a dozen different types of what he called discrete calls. These calls typically are less than two seconds long and are variations of high pitched squeals and screams, rather like the squeak of a rusty hinge on a slammed door. Killer whales appear to use calls to coordinate group behavior and maintain contact with others. All whales within the pod emit most or all of the pod's call repertoire, and no call appeared to be used exclusively in one context. On the contrary, Ford heard all calls in the pod's repertoire whether the group was foraging, traveling, or socializing.

A killer whale calf is probably a member of a small group of mammals (including humpback whales and bottlenose dolphins) whose vocalization is learned rather than genetically determined. Studies have shown that a young killer whale, which rarely leaves its mother's side during the first year of life, probably learns to "speak" by mimicking the mother. The calf continues to live within its mother's group for its entire life, and as a result the call repertoire stays the same.

Ford found that several of the pods he studied had some shared calls, although the accent was noticeably different between pods. He called these similar vocal groups clans and theorized that they descended from a common ancestral pod. Years ago, the scientist speculated, a pod arrived on the coast, bringing its own unique set of calls. The pod eventually grew and slowly began to divide. As the new pods spent more time apart from the old, they developed their own call repertoires through the process known as cultural drift.

If this theory is true, pods with somewhat similar dialects probably split from the same group in more recent years, while those whose calls have little in common severed their ancestral ties in the distant past, perhaps, as Ford suspects, centuries ago.

What, if any, advantage there is to a distinct call dialect remains unknown. Pods typically travel with other pods, and some superpods of more than one hundred whales have been spotted. If calls are used to maintain contact with the group, in some situations having one's own dialect might serve a whale well. The dialect also may aid in breeding, enabling an animal to distinguish between a relative and an outsider.

Transients are definitely outsiders. After his study on the residents, Ford set out to record the transients, which travel farther, faster, and in smaller groups. He recorded transient pods from California, British Columbia, and Southeast

Alaska. The transient pods are usually silent as they stealthily try to sneak up on seals and whales, but they often call during or just after a kill. Ford found that transient pods have fewer calls than residents but the real shocker was his discovery that all transient pods shared at least one call type. If transient calls evolve the same way that resident calls do, then the transients belong to one community with a coastal range of more than two thousand miles!

As to whether a whale from one pod can communicate with one from another group, Ford believes that because pods from different clans so frequently interact, there must be some communication taking place. Individuals are no doubt able to identify others as members of a different pod on the basis of dialect. As to whether they can tell more than this, try this experiment. Turn the dial on your television set to one of the stations that broadcasts programs in another language, one that you understand not a word of. Watch for a moment and then ask yourself how the characters are feeling. Chances are that without understanding what they are saying, you can see their anger, excitement, happiness, or pain. Perhaps a killer whale communicating with another that speaks a "foreign language" nevertheless has a feel for the other's mood.

Do Dolphins Have a Natural Language?
There is little doubt that many dolphin species have a rich vocal repertoire of whistles, squeaks, pops, squawks, groans, clicks, and other sounds, many of which are used to pass on some general information to fellow dolphins, as well as to communicate mood. And the large-brained dolphins are clearly intelligent animals, probably among the most intelligent in the animal kingdom. Captive bottlenose dolphins have astounded researchers with their amazing talent for mimicry. One such dolphin was trained to mimic computer sounds. It wasn't unusual for the animal to hear a new sound only once and yet be able to reproduce it perfectly.

Yet despite widespread stories that celebrate the "talking" dolphin, there is no scientific evidence to support the conclusion that dolphins talk to each other the way we humans do. That is, they do not pass abstract information and ideas by using a language made up of word sequences, each with a specific meaning.

On the other hand, dolphins may be capable of one of the basic elements of language, using specific sounds to represent objects. Vervet monkeys have different alarm calls for aerial and terrestrial predators. A playback of an alarm call made in response to an eagle caused the monkeys to look up, while a playback of an alarm call made in response to a python caused the monkeys to look around on the ground. If dolphins do mimic each other's signature whistles, they may be capable of representing each other in the same way vervet monkeys represent different classes of predators.

In searching for a natural language in dolphins, scientists have attempted to analyze the informational content of dolphin vocalizations. Even if the code cannot be deciphered, it is assumed that if a language exists, there would be a diverse and varied number of vocalizations. But this is not thought to be the case. Dolphin vocalizations, while certainly varied, aren't thought to be any more so than those of other highly social mammals. But the jury is still out. One thing that quickly became clear when we recorded bottlenose dolphins in Shark Bay is that they make more kinds of pulsed vocalizations than we had suspected. The vocalizations of wild dolphins present a rich area for future research.

In one experiment, scientists sought to discover whether dolphins could create arbitrary symbols to represent new events or objects if a situation required them to do so. A reward of food for a male and a female bottlenose dolphin was contingent upon the transmission of information between the pair. The dolphins were housed in the same tank but separated by a net across the center and an opaque screen during training and testing. To receive their rewards, each dolphin had to select the correct paddle from a pair located in its half of the tank; both animals had to choose correctly for either to get food. The female was trained to press her paddle before the male pressed his. With the screen in place, the male had to rely on acoustic cues from the female's paddle press to time his response. The correct paddle was signaled by a cue light. If the light flashed, a response on the left paddle was correct; a steady light meant that the pair needed to press the right paddle. Initially, the male had a cue light on his side as well, but later that was withdrawn, leaving him dependent upon some form of vocal information from the female.

Those who designed the experiment speculated that such information would imply an ability to use vocalizations to indicate something as arbitrary as the state of the light, a sign that dolphins might have an open language system similar to humans.

In trial after trial, the male chose the correct paddle even though he could not see the cue light. The female, for her part, was heard to vocalize prior to most of the trials. At first it seemed that the female knowingly transmitted acoustic information to the male—in essence, that she developed symbols for transmission and understood the need to communicate the information, as well as its value to her and to the male.

Further studies, however, did not support this conclusion. The female's pretrial vocalizations persisted even after the visual screen was withdrawn and the male could see the cue light, and in fact, even when the male was removed from the tank. Moreover, when the paddled response required for each cue light was reversed, the animals became confused, as they did when researchers attempted to switch the animals' roles.

The scientists concluded that the dolphins' initial high performance was probably due to independent learning by each animal. The sender probably developed different postures during the vocalizations that tipped the receiver off.

There wasn't any evidence that the dolphins were using any natural language in their dealing with each other.

The undersea world of dolphins and whales, however visually limited, is an acoustical gold mine both for its inhabitants and for the humans equipped to eavesdrop on them.

Great strides have been made in recent years with the advent of better methods by which to track, identify, and listen to the sources of these myriad sounds. Perhaps with time and patience, scientists will be able to unearth more clues about what these creatures are saying and, more importantly, what it means.

5

The Social Lives of Whales and Dolphins

As strandings go, this one was not typical.

Thirty false killer whales had gathered in the shallow water along the shore of the Dry Tortugas, a small clump of islands off the Florida coast. Although many of the animals bore the bites of sharks as well as other lesions that are common in a whale's life, only one, a large male, was clearly sick. Blood oozed from his right ear as he lay on his side, with the rest of the group flanking him.

Mass strandings—the usually fatal phenomenon in which a group of whales swims onto a beach—are relatively rare, primarily affecting odontocetes such as pilot whales, sperm whales, pygmy sperm whales, false killer whales, and melon-headed whales. Theories abound as to why whales strand. In some mass strandings, scientists who have autopsied the whales' bodies have found brain lesions caused by a parasite in most of the victims. They speculate that such invaders adversely affect the whales' sense of balance or echolocating abilities, driving them ashore.

Other strandings have been attributed to entrapment caused by a change in tide. In such a scenario, the whales enter an estuary to feed, only to be trapped by sand bars that become evident when the tide ebbs. Slowly, the trapped water drains out of the tidepool, draining the life out of the trapped cetaceans.

Other whale strandings occur in different geographic conditions but also as a result of a retreating tide. Some speculate that since the whales most likely to strand are basically open-sea animals, when these species do venture close to the coastline, their ability to navigate may be confused by shallow sandbanks, an unfamiliar landscape, or magnetic anomalies. Some strandings are made in the pursuit of food, as sometimes occurs when a bottlenose dolphin or killer whale flings itself onto the beach, then slides back into the water, almost effortlessly. Yet when these species strand in a mass, they seem to forget how to slip back into the protective comfort of the sea and, like most stranded cetaceans, die.

But the false killer whales that stranded near Florida did not precisely fit any of these molds. True, the sick whale, when autopsied after his death, turned out to be hosting a large clan of nematodes, a parasitic worm. More than two hundred of the creatures had invaded his ears. There is some evidence that in certain species such infestation can impair an animal's echolocation, and interfere with its feeding. That explains how the whale may have come to rest in less than two feet of water, weak from near starvation, and no doubt in pain. But it does nothing to help us understand why his healthy companions had chosen to share his predicament.

Even more compelling is the fact that, unlike most strandings where the whales are actually beached, the false killers were still in water, albeit shallow. With the exception of the dying whale, the whales could have left at any time. Instead, they chose to stay, even though the sun was making their own wounds worse. Why?

Many people, among them scientists who witnessed the event, believe that the social bonds between the members of some groups are so strong that if one individual strands, the others follow. And it is interesting to note that most species that strand en masse, in fact, exhibit some of the most stable social bonds found in the cetacean world. The stranded pod may have been one large clan of close relatives; the bleeding male may have been an uncle or brother to many of the others. For these animals, family values permeate every aspect of their lives, from reproduction to feeding to the care of offspring. Survival itself may hinge on group solidarity. This dependence upon others may be so strong that even the risk of dangerous and often fatal events such as strandings may seem preferable to separating from one's companions. In short, the risk of dying with one's group may be a more palatable alternative than the risk of living alone.

It is impossible to know what was going through these animals' minds as they followed the ailing male toward the beach. They were certainly vocal, making an astonishing variety of sounds. One thing was clear: the others were not about to leave him.

For three days—until the whale died—the others pressed around him, moving closer with time, their noses pointing toward the beach. The wounds on the healthy animals' backs festered and grew in size as exposure took its toll. Observers rubbed suntan lotion on the whales' backs, a gesture that was met as benignly as that of a master stroking a kitten's fur. The only threat issued was by a mother who bared her formidable teeth when one of her would-be rescuers ventured too close to her infant.

Several times humans attempted to push the healthy animals back to sea, a monumental effort that proved futile. If a whale became separated from its group, it became agitated, calming only when it had returned to the group and could touch one of its own kind.

By the time the sick whale died, several of the others had left, probably the night before. The remaining whales broke ranks and, emitting high-pitched whistles, retreated to the life-sustaining deep water from which they had come.

The bonds that link the members of a whale or dolphin society together come in all strengths. Some relationships are fleeting, transitory occurrences that seem of little consequence. Other societies such as false killer whales, the species just described, pilot whales, and killer whales form cohesive groups that may endure over many years and, in some cases, possibly for a lifetime.

For the most part, odontocetes are highly social creatures, some in large stable groups, others in small. Even some baleen whales are showing more evidence of long-term social bonds than we had previously suspected. Membership in a group may mean feeding together, as well as joining together in the avoidance of or defense against predators. Males in a group may cooperate with each other to find mates; for females, group life may entail living with other females and infants in nursery schools.

Belonging to a social group has its rewards, but it also carries some costs. Your fellows may help you find food and avoid sharks, but they may also compete with you for mates or a favored food item, and pass along parasites. Yet the fact that individuals live in groups is testimony to their overiding importance, and incidents such as the false killer whale stranding tell us that group living in the ocean may have been taken to extremes not found on terra firma.

In this chapter we will look at the ways in which cetaceans group together, the reasons that life in a group may be advantageous, and some examples of such groups. Finally, we will examine altruistic behavior among dolphins and whales. When a dolphin can't swim, others may support it. When a whale has been harpooned, others stay close to the victim, circling and even swimming close to the capture vessel.

Though admirable, these behaviors are risky, and in the case of the harpooned whale, only served to get more animals killed during the days of active whaling. Why then do they do it?

Group Size

The groups in which a dolphin or whale moves are as diverse as the species themselves. Many of the large baleen whales are rarely seen in the company of more than one or two others, while some dolphins travel in schools containing hundreds of animals. Moreover, the size of a group or aggregation can vary depending upon the type of activity. Hundreds of bowhead whales may be spread out in a feeding area but groups that actually feed together in a coordinated fashion will number fewer than fifteen individuals.

Determining the size of cetacean groups is not easy for even the most highly trained humans. There are, of course, the obvious physical restraints. It is difficult to estimate a group's size when most of its members are underwater and may not choose to surface until they are too far away to be counted. Even when a whale is visible, looks can be deceiving. Some baleen species, for example, may not be sighted together and consquently not recognized as a group because the individuals are spread out over a several mile area. Yet the whales may be constantly calling to one another, maintaining contact even when separated. At the other end of the spectrum are the thousands of dolphins that may congregate where fish are plentiful. Which ones form part of a group, and how many groups are feeding? It is impossible to know.

Because of these variables, both between species and within a species itself, it is difficult to establish rules about group size. However, we can give you some general information as well as some insight into differences between mysticetes and odontocetes.

Mysticetes. If you are ever lucky enough to see a baleen whale, it will probably be traveling alone or with no more than four or five others. That doesn't mean, however, that it isn't part of a larger social group. If one definition of a group is "individuals who are in contact with one another," and in many species—at least some of the time—individuals may form part of an aggregation of tens or even hundreds of whales. These larger groups are especially prevalent on the feeding or mating grounds or often during migration between the two.

Typically, bowhead whales can be found feeding in groups of anywhere from two to ten, while gray whales migrate in groups ranging from five to fifty, with each group further subdivided into pairs of mothers and calves. Right whales normally are found in groups of up to twelve, while fin whale groups usually number no more than ten members.

Evidence suggests that most of these baleen groups are transient, with members coming and going, often never to be seen again with the same individuals. Until recently, we thought that the only close bonds in the baleen world were those between mother and calf, and that they lasted only until the youngster was able to live on its own. It now looks as if there may be more substantial bonds between adults of some species such as the humpback whale, but baleen societies do not seem to be organized into the structurally complex units of many of the odontocete species.

Odontocetes. Group size within the toothed whale species runs the gamut from the little known boto, a river dolphin that is observed alone or with a few individuals, to many of the pelagic or open-sea dolphins, which are often seen in groups of thousands. Again, like the baleen whales, such huge groups usually come together only for specific activities. The rest of the time groups generally number anywhere from five to one hundred animals. Some of the odontocetes form stable groups that may last a lifetime.

But group size can give us only limited information about cetacean societies, and sometimes it can be downright misleading. Societies are built upon individual social relationships, the bond between a mother and her infant, two sisters, or two cooperating males. As we have seen, the boto is thought to be relatively solitary. However, in Shark Bay a female bottlenose named Yan is also very solitary, but she still has a number of social relationships and forms part of a huge and complex society of more than three hundred and fifty individuals. Perhaps the *boto* lives in a more complex society than can possibly be revealed by our brief glimpses of nameless individuals.

Researchers began putting names to individual dolphins and whales in the early 1970s. By taking pictures of distinctive markings on fins and tails, biologists can build up a long-term record of individual association patterns. This is how we learn whether groups are fleeting aggregations of mating or feeding animals or stable entities that reflect long-term social bonds.

Once we find that individual dolphins or whales have stable associations, we want to know why. We want to discover the nature of cetacean social relationships. To accomplish this we need to watch and listen to the daily lives of individuals, to observe them as they feed, play, fight, and mate.

Around the world, scientists are peeking into the worlds of dolphin and whale societies. In Shark Bay we follow individual bottlenose dolphins in our small dinghies for up to ten hours at a time. We watch as groups join and incredible social interactions unfold. Such observations are priceless when it comes to learning about social behavior, but they cannot tell the whole story. For that, we have also come to rely upon DNA testing. The DNA in a bit of whale skin can tell us if two individuals are closely related or if a particular male fathered a female's infant. Tissue containing DNA can be collected from stranded animals, with small darts, or, in the case of sperm whales, from sloughed-off skin found floating in the water after a whale dives.

Before we learn more about cetacean societies, we will consider why whales and dolphins live in groups.

The Advantages of Life in a Group

While a solitary life may hold a certain allure for those of us weary of inching our way home along car-clogged freeways, we go on living among others despite all the inconveniences. Most cetaceans, like humans, are basically social animals who find more advantages than disadvantages to living within a group, no matter what the size.

For the whale or dolphin, membership in a group offers three possible advantages: it may be helpful to have friends for protection against predators; foraging may be easier in a group than singly; and the group may serve as a meeting place for males and fertile females.

Let's explore each one of these possible advantages.

Defense Against Predators. Probably the fundamental reason whales and dolphins form groups is the protection a group offers from predators. As we have seen, even the largest baleen whales can fall victim to the cunning of a hungry pack of killer whales. Some species of baleen such as right, bowhead, and gray whales have been seen forming a defensive circle, similar to the defensive posture used by some African plains ungulates such as the wildebeest. When under threat by killer whales, these species of baleens flail their formidable tails, pointed outward from the circle.

Until humans came along, river dolphins had it relatively easy, tucked safely away from the large predators that hunt the oceanic species. The minimal threat from predators in their murky environment may explain why river dolphins travel alone or in small groups.

Small dolphins that dwell in the ocean well know its perils, namely, sharks and killer whales. Schooling dolphins are alert to the slightest change in the environment, which is likely to cause the group to avoid the disturbance and tighten ranks. Nearshore waters may provide some respite from threat. Argentine dusky dolphins hide in the shallows when killer whales cruise by. Shallows are not always safe, however. In Shark Bay we saw a twelve-foot-long tiger shark cruising in water only three feet deep.

Caught in the seines set for yellowfin tuna, a group of Pacific spotted dolphins packed together into a disk-shaped group that moved as far away from any disturbance—motor and winch noises, nets, and swimmers—as it could. Mothers, calves, and young dolphins were segregated in the center of the group. As for the dolphins on the periphery, they moved about, diving, surfacing, full of activity, all of which served to keep the most vulnerable members of the society in the center, cushioned on all sides by the stronger animals.

The protection of the group is an important advantage for the cetacean mother and her calf. A sperm whale must dive to the ocean's depths to find squid yet her calf may not yet be capable of executing such a deep dive. A dilemma is born: the mother must find food, but a lone calf is an open invitation to a shark or killer whale. Perhaps that is where the "babysitter" comes in. Within the sperm's female group there are several close and long-term associates, some of whom are between pregnancies. These so-called aunts show a great deal of interest in the calf and may stay close to the mother-calf pair. When the mother is feeding, the calf remains under the watchful eye of the surrogate.

In many cetacean species, mother-calf pairs form nursery groups away from the males, who could pose a physical threat to the infants. Some unisex schools have been reported among narwhals, common dolphins in the Black Sea, and beluga whales, usually during migration.

In the society of killer whales, the males appear to protect the females and their calves. Scientists aboard a research vessel encountered a school of fifteen killer whales. Upon seeing the ship, the adult males positioned themselves on the outside of the school, presumably guarding the females and young in the center. The boat followed the killers for more than six hours, during which the males maintained their protective positions.

Hunting for Food. Many cetacean species travel in groups to find and capture food. Dusky dolphins feeding on schools of anchovies can feed for longer if more dolphins participate in herding the fish. Bernd Würsig of Texas A&M University suspects that dusky dolphins leap out of the water while in such feeding groups as a means of attracting others to the group and its activity.

The reason baleen whales travel alone or in small, widely dispersed groups may also be related to feeding. These whales have such enormous appetites that a single area could not begin to meet the food demands of a large group. Even among baleen whales such as the humpback, however, there is some evidence of group foraging.

One working hypothesis is that some of the prey that one whale misses will end up in the mouth of a neighbor whale. The corraling of large fish schools and pack-hunting are two other ways in which a small group may forage more effectively than a lone whale. (See Chapter 3, "The Endless Search for Food," page 49, for a more detailed explanation of group feeding patterns.)

In some primate species, groups defend food from other groups, and it is possible that some dolphins may cooperate to guard their food supply against others. Dolphins in Shark Bay sometimes go speeding toward a group that is feeding on a school of fish, only to pull up suddenly and just watch from twenty to thirty feet away. It looks as though they've somehow received the message that their presence is not welcomed.

Bringing the Sexes Together. The urge to mate may bring solitary cetaceans into a group or bring groups together into larger groups.

The more solitary baleen whales often have to travel hundreds or even thousands of miles to meet whales with whom to breed. These whales spend part of the year feeding, then they migrate to the breeding grounds. Like migrating birds, the whales appear to be faithful to the same grounds each year. On their breeding grounds in Hawaii, humpback whales often form groups of several males competing for a female.

A baleen whale that may be miles away from the closest of its kind will make low-frequency sounds that can be heard at distances of more than one hundred miles and may, some scientists suggest, serve to bring the whales together.

A male killer whale is unlikely to find many receptive females in his group because he is probably related to all of them. So sometimes pods of killer whales in British Columbia get together in big powwows called superpods where lots of social and sexual behavior takes place. Researchers have suggested that males may find opportunities to father offspring in these superpods.

Dealing with Friends and Foe

Whales and dolphins love to touch and be touched. At times it seems they can't keep their flippers to themselves. Touching, stroking, rubbing, even mounting another animal are all ways in which cetaceans maintain and strengthen their affiliative ties with one another.

One bottlenose dolphin may swim alongside another animal, pressing the length of its body against the other's pectoral fin. The rub may be brief, lasting three or four seconds, after which the dolphins part. Other times, though, there is a reciprocal arrangement, almost like our, "You scratch my back and I'll scratch yours." Then the animals take turns rubbing each other, an apparently enjoyable pastime that can go on for five minutes or more. In Shark Bay, one dolphin may swim right next to but slightly behind another, resting its pectoral fin against the other dolphin's side for minutes at a time.

Young whales may stroke one another with their genitals, swim belly to belly, or touch flippers in a manner reminiscent of young lovers holding hands. It isn't uncommon to see male bottlenose dolphins mounting each other. Such behavior is common and occurs in both reproductive and social contexts.

Not all cetacean touching, of course, is friendly. Like all creatures, whales and dolphins clash with even their closest associates. Head jerking, charging, tail slapping, tail swishing, pushing, shoving, and raking one's teeth over the object of one's displeasure are all signs that a cetacean has a score to settle. In captivity, killer whales and bottlenose dolphins have been known to punish their calves by holding them underwater, a behavior that has also been directed at their trainers on more than one occasion.

Vexed bottlenose dolphins in Shark Bay will line up head to head, squawking in a comical burst of highs and lows that brings Donald Duck to mind. Sometimes these verbal in-

Dolphins engage in lots of social sex. Here, one dolphin pushes another along by placing its beak in the other's genital slit.

sults escalate into a brawl, but often it seems that the dolphins squawk themselves out and go their separate ways. Bottlenose dolphins also scream, growl, and even bray like donkeys when they are miffed. A head-jerk will often be accompanied by a loud crack that sounds like a rifle shot. One humpback whale actually screamed as it charged a research vessel, and the male's song, while attractive to females, may communicate "get lost" to other males.

The most serious aggression in whales involves hitting with the tail; some dolphins will ram an adversary. Dolphins in captivity have killed each other by hitting and ramming. Even in killer whale skirmishes, hitting may be more dangerous than biting. In a lethal battle between two killers at Sea World, the fatal blow was delivered by the tail.

Sex can be used to express friendship or aggression in dolphins. A Shark Bay male bottlenose dolphin may mount his buddy in a relaxed friendly manner, after which they will change positions. Or sexual behavior may occur in an aggressive context, with one alliance herding, harassing, and mounting the other. Less often, we see females mount each other in social circumstances.

Male bottlenose dolphins "fence" with their penises in Sarasota Bay. Groups of young and old male killer whales engage in rough-and-tumble play, which includes erections. Courtship behavior has been observed in all-male groups of gray whales along their migration route.

If social animals are going to live together, they need a way to communicate status. Even if you are a dominant individual, it would be very costly to have to prove the point every time you encounter a subordinate. With five years' experience of watching baboons in Kenya, Amy Samuels set out to learn how bottlenose dolphins communicate status. At the Brookfield Zoo in Chicago, she spent endless hours videotaping the minutest details of dolphin social life and found that status communication was often subtle, and was more reliably communicated by the submissive individual. When a dominant dolphin came cruising by, the subordinate dolphin would flinch or flee. Male dolphins were always dominant to females. A female's place among females was fairly stable and rarely an issue, unlike the relationship between the two males, who often reversed their status after periods of intense rivalry.

Predators and Parasites

The dolphin you see from a distance may appear a picture of grace and perfection as its streamlined body torpedoes through the water. But looks can be deceiving. Up close, that same dolphin's body may be cruelly decorated with a vast assortment of scars, tooth rakes, wounds, and skin lesions. And these visible markings don't begin to tell the whole story, for a host of worms and other microscopic parasites may be nesting within the dolphin's tissues.

Like all creatures, dolphins and whales are susceptible to a wide variety of tormentors. Although many may be minuscule in size, their impact is greatly felt as they burrow within the cetacean body, attacking, impairing its function. Others like the shark, a dangerous predator, leave their mark in a more obvious manner, tearing mouthfuls of flesh from their victims.

Birds have succeeded in making life miserable for more than one whale. Sea birds often land on whales' backs and peck at the crabs, shellfish, and other small hitchhikers attached to it. A whale with a gull on its back is not a happy whale. Often the animal's back is sunburned and beginning to peel and its bird rider begins to peel the layers of skin like an onion, gouging with its beak into the delicate deeper layers. If a whale could literally be driven crazy, this might do it.

Probably the most visible parasites are the species of barnacles that encircle the heads of some whales like a wreath. Ironically, these readily apparent parasites, unlike many others that can't be seen, do not appear to cause any infection or inflammation in their host; they simply hitch a ride and filter food from the water. Typically, the barnacles adhere to the skin around the head, flippers, and tail flukes. Many of the large whales such as the humpback, gray, right whales, and occasionally sperms are often seen swimming with large colonies of barnacles covering their heads.

The faster-moving whales and dolphins usually are less susceptible to barnacles. Some barnacles reach their peak density in cold water and drop off as the animal moves into the tropics. By the time a humpback leaves its polar feeding grounds it may be wearing as much as half a ton of barnacles. If having an armor of barnacles helps whales in aggressive interactions, then their relationship may be more mutualistic than parasitic.

All kinds of other external parasites prey on dolphins and whales. Whale lice feed upon cetacean skin and a large parasitic crustacean called *Pennella* anchors itself into the whale's blubber, its protruding abdomen hanging down from the skin. Many of the baleen whales who summer in polar waters acquire a thin yellow-green covering of diatoms, a minnute kind of algae. These parasites certainly don't enhance a whale's beauty, but apart from a little local irritation, they don't appear to pose a major health hazard.

The same cannot be said for some internal parasites. Some of the tapeworms that inhabit the stomach and intestines of both baleen and toothed whales may reach a length of more than forty-five feet. Some species of lung nematodes (worms) are associated with pneumonia, a common cause of death. One sperm whale's stomach contained one hundred ten pounds of nematodes. And a species of flatflukes that invades the brain has been known to cause brain lesions. Parasites also have been found to colonize the mammary glands of some dolphin species, in severe cases even impairing the female's ability to produce milk.

How detrimental are these parasites? Post-mortems on stranded dolphins and whales along the Washington and Oregon coasts revealed bacterial infections and parasitism to be important causes of death, each accounting for about a quarter of the dead animals examined. In one study scientists found that one worm parasite, *Crassicauda*, was responsible for 10 percent of spotted dolphin deaths. And another scientist found that eighty-two out of a study population of eighty-seven fin whales were carrying this same parasite; those with severe infections would probably die of renal failure, he concluded.

At least two fish are occasional parasites on dolphins and whales. Remoras hitchhike on the bellies of whales and dolphins. The most acrobatic dolphins are spinners, whose midair twirls have long amazed and puzzled scientists. Why do they spin? A close look at photographs of spinning spinners often reveals a remora being flung off. Spinning may be the best way for the dolphins to rid themselves of these uninvited guests.

A much nastier parasitic fish, the cookie-cutter shark, is a nightmare come true for spinners and many other warm-water dolphins. Rather slow and not quite two feet long, this shark doesn't look very threatening. But looks can be deceiving. As its name suggests, this shark's specially adapted mouth enables it to form a vacuum against the side of a whale or dolphin. As the shark closes its mouth, a line of razor-sharp teeth in its lower jaw scoop out a silver dollar-sized disk of flesh from its unfortunate victim. Some tropical dolphins have several scars from attacks by cookie-cutters.

If it isn't bad enough having to contend with a plethora of parasites, dolphins and whales are also vulnerable to some predators. Granted, given the size of most cetaceans, their predators are few. The hunting methods of killer whales were explored earlier, and they probably apply to pygmy and false killers also. That leaves sharks.

Fishermen along the coast of Florida call dolphins and sharks the dogs and cats of the sea and tell many a tale of battles between the two animals. Sometimes the dolphins win, as in an eyewitness account of an incident in the Gulf of Mexico when bottlenose dolphins were seen beating a shark with their snouts with such force that the shark shot from the water. If dolphins attack sharks, it is only because sharks are their worst enemy.

Actual observations of contests between cetaceans and sharks are limited. But if one examines a group of dolphins, judging by the number of scars from healed shark bites, it appears that the shark threat is a very real one.

Great white sharks, bull sharks, and tiger sharks are often implicated in attacks on dolphins. Some of the wounds are massive. One freshly healed shark bite described by researchers was ten inches by ten inches on a slightly over six-foot-long bottlenose dolphin. In one study, between 3 and 18 percent of the cetaceans examined showed evidence of having survived a shark attack.

Scientists are able to determine the source of the scars by examining the size and shape of the laceration. In Sarasota, 20 percent of the bottlenose dolphins examined had shark-bite scars, while in Moreton Bay, Queensland, 37 percent of 334 dolphins bore the marks of sharks. And these are the ones that got away. Dead sharks are frequently found with the remains of dolphins in their stomachs.

Like most predators, a shark may be more likely to go after the young or weak. Sharks undoubtedly claim a fair number of newborn cetaceans. Mothers also are at greater risk, presumably because they are protecting the calf. Of twenty-one dolphins with fresh shark bites, an observer noted that five were females with young calves.

A shark searching for its next meal may use a "bite and spit" method of attack. After it injures its prey, the shark retreats a short distance away, waiting for the victim to bleed to death or lapse into a state of shock. Then it moves in to eat. Other sharks just rip and tear, grabbing the victim and shaking it like a dog shakes a bone.

Living with One's Group

Females form the core of most mammal societies. Saddled with the chores of parental care, their major concern is to find food for themselves and their offspring. Females often form groups with their female relatives to aid in foraging and in protection against predators.

Males, on the other hand, devote their energies to finding and competing for mates. With the exception of killer and pilot whales, most male cetaceans leave home, because their female relatives are not viable mating partners. A male's mother may boot him out anyway, rather than have him continue to pilfer her precious food supply. In only a small minority of mammals are things reversed, with males staying at home and females dispersing. Chimpanzees are an example of such a male-bonded community. Related males defend the community range from other males while females disperse to neighboring communities.

Any mother who has ever lamented her empty nest should have been born either a killer or pilot whale. Both male and female pilot and killer whales stay with their mother's group throughout her life. Matings probably occur when a number of pods get together.

As for the pilot whales, generations of related individuals live together in pods that may contain as many as one hundred animals. Pilot whales are one species prone to stranding en masse, a fate that, at least in part, is probably related to the pod's cohesiveness. The not-quite-stranded false killers that we met at the beginning of this chapter are closely related to pilot and killer whales and may have a similar social system.

While killer whales and pilot whales have no counterpart on land, other cetacean societies show intriguing similarities to those of some land dwellers. Consider the sperm whale. Male sperms typically leave their mothers after several years to form bachelor groups with other young males. The young males slowly move into higher latitudes, returning to the tropical waters inhabited by females and their young only when they are mature and ready to breed, typically at about the age of twenty-seven. The big males roam among female groups, apparently seeking opportunities to mate. The females, on the other hand, spend their lives with other females and their calves. In a four-year study of sperms off the Galapagos Islands, researchers found that females lived in stable groups of around thirteen individuals. These stable groups may well be related females and their calves, which would explain why females in the same group tend to be similar in appearance. So stable are these associations that four pairs of female sperms marked in the North Pacific were still together when they were killed up to ten years later. Female groups form temporary, casual foraging associations with other similar groups, so you usually find groups of around twenty whales.

This description of sperm whales will strike a familiar chord with anyone who has watched elephants. Female elephants also live with other females. They travel in groups of closely related females but sometimes interact with more distantly related female groups. Males often associate in bachelor groups. Solitary male elephants, like sperm males, roam from group to group, seeking females in estrus.

Some dolphins such as the bottlenose, humpback, and dusky dolphin live in fission-fusion societies similar to those of chimpanzees and spider monkeys. This is a fluid system in which the size and membership of groups may vary from day to day or hour to hour, with some members coming while others are going. Never are all the members of the group together at one time. This is not to say that stable relationships are not formed in such a society. Often there are long-term associations between particular individuals. Mothers and their offspring, of course, may remain together for many years. Males in some dolphin societies have been known to form close ties with one or two other males. Females, too, may have a network of female associates. Other small cetaceans such as the harbor and finless porpoises usually are found in small groups of fewer than ten animals. Perhaps they live in fission-fusion societies also; we won't know until some enterprising young researcher sets his or her mind to discovering the answer.

Now let's look in more detail at two cetacean societies, one baleen whale and one odontocete, that have been studied in more detail than any other.

Humpback Males: Singers and Sluggers

When you see a group of humpback whales together, it is a safe bet they are breeding or feeding. Humpback whales on their feeding grounds feed in small groups, usually of three or fewer, although larger groups have been sighted. As with most baleen whales, the small groups may be related to the large amounts of prey required by each whale.

Females, the more sociable of the sexes, usually feed with at least one other animal of either sex—whether juvenile or mature it doesn't appear to matter. Adult males, on the other hand, are more frequently found alone. When they are in the company of other whales, those individuals are generally two or more females. In the event that two males happen to frequent the same place at the same time, it appears their tolerance of each other is low; they usually swim their separate ways within ten minutes. Mason Weinrich, who studies humpbacks on Stellwaggen Bank off the coast of Massachusetts, speculates that males may be so antagonistic toward one another on the breeding grounds that this hostile relationship carries over, causing them to avoid each other whenever possible. Group feeding is thought to be a cooperative affair, and you don't want to help the competition.

The females' lack of sexual competition may account for their more gregarious nature. Recent studies have shown that females with calves may have some relatively stable relationships with other adults, most of which are formed during pregnancy, a factor that may be related to the whale's need to optimize its foraging through cooperation. In the Gulf of Maine, for example, some female associations have been known to last as long as seventy-nine days and may recur year after year. Weinrich points out that, although we don't see the strong, consistent bonds that typify many odontocete societies, humpbacks may still have long-term social relationships with many other individuals.

When the humpbacks leave their feeding grounds they migrate thousands of miles to the tropics. There, in warm, sunlit island waters, they court and mate. Females who are in the tropics to mate don't seem to linger. They are rarely resighted more than once and, once pregnant, are among the first to begin the journey to the high-latitude summer feeding grounds. Males probably remain as long as there are opportunities to mate with more females.

Singing males are loners and usually keep at least three miles between themselves and neighboring crooners. Singing is probably a strategy to attract a mate and, like some bird songs, may be the way a male advertises his health and vigor to interested females. Possibly because there are fewer fertile females left to respond, males sing for longer periods as the breeding season progresses.

On the breeding grounds, whales may be found in groups of up to fifteen adults. It is the structure, however, and not the size of such groups that is interesting. In a study of two separate populations of humpbacks that winter in the Caribbean and off Hawaii, researchers found that in each group one humpback, a fertile female, was the nuclear animal around which the others moved. One male, the so-called principal escort, swam close to the female, who sometimes was with a calf. Other males, known as secondary escorts, maintained positions around the couple.

Now and then a secondary escort would make a move toward the female. The female appeared blasé, but her consort was anything but. He raced into position, throwing his body between the female and the male challenger, who turned, lunged, thrashed, and dived, apparently all in an attempt to oust the principal male from his post. Fighting males will violently beat each other with their huge flukes. Even when a challenge was not evident, the atmosphere was tense. Often the principal male would blow a stream of bubbles, a transparent curtain between his prize and those who sought to capture it.

Clearly, being an escort takes its toll. Observers noted that it wasn't long before the competing males' dorsal fins and heads became abraded and bloody. The nuclear animal, on the other hand, seemed to be untouched.

The road to victory is not without its roadblocks, however. A challenge lasted anywhere from thirty seconds to ten minutes. Some whales needed only one challenge to win the position closest to the female; one animal made ten attempts to unseat the reigning principal, all of them unsuccessful. In some instances, larger whales replaced smaller ones; in others, the opposite was true. Stamina more than size appeared to decide the battle's outcome.

A defeated challenger simply resumed his place in the formation. But in ten cases where the principal escort was replaced, seven losers left the group within forty-five minutes.

Sometimes the defeated humpbacks went off alone and started singing.

Humpbacks moved in and out of groups readily. Large groups in particular rarely maintained a stable membership for more than one hour. Singing male humpbacks, whose songs are thought to be related to reproduction, often broke off their song to join a group. Singers evidently scrap their sing-and-wait strategy to compete for any mating opportunity at hand. Moreover, the addition of an ex-singer to a group acted like a magnet, pulling more whales in.

While males escorting a female don't sing, the groups are noisy affairs. Peter Tyack, of the Woods Hole Oceanographic Institute, wondered what would happen if he recorded one of these mating groups and played the sounds back to a singer. He found out when thirty tons of humpback whale came charging at his boat. Fortunately, the whale veered off, leaving the startled researchers bouncing in its wake.

Although there were often other groups of humpbacks in the area, most of the time there was little contact between groups. One exception was the sole escort to a mother-calf pair who defected to join a group that already contained three escorts. It soon became clear to those watching the whales that all females were not considered equal. Presumably, a female humpback's attractiveness is a function of where she is in her reproductive cycle.

As to the end result of all this effort, it is clear that all the males were anxious to mate with the female. Although no one has ever seen humpbacks mating, scientists believe that by being a principal or lone escort to a female, the male enhances his chances of copulating with her.

The Dolphins of Shark Bay

Thousands of visitors every year go out of their way to journey to Monkey Mia campground, an obscure outpost near Shark Bay in Western Australia, and, until recently, the only place in the world where an ordinary person can have the thrill of feeding a fish to a wild bottlenose dolphin. The dolphins swim into the shallows, delighting an awed crowd of tourists, many of whom wade out to feed and stroke the animals. Parents who wouldn't think of letting their toddler near an unknown dog, help hold tiny hands out to pat the dolphins' smooth skin as they maneuver between the endless pairs of legs. It isn't difficult to see how these creatures, with their mouths frozen in what appears to be a continuous state of mirth, could make even the most cautious forget that they are neither cute nor cuddly playthings but wild animals, probably among the most intelligent in the world.

On the contrary, as those of us who arrived in Shark Bay in 1982 would later discover, however good-natured these bottlenose dolphins, they are also devious, clever, and yes, even brutal in their dealings with other dolphins. Male dolphins travel in pairs or triplets (first-order alliance), herd females, and are not above enlisting the aid of another male alliance to form a second-order alliance, for the purpose of snatching a herded female from a rival group or protecting a fertile female that the alliance currently holds.

In the early 1980s, when our team began what would prove to be the most detailed study of cetacean social relationships to date, we knew little about the social lives of wild dolphins. Several pioneers had shed light on the social architecture of a few coastal species by boating from group to group and recording who was swimming with who. In Sarasota, Florida, Randy Wells and his colleagues were assembling a detailed picture of bottlenose dolphin society. Recording the composition of groups provides a snapshot of dolphin society, but to really understand social relationships you need a film to study. The clear waters of Shark Bay and the tameness of its dolphins allowed us to get that film, by following individual dolphins for hours on end. Of the social dramas revealed to us over the next few years, none were as complex and fascinating as the alliances forged by the male dolphins of Shark Bay.

We had long wondered why males formed such strong bonds with one or two other males, traveling, foraging, and socializing together. Three males called Snubby, Sickle, and Bibi provided the first clue one day when they swam near the shore escorting a stranger. The newcomer, a female with a small infant, suddenly bolted away from the trio, with the males in hot pursuit. After much splashing and thrashing, the female returned near shore with the males, only to try her escape again a moment later. The males gave chase a second time and brought her back, flanking her like guards around a prisoner.

During more than two years of observation, we found that the males often threaten a herded female by emitting a loud popping sound. Pops mean "stay close" and are backed up with overt aggression such as hitting and biting.

Herding begins when the males rush up to a female. Then the chase begins and it can cover more than a mile. In one record chase, the female eluded her captors for eighty-five minutes in a fast-moving pursuit that spanned almost five miles. The males often engage in displays around the female that may involve aerial feats such as leaping from the water in opposite directions. We don't know whether they are trying to impress their captive or each other. Females sometimes try to escape from the males by bolting away from them at full speed. Sometimes the males may not follow the escaping female, but often they do. Females successfully get away about 25 percent of the time.

Lest you think that all dolphins are like the much beloved Flipper who warmed the hearts of a generation of television viewers, consider these animals in pursuit of an elusive female. There is nothing gentle or sentimental about them; they can be downright mean, chasing, hitting, charging, biting, and slamming into a female who doesn't cooperate. Those who have observed the dolphins in action acknowledge that from the way things look and sound, the recipient of this attention is probably not having a good time; many a female has emerged from such a chase sporting a fresh collection of tooth-rake marks.

What happens after a female is herded by a male alliance is open to speculation. Presumably, male dolphins, like several other animal species, herd in order to copulate with a fertile female, a relatively rare prize since female bottlenose dolphins give birth only once every four or five years. It is difficult to observe these wild animals mating, so we can't say with certainty that the end result of herding is copulation. Do the males force the herded female to copulate with one or more of them? If not, then do herded females mate with the males because they are prevented from mating with those whom they might prefer? Perhaps the female wants to mate with *all* the males available, and herding is an attempt to monopolize her. And, if the purpose of herding is reproductive success, why in several instances have males been observed herding females who were not fertile, such as those in the latter stages of pregnancy? These are intriguing questions that as yet have no answers.

One major difference between these herding male dolphins and other mammals is that for the latter herding is thought to be a strategy used by a single male to increase his chance of being the one to impregnate a female. What makes the Shark Bay dolphins' behavior so unusual is their group approach. We don't know why males work together to herd females or how each individual benefits from the association. It may be a matter of practicality: a single male may not be capable of herding a similar-sized female who is equally capable of fancy maneuvering in the three-dimensional aquatic world. Or a lone male attempting to herd may not stand a chance against male alliances who are on the prowl, waiting to snatch a female from a weaker adversary.

The formation of gangs is not uncommon in the animal world. Several primate species including chimpanzees and baboons have been known to band with others to attack an enemy camp. What is unique about the Shark Bay male alliances is their solicitation of other male alliances to attack yet a third group. Sometimes these skirmishes have become major battles that drag on for more than an hour, as one alliance and its ally attacks another group, which is then defended by yet a fourth alliance.

For those of us involved in the Shark Bay project, August 19, 1987, stands out as the exciting day we discovered the "alliances of alliances." Snubby, Sickle, and Bibi were herding one of the tame females, Holey-fin, when a rival alliance,

Trips and Bite, minus their usual partner Cetus, paid a visit to Monkey Mia. That was unusual enough in itself, so we expected fireworks immediately. But nothing happened. Trips and Bite just looked on as Snubby, Sickle, and Bibi continued their excited displays around Holey-fin, then left. We followed.

Nearly a mile offshore, they had joined up with their buddy Cetus, in addition to Real Notch and Hi, who were archenemies of Snubby, Sickle, and Bibi. Real Notch and Hi were already herding the female Munch, but that evidently wasn't enough to keep them out of a good fight with the males of Monkey Mia. Toward the park the two alliances traveled, and there, in front of startled tourists, they attacked and captured Holey-fin from their archrivals. It was a scene of pure chaos, with dolphins charging all around the small boats moored by the park. When the exuberant victors emerged from the park shallows with Holey-fin, Snubby, Sickle, and Bibi charged up from behind in a tight group as though they were determined to press the issue. But their bravery was a façade. All the others had to do was turn around—and Snubby, Sickle, and Bibi beat a path the other way. Outnumbered five to three, they were excited but not stupid.

Given such a society, it isn't surprising that male alliances spend so much time engaged in friendly discourse with other alliances; in this world it pays to cultivate friends. During mating season in particular, it is common to see two friendly alliances shadowing each other as one or both herd a female. When one changes course, so does the other.

Of course, in the world of the Shark Bay males, these second order alliances can shift as quickly as the wind and the subject of yesterday's aggression may today be more useful as a friend. On a different occasion we saw Real Notch and Hi, in the company of Chop, Bottomhook, and Lambda, turn on their former allies Trips, Bite, and Cetus. So much for friendship.

Social Relationships Among Female Dolphins. A female bottlenose dolphin's association with other females appears unfettered by hard-and-fast rules. Take Yogi, a Shark Bay female. Yogi is a loner who rarely has anything to do with

other adults. Square, on the other hand, has stable relationships with several females. Uhf was a social butterfly,
associating with a wide variety of her neighbors, both before
she gave birth to a calf and then again after the infant died.
But during the two years in between when she was nursing,
she was more of a recluse.

While we have made considerable headway in understanding how males relate to one another at Shark Bay, female
associations remain a puzzle.

One reason it may be harder to understand the relationships females have with each other is that, in contrast to
the males, association patterns between females are inconsis-
tent. Age, the female's reproductive cycle, the status of the
female's mother, and her circle of kin all may influence her relationships with other females.

In general, female dolphins, both at Shark Bay and in
the waters off Sarasota, Florida, tend to associate with other females, if they socialize at all. These relationships are nowhere
near as consistent, though, as the male alliances discussed in
the previous section. Scientists studying the Sarasota dolphins
found that up to three generations of female dolphins swim
together in loosely associated bands. However, genetic analyses
indicate that some females swimming in the same social band
are not closely related. While a similar study has not been
done at Shark Bay, researchers know of two mothers and
daughters who remained close after the daughters grew up.

A social female dolphin tends to form a network of associates, in which a female is connected to many other females
in the network by a chain of consistent associates. Thus,
Dolphin A associates with Dolphin B who associates with
Dolphin C, but A does not associate with C.

One possible benefit of such associations between females has been observed a few times when a female is being
harassed by an alliance of males. Two other females have been
seen "hiding" the victim from the herding males. We observed
more overt cooperation when the male alliance Wave and
Shave swam up to a group and began chasing a female with a
small calf. A half-mile into the chase, they all turned sharply as

another group came charging up, and suddenly the pursuers were being pursued. Wave and Shave gave up the chase and found themselves surrounded by six females. Even if they are unable to chase off the males, females sometimes offer support by allowing a harassed female to rest a flipper against their side.

Cooperative and Helping Behavior

Dolphins have a reputation for being cooperative and altruistic, second only to our own kind. Everybody has heard stories of dolphins helping their sick or wounded fellows to the surface, or pushing drowning people to the shore. But before we talk about such behavior in dolphins we need to understand what we mean by cooperation and altruism and how such behavior can evolve.

Two dolphins cooperate to chase a school of fish. The fish, attempting to avoid the dolphins, cooperate by synchronizing their movements. In both of these cases, individuals cooperate to eat better or better avoid being eaten. The evolution of this kind of cooperative behavior is easy to understand. An individual who doesn't cooperate loses out; a fish that leaves the school becomes an immediate target for one of the dolphins.

Now consider some different behaviors. A sperm whale pulls a harpoon out of one of her schoolmates. A Belding's ground squirrel gives an alarm call to warn her neighbors of an approaching badger. A stranger bolts into a burning building to rescue a small child.

These are examples of altruism. The altruist in each case suffers a cost or takes a risk: the alarm-calling squirrel might get caught by the badger, the stranger might die in the burning house. It would be nice to believe that creatures perform acts of kindness because they are the right things to do. But evolution doesn't tolerate animals taking such risks unless there is a genetic profit to be had. Biologists have developed several theories to explain how altruism in humans and animals can evolve.

Kinship or Nepotism. A famous biologist once remarked that he would give his life for two brothers or eight cousins. He realized that the chance that any one of his genes is present in his brother is one half but there is only an eighth of a chance that it will be present in his cousin. This is the mathematics of nepotism. Evolution has shaped animals to behave altruistically toward their relatives according to how costly the act is, how much the relative will benefit, and how closely related they are. Nepotism is found all over the animal kingdom. The ground squirrel, it turns out, calls her alarm because her female relatives live around her. The risk to herself is outweighed by the benefit her kin receive from the warning.

Exchanging Favors. Relationships based on reciprocal altruism are mutually beneficial. The friendships we enjoy are usually based on reciprocity. You lend your friend your car today, she lends you money next week. But reciprocal altruism is vulnerable to cheaters. If your friend wrecks your car and doesn't pay you for the damage, you've lost out. This problem of cheating means that reciprocal altruism can only evolve when there are stringent checks and balances—when we are constantly monitoring our relationships and carefully examining our exchanges with others to make sure we are not getting the short end of the stick. Unless other animals have the smarts or some other way to check cheaters at the gate, reciprocal altruism can't work.

Reciprocal altruism is, at best, considered rare in animals. More common are cases that look like reciprocity but aren't. Sometimes animals benefit each other incidentally. A bird who startles and flies off when a cat approaches has inadvertently informed its neighbors that a predator is nearby. Now, if a bird spies a snake crawling up toward a neighbor's nest, it might behoove it to warn the other bird. If it doesn't, and the neighbor gets eaten, our selfish bird will be more vulnerable the next time the cat comes around.

Socially Enforced Altruism. Human friendships don't occur in a vacuum. If your friend wrecks your car and does not make restitution, it's a good bet the news will travel fast, making it nearly impossible for this cheater to borrow a car or anything else in the future. We are all concerned about our reputation. That concern may motivate us to perform altruistic acts even when the recipient can't reciprocate. Society may demand it. Imagine for instance, a selfish man who walked by a burning house with children trapped inside and did nothing. Our man didn't run inside to save them, nor did he even bother to call the fire department. He just kept on walking, minding his own business. How would society view such a person? Not very well.

This is not to say that we are conscious of our motivations or sit around calculating when we should do this or that (although sometimes we are and sometimes we do). Simply, evolution has shaped our emotions to motivate us to behave altruistically under the culturally appropriate circumstances, and to indignantly punish or criticize those whom we catch cheating.

What about altruism in dolphins? Their altruism comes in many forms. Dolphins have been known to help a mother during birth by removing her stillborn calf or the afterbirth. At Florida's Marineland, a pilot whale removed the placenta from a Pacific whitesided dolphin (dolphins don't eat the placenta like some mammals). And one well-intentioned captive roughtooth dolphin pulled a hypodermic needle out of a tankmate who was undergoing medical treatment and became aggressive toward the veterinarian.

Whales and dolphins have also been observed throwing themselves into a confrontation between an animal on the verge of capture and whaling or fishing boats. The intervening cetacean will attempt to bite and attack the boat with its body, while trying to push the victim away from the threat.

A more passive form of support involves standing by a whale that is fighting capture. Cases have been reported where the animal under siege belonged to a different species than those who stood by it, literally to the end. In one such instance, a group of Pacific striped dolphins stood by a Pacific pilot whale even after she was taken aboard the ship.

Cetaceans have frequently been seen supporting a distressed schoolmate to the surface. The helping animal positions itself beneath the sick one, holding it upward so that it doesn't drown. The supporting whale or dolphin in the midst of such a task neglects its own need to feed, leaving only for a few moments at a time in order to breathe itself. This supportive behavior ends only when the sick animal is able to take care of itself or dies.

Where does dolphin altruism fit into our scheme? Let's consider the possibilities.

Cooperation. We have already encountered fascinating examples of dolphin cooperation in the killer whales that washed the seal off of the ice floe with a wave of their own making, and in cooperative fishing by dolphins. Male bottlenose dolphins in Shark Bay probably join in herding females because they can't do it as well by themselves.

Kinship. Altruism directed toward kin other than offspring is probably common in dolphins and perhaps even baleen whales. As we know, groups of female sperm whales and groups of male and female killer and pilot whales are all made up of relatives. A probable case of nepotism in killer whales was reported by Juan Carlos Lopez from the Patagonian coast of Argentina. Adult male killers apparently teach youngsters how to catch seals on the beach. The males have not only been observed charging the beach with a toddler in tow, but actually tossing a seal they caught to their trainee. Female bottlenose dolphins spend a lot of time with their relatives and some male alliances may be made up of relatives. In Shark Bay older siblings often play with and babysit youngsters.

Reciprocal Altruism. Given that all of the observations of dolphin altruism are anecdotal, we have not yet determined whether dolphins engage in reciprocal altruism.

The puzzle to be explained is dolphins' unusual penchant for behaving altruistically toward members of other species and genera. Although claims of altruism toward humans are often made, we are aware of only two cases that may fit the bill and were observed by biologists. Those false killer whales who were almost stranded in Florida exhibited some interesting behavior toward biologist James Porter. When he

*An Amazon river dolphin in distress is helped
to the surface by its mates.*

entered the water with a snorkel, the flanking whale broke
away from the group and pushed him toward the beach.
Astonished, he tried it again, three times on each side of the
group, and every time the flanking whale broke away and
pushed him toward shore. When he swam without the snorkel,
however, the whales did not respond. Did the snorkle sound as
though he had a clogged blowhole and was in need of help?
Or did the sound simply irritate the whales, so they were encouraging him to leave?

National Geographic photographer Flip Nicklin was taking pictures of false killer whales off Hawaii when one swam
up to him with a large mahi-mahi in its mouth. It let the fish
go in Nicklin's face and backed away. The photographer, surprised as you might imagine, accepted the fish, but gave it
back to the whale, who then swam off.

Some scientists have tried to explain these anomalous
behaviors as automatic, instinctive, stereotyped responses to
distress signals. This explanation could work if the animals
spent their entire life surrounded by close relatives. But that is
not always the case. Nor does it explain why one species would

exhibit such behavior with another. These behaviors were not stereotyped; rather, the animals appeared to be able to improvise, adapting their actions to meet the needs of the occasion. Consider the case of a pilot whale that had been shot by men aboard a ship. The dead animal drifted toward the ship but when it was just a few feet away, two other pilots suddenly appeared on either side of the body. Pressing their snouts on top of the dead whale's head, the whales dragged the body under the surface, away from the ship—never to be seen again. This was not typical supportive behavior but rather the opposite, in which the animals apparently improvised in response to a specific situation.

Most of the cases of interspecies dolphin altruism are from captive situations. Are they simply misplaced bonds, the sort you get when a cat who loses her litter attempts to mother puppies? What, then, do we make of the whales' odd behavior toward James Porter? Even more puzzling is the way they behaved to the bleeding male. Even if he were a relative upon whom they were dependent and to whom they owed a bushel of favors, how could their continued association be worth the grave risk of stranding? As much as anything, observations such as Porter's tell us that we have a lot to learn about dolphin and whale societies.

One thing those of us who study dolphins *have* learned is that despite their penchant for violence, dolphins can be remarkably restrained. That much is obvious when you see the poking and pawing they put up with every day from well-intentioned tourists at Monkey Mia. These dolphins are accustomed to humans who are too excited to observe proper etiquette. But what of dolphins that have had no close contact with people before?

About a mile from Monkey Mia, we came across a semi-stranded bottlenose dolphin of a different type from those we study—longer, more robust, probably from a population that spends more time offshore. Only his back was exposed, and he was arching head and tail up in the air as we approached in a dinghy. Parking the boat some twenty-five feet away, we slowly waded over. When we got beside him, we saw that he was looking up, eyes large, whites showing. What to do? A gentle stroke seemed as good as anything. And with that, he closed his eyes most of the way and visibly relaxed. What would any wild animal—lion, deer, or rabbit—do in that situation? Bite, hit, flail, kick, struggle—but not relax. We were left to wonder whether that single stroke had somehow communicated reassurance to the distressed animal.

Fortunately, this stranding had a happy ending. We retreived some fish from the park. The dolphin eagerly took the first one and was still happily stuffing them in fifty fish later. Then the tide came in, and after he had slowly regained his ability to swim in a straight line, he left.

Whale and dolphin behavior, like that of all social creatures, is shaped by the societies in which they live. Among many dolphins and some species of whales, the high risk of predation has produced societies whose members are highly dependent upon each other for survival. Cetaceans get on each other's nerves, just as we do. They may squabble, clash over a potential mate, draw a neighbor's blood, or worse. But they are also capable of profound acts of kindness, not only to members of the group but sometimes to strangers as well. And in some cetacean societies, as we have seen, members will go to great lengths to maintain these tight bonds. Sometimes even death is a risk worth taking.

6

Courtship and Reproduction

The force that guides the lives of all animals is the creation of offspring. Feeding, socializing, and communication all are simply a means to an end, the end being the spread of one's genetic heritage. Animals strive to reproduce—a long history of natural selection has seen to that. But there is more than one road to reproductive success and different species travel different paths.

At one end of the spectrum is the "live fast and die young" strategy: individuals mature early and reproduce like there is no tomorrow. That's because there *is* no tomorrow for them, the cost of high early reproductive effort being early death. Other species take it slow and easy, maturing late, investing heavily in each offspring and, as a consequence, living longer. In contrast to rabbits (which reproduce like, well, rabbits) and most other mammals, all cetaceans take the slow road, producing one offspring at a time after a long period of maturation. But there is still considerable variation within the order of Cetacea, as we shall see. We will also explore how whales and dolphins go about the business of procreation, from courtship to birth.

Like so many elements of cetacean life, reproduction in the wild is seldom witnessed by humans. A cetacean's genitals are invisible most of the time, housed within slits under the animal. Because whales and dolphins spend most of their lives underwater, it is a rare event when a person actually witnesses the act of mating.

Even when scientists observe what is suspected mating behavior, it is difficult to know for certain. A male may assume a courtship display. His penis may be erect. And it may appear to make contact with the female's genitals. But these encounters are very brief—often lasting only a few seconds. And even close human observers are rarely in a position to know whether the male actually ejaculates inside the female. And to complicate matters, so much of sexual behavior, in dolphins at least, is not intended for reproduction but as a way of making social contact.

So it can be confusing. Not for the cetaceans, of course, who know exactly what they're doing, but for the humans who spend their days trying to piece together clues to solve the mystery of how the world's largest creatures reproduce.

We can find out when offspring are conceived, if we know when they are born and how long gestation lasts. In general, cetacean reproduction is a seasonal affair. In some species there is a well-defined breeding season, while in others there are one or two peaks in breeding activity even though some breeding may occur at any time of year.

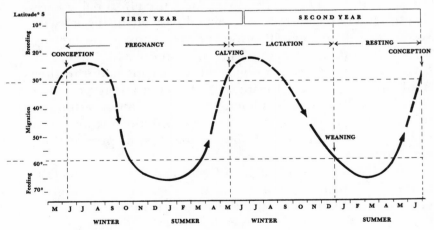

The breeding cycle of the fin whale. During her pregnancy the female may spend five months feeding in the high latitudes, then travel back to warmer waters to give birth. The infant is weaned before its mother returns to colder waters to recover and feed before the cycle begins again.

The behavioral studies of coastal species described in Chapter 5 have also taught us much about when cetaceans breed in the wild. However, most information on breeding schedules has been constructed from captive studies and the scientific examination of dead whales and dolphins. Whether a female is carrying a fetus, whether she is lactating, or is reproductively inactive all can provide insight into the time and duration of a species' peak breeding times, length of gestation, and how long a mother nurses her offspring. Moreover, reasonable estimates of age combined with detailed examination of the ovaries of females can tell us the age at which a female first reproduces, and whether individuals reproduce at different rates as they grow older. Captive studies of bottlenose dolphins and killer whales have taught us much about reproduction in these species, including the pattern of hormonal fluctuation during the reproductive cycle.

Because reproduction in the baleen whales is often tied to their yearly migrations between the tropics and high latitudes, breeding usually occurs during a period of a few months. The Hawaiian humpback whales we met in the previous chapter mate and give birth between January and March. For southern right whales, conceptions occur from August to October, while most gray whale conceptions appear to take place from December to February. By baleen whale standards, the Bryde's whales that live close to the coast of South Africa are relatively sedentary, remaining in warm climates where breeding activity may take place year round. A distinctive offshore form of Bryde's whale along the same coast engages in greater seasonal migration and seasonal reproduction. Scientists believe that most successful baleen matings occur while the animals are on or near the areas where females give birth, the winter breeding grounds. It is there that some whales, rather solitary much of the year, come together to form large aggregations, apparently for the purpose of reproduction.

Seasons are reversed between the two hemispheres so when leaves are falling in the Northern Hemisphere spring flowers are budding south of the equator. This means that some baleen whale populations on either side of the equator might be breeding during the same season, spring, for example, but six months apart. Thus, Northern Hemisphere humpback whales are feeding while Southern Hemisphere humpbacks are breeding.

Odontocete reproduction is also seasonal, but more variably so. Even in a resident population of dolphins, factors that may promote seasonal breeding are evident. With a twelve-month gestation period, the bottlenose dolphin mates during the same season that births occur. Perhaps May to July are the favored breeding months in Sarasota Bay because their warm temperatures are less stressful for a newborn than the winter chill. By the same token, the same season may be favored in Shark Bay because a steady supply of fish is available to relieve the stress of lactation on new mothers. Harbor porpoises in the Bay of Fundy may have the most focused birth season of all: late June. Sperm whales mate in the spring, between March and May in the Northern Hemisphere, September to December in southern waters.

So in virtually all the world's main bodies of water, over a broad span of months, whales and dolphins of every known species come together for the purpose of strengthening their genetic hold on the future. It is usually a brief coupling, sometimes between strangers, and sometimes between individuals that have known each other for most of their lives.

Meeting and Wooing a Potential Mate

A courting male needs a receptive female. Male land mammals are usually attracted to a female in estrus (heat) by the scent of the secretions that she produces. Just how male whales and dolphins find ready females is unclear. Unlike female primates whose sexual organs swell during estrus, female whales and dolphins do not appear to have consistent anatomical changes that are dead giveaways of their sexual readiness.

Perhaps searching males taste the water for chemical signals delivered by urine and feces. Massive trails of feces are commonly seen around groups of breeding whales. Behavioral changes in a female may indicate a readiness to breed. Or it is possible that the female communicates her desire by sending an acoustical message to nearby males.

In Shark Bay, male bottlenose dolphins inspect the genitals of females. During a genital inspection, the male approaches the female and angles his rostrum or beak near her genital area. Often two males perform the inspection together, each one approaching from a different side. We have recorded the males emitting a high pitched echolocation buzz as they jockey into position. This may indicate their ability to detect subtle tissue changes that occur during estrus. They also may be attempting to taste any chemical indicators of estrus that may be evident in the female's urine. Sometimes after such an inspection the males will become very excited around the female; at other times they appear blasé and simply move on.

Elements of courtship have been observed in a number of cetaceans. Right whales engage in energetic and highly visible mating bouts in which several males simultaneously pursue and attempt to mate with a single female. She will often roll belly-up and the male's almost prehensile penis curls up over her, probing for her genital slit. One researcher watched as two males, flanking a belly-up female, copulated with her at the same time! Only the larger of the two males ejaculated, as indicated by waves of contractions traveling the length of his eight-foot-long penis.

A group of courting male gray whales will pursue a female whale for a couple of miles, lunging through the sea in a high-speed chase that stirs up crashing waves before the female begins to mate, usually with several of her pursuers. Humpback males have been seen blowing bubbles around the genitals of receptive females and lying at the surface belly-up, slapping the water with their flippers. Whether or not this is done to sexually excite the female is not yet known. And as we saw in the previous chapter, male bottlenose dolphins in Australian waters form alliances to herd females, presumably to monopolize them for mating.

Naturally, it is easier to study elements of animal behavior when that animal's environment is not the open sea but a

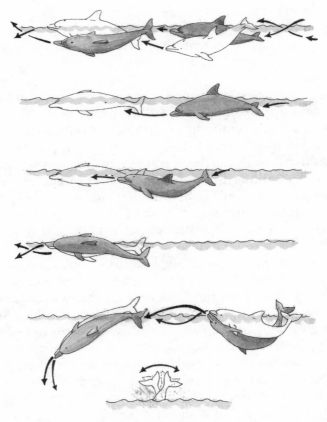

A sequence of mating behavior in bottlenose dolphins, as observed off the coast of Portugal.

confined space, easily accessible to all eyes that wish to pry. For a more detailed look at cetacean courtship, we must turn to captive studies on bottlenose dolphins, the species most often held in captivity. Captive animals may behave differently from how they behave in their native environment, however. Thus it is important to understand that captive studies, while insightful, may not always give an accurate picture of what happens in the wild. Further, what one or a few individuals do may not reflect the true range of a species' behavior. Just as dolphins are highly individualistic in their foraging behavior, they may also have individually distinctive courtship behavior.

Researchers spent three years watching the courtships of a group of bottlenose dolphins in a large tank at Marineland in Florida. In the springtime, the scientists noticed that the adult male in the group, who had changed his swimming partners frequently during the rest of the year, began to show a preference for one female, remaining with her for extended periods. The male was ardent in his pursuit. If she strayed from his side, he chased her down; as she fed, he hovered. In short, he made his intent clear. After a few days—occasionally even weeks—the relationship either progressed to the next stage or the couple parted.

When the male and female were still together after this initial round of courting, the behavior sometimes turned more aggressive. Like male mammals of many other species, the dolphin couldn't keep from touching his partner's body. No shrinking violet, the female, too, got her fair share of strokes in, nuzzling, rubbing, and mouthing her partner.

In one of the first indications that the animals would soon mate, the male swam toward the female and positioned himself in front of her, bending his body to form an S-curve with his head up and flukes down. He held the shape for a few seconds, then resumed normal swimming, and later repeated the position. In instances where a female seemed unresponsive or when there were other activities going on in the tank, the male sometimes gave up after posturing only once.

Dolphins love to touch and be touched, whether by fellow animals, humans, or even inanimate objects. Since so much of a dolphin's social life revolves around physical contact, it isn't surprising that courtship is so tactile.

At Marineland, when the courting pair swam, the male would position his body just behind and below the female. The female then would often move her flukes in such a way that she stroked the male's head. Sometimes the two reversed their positions and the male stroked the female's head. At times the two swam so that their flippers stroked the other's body, or one animal used its head to softly stroke the other.

Rubbing, a much more vigorous tactile stimulation than stroking, also was used to advance the relationship. One animal—usually the male—might swim head-on toward the female as though he was going to run her down. Seconds before the "crash" the male would turn slightly, just enough to avoid a full-impact collision but not enough to keep his body from rubbing against the object of his desire. This behavior usually was repeated several times. For her part, the female either swam toward the male as he rushed toward her, an action that served to increase the friction or literally leaped out of the water. When the female reentered the water, the male was right there to greet her, rubbing her enthusiastically.

As the courtship continued, the pair nuzzled each other's genitals. Or one animal would take the other's flipper or even its entire head between its teeth and then close its mouth. Luckily for the subject of such explorations, the grasp was always gentle. When the imprisoned dolphin pulled away, not one gash or toothmark could be spotted on its skin.

Aside from their love of touch, dolphins are also very vocal creatures, emitting a vast array of sounds. This too can be seen during courtship. The male produced a series of high-pitched yelps as the courtship moved closer to culmination. The male normally did not yelp when the female swam by his side; the sound seemed to be reserved for times when she had wandered away. That was all it took for the male to yelp his displeasure. If another female responded, the male ignored her, continuing to yelp. The only thing that would silence him was the return of the courted female. Perhaps yelping is a plea or even a demand for the female to return.

It should be understood that the male's prelude to copulation was not always consistent. One day his behavior might run the gamut of all these actions. Another day he might devote most of his time to one activity, nuzzling, for instance.

Copulation often followed a period of strong rubbing or the female's leaping (escape) behavior previously described. The male, who often had an erection during various stages of courtship, approached the female's right side, and partially rolling onto his right side, brought his penis close to her genital slit. The ball was then in her court.

A killer whale surveys its sur-
roundings, a behavior called
spy-hopping. Arctic killer
whales often spy-hop as they
search for seals on ice floes.
G.L. Kooyman / Animals Animals

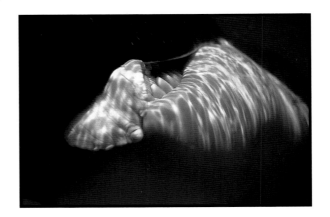

Unlike many other dolphins,
killer whales can stick their
tongues out. Note the large
teeth of this formidable
predator.
Henry Ausloos / Animals Animals

◄ *Overleaf: A miffed bottlenose*
dolphin may express its feel-
ings by jerking its head,
rapidly opening its mouth,
and blowing bubbles.
Gerard Lacz / Animals Animals

This young humpback whale has a formidable forty-five-foot-long mother to protect it from dangerous predators.
James D. Watt /
Animals Animals

One way dolphins express friendship is by stroking and petting each other with their flippers.
Rachel Smolker

Atlantic whitesided dolphins are a very social species that live farther offshore than the more familiar bottlenose dolphin.

John Chellman / Animals Animals

Large patches of rough skin called callosities decorate the head of this southern right whale. Whale lice, a type of crustacean, live on the callosities, making them look white. The large callosity on top of the whale's jaw is known as a bonnet.

Joe McDonald / Animals Animals

This Gervais beaked whale was beached on Cumberland Island, Georgia. Beaked whales are an enigmatic group, distantly related to other toothed whales.
Fred Whitehead / Animals Animals

The boto of the Amazon and Orinoco river basins of South America. Note the long pincer jaw, which is characteristic of many species of river dolphins.
Zig Leszczynski / Animals Animals

◄ Overleaf: A hunter admires the tusk of a male narwhal. The narwhal tusk, which can exceed nine feet in length, is a formidable weapon in conflicts between males.
Tony Martin, OSF / Animals Animals

*A pod of melon-headed
whales, relatives of killer
and pilot whales, cruises
near this humpback whale.*
James D. Watt /
Animals Animals

This pygmy sperm whale had the misfortune to venture into a shrimp net. Pygmy and dwarf sperm whales, a mere twelve to thirteen feet long, are petite cousins of the massive sperm whale and rarely seen at sea.
Fred Whitehead / Animals Animals

Right whales feed by skimming the surface with mouths agape. The baleen trap their planktonic food.
James D. Watt / Animals Animals

*Playing or fighting, kiss-
ing or biting? That is the
question that the scientists
who study cetacean behav-
ior constantly ask them-
selves. As in the case of
these two belugas, it is not
always easy to tell.*
Richard Kolar /
Animals Animals

For three days, a pod of false killer whales floated in close formation around an old male in the shallows of the Dry Tortugas Islands off the west coast of Florida; only the lack of tidal movement kept it from stranding. Why whales engage in such high-risk behavior is a mystery.
James W. Porter

The whales were remarkably relaxed and allowed people to stroke them, but they became agitated when the group was separated by humans attempting to push the whales offshore. The only other sign of displeasure came when this female bared her teeth at a person who ventured too close to her calf.
James W. Porter

*Male bottlenose dolphins
in Shark Bay perform
elaborate and beautiful
synchronous displays
around females. Here, two
males execute simultaneous
belly-slaps on either side of
the female.*
Richard Connor

It may look as if this bottlenose dolphin is smiling but that's just the way the animal's mouthline is formed. A dolphin does not reflect its emotions on its face, as a human being does. The clues to whether this dolphin is happy, angry, or just plain bored are found not in its face, but in its behavior.
Henry Ausloos / Animals Animals

A spinner dolphin doing what it does so well—spinning, of course. Why do spinners spin? Some scientists believe the centrifugal force of spinning enables the dolphins to fling off the pesky remoras who hitchhike on them. Spinning also may have been incorporated into this species' social behavior.
Kula Nai'a Project

Tool use in dolphins? In Shark Bay, Western Australia, several bottlenose dolphins routinely wear cone-shaped sponges over their beaks, possibly for protection as they nose along the bottom in search of prey.
Rachel Smolker

These humpback whales are engaged in some boisterous socializing.
James D. Watt /
Animals Animals

This pygmy sperm whale bears wounds from a shark attack. Survivors of such attacks often have crescent-shaped scars as testimony to their brush with death.
Fred Whitehead / Animals Animals

This unfortunate fin whale is being hauled in at a shore factory for processing. The long black-and-white stripes are actually pleats, which enable the animal to expand its mouth to take in enormous quantities of food-filled water.
Tony Martin, OSF / Animals Animals

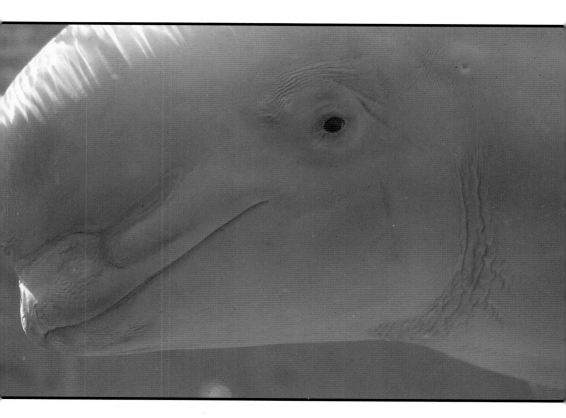

*The beluga, also sometimes
known as the sea canary,
has a large repertoire of
sounds.*
Margot Conte / Animals
Animals

➤
*Overleaf: A pilot whale
leaps out of the water, a
behavior that still isn't fully
understood by the scientists
who study cetaceans.*
Lewis Trusty / Animals Animals

As he approached, she did one of three things. Sometimes she swam away or simply continued swimming at his side. In either scenario, it was impossible for the male to enter her and after awhile he usually gave up and swam away rebuffed. A happier ending was when the female rolled over onto her left side and presented herself to the male, meanwhile slowing her swimming speed. The male was then able to bring his erect penis to her vagina. While this may sound elementary, copulating and swimming are not always easy to do at the same time. Water currents often forced the mating animals apart. Not one to be deterred, however, the male finally succeeded in inserting his penis into the female. The scientists who were watching from outside the tank observed a few thrusts; not more than ten seconds later, the animals separated.

The female didn't show quite the enthusiasm the male exhibited during courtship, but that may simply have been because she didn't need to. In some primate species, a female's interest in sex may be masked by the overt behavior of the male. Indeed, another female in the same tank was ignored by the male, in spite of her posturing, stroking, rubbing and approaching him from all angles. If the male continued to ignore her, she sometimes sought the affections of an immature male or rubbed her genitals against the gravel bottom or brushes that were ostensibly for the dolphins to scratch their backs on. In Shark Bay, a young female who was unable to stir the interests of several young males finally "mated" with one of the reluctant males' flippers.

Mating Systems

Mating systems are generally divided into four types: monogamy, polygyny, polyandry, and promiscuity. In a more accommodating world, researchers would be able to identify a species' mating system by determining which animals were mating, with whom, and how often such matings resulted in the creation of a new life.

Unfortunately, our window into the cetacean world has been far from crystal clear. In the past it has been almost impossible to know which animals were mating with whom and to determine paternity in live wild whales and dolphins. A new technique called biopsy darting may help shed more light into the darkest corners of cetacean reproduction.

With this technique, a dart is shot from a crossbow at the animal. The tip of the dart removes a small plug of its skin and blubber, which is then retrieved with a line. Contained within this tiny sample of tissue is the individual's DNA, a genetic blueprint that can then be used to determine the animal's genetic heritage.

In certain colonies of smaller cetaceans such as the bottle-nose dolphins in Sarasota, scientists periodically net and capture individuals to determine sex, age, size, weight, reproductive status, and general physical health. Blood samples also are taken for genetic analysis. Improved access to this critical genetic information along with additional behavioral observations cannot help but clear the way for a better understanding of how cetaceans breed.

Among some better understood species, scientists have logged enough observational hours to feel relatively comfortable in categorizing their sexual behavior. However, many of the lesser-known species such as river dolphins are so poorly understood that it is difficult to even speculate about their mating system.

In a monogamous breeding system, individuals mate with only one partner during the breeding season. In some cases the bond is broken at the end of the season; in others the pair remain together for years and, in some cases, are devoted for life. At one time a popular (and somewhat romanticized) notion held that some whales were monogamous, remaining together until death did them part. However appealing this idea is to humans who wish to humanize animals, it is highly unlikely that most whales and dolphins are monogamous.

In the avian world, monogamy is common among many of the smaller birds. Generally, such a system evolves because the care of both parents is vital to the survival of the young. One parent bird sits on the nest while the other forages. Subtract one from this rearing equation and the nestlings are doomed.

Male whales and dolphins, on the other hand, don't appear to be necessary to the successful rearing of offspring and in some species they may even pose a threat to the young. The mother satisfies her infant's nutritional requirements with her own milk for months, and in some species, even years. In the bird world, many cases of believed monogamy have collapsed under the scrutiny of DNA analysis. It turns out that females of many so-called monogamous birds sneak copulations with neighboring males.

Polyandry, a system in which a single female mates with several males, is practiced by a small number of animals. Unlike males who, at least theoretically, have no limits to the number of offspring they can sire, females are only capable of producing a given number of young at any one time. Among mammals, polyandry is very rare, and there is no evidence that any cetaceans practice it.

In a polygynous mating system, one male mates with several females. Polygyny is one of the most popular mating systems in the mammal world and it is safe to say that polygyny is the favorite strategy of male cetaceans. Females, however, may have other ideas.

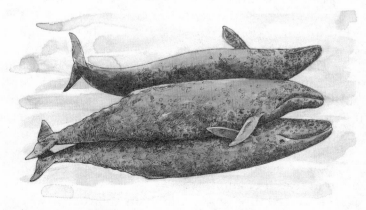

A mating ménage-à-trois of gray whales, with the female in the center. Gray whale females mate with more than one male during a breeding cycle.

Males and females belonging to species with polygynous systems tend to be markedly different from one another, in size, color, or other characteristics, a condition known as sexual dimorphism. Thus whale species that exhibit striking sexual dimorphism, such as sperm whales, killer whales, and narwhals, are thought to be polygynous.

Many animal species are promiscuous, which means that both sexes will mate with more than one individual. Promiscuity may be an unfortunate name for this category because it implies that everybody mates willy-nilly. This may, in fact, be the case. But females may also have preferred mates in a promiscuous system. Among most baleen whales and many dolphins, promiscuity appears to reign. Species considered to be promiscuous include southern right whales, bowheads, gray whales, and spinner, dusky, and bottlenose dolphins. Many of the species that are currently thought to be polygynous may also turn out to be promiscuous.

One cetacean thought to be highly promiscuous is the gray whale. Some scientists have described promiscuous mating systems as occurring in situations where both sexes congregate for a short but highly synchronized mating period, a description that is certainly on target in the case of the gray whale. Toward the end of their long migration males and females without calves gather in lagoons to court. Females are out of breeding commission every other year because they are nursing offspring, so the ratio of males to females is two to one and as the season progresses, the number of eligible females is reduced as they become pregnant.

After a high-speed chase that typically involves more than one male pursing a female, mating begins. Mating groups of anywhere from two to eighteen animals have been seen. Bouts may last as long as two hours, with animals leaving the group while fresh sexual recruits move in. At the end of a mating bout, the female will have copulated with several males. When the males are finished with one female, they head out in search of another.

There are three basic problems that occur when you try to pigeonhole sexual behavior into one of four categories.

Using their spiral lances, two narwhals joust above a third whale.

Mating systems really constitute a continuum and the range of behavior within a category may be more complex than the simple distinctions between categories.

First, in some promiscuous species, male-male fighting over females may be virtually nonexistent while in others, such as the bottlenose dolphin, males may put considerable effort into monopolizing females. Second, different populations of the same species may exhibit different tendencies toward one mating system or another. Females may be distributed differently because of what they eat. Resident female killer whales in British Columbia feed on salmon and travel in larger groups than transient females, which hunt for other marine mammals. This difference in grouping may also affect male mating strategies; do males stay with one group and defend it or roam between groups? Third, even within the same population, individuals may pursue different strategies.

In Shark Bay, one trio of lethargic older males didn't herd females as much as the younger more energetic males, seeming instead to spend more time in friendly interactions with females. Perhaps "being nice" becomes the best option for males who are no longer able to compete directly with the younger crowd. Females may even prefer nice old males, whose longevity may indicate a good genetic constitution.

Sexual Politics

Whatever the mating system, it is incumbent upon males to compete for females if their genetic heritage is to flourish. That is where certain strategies, honed by natural selection, come into play, enabling individual females to mate with the best male possible and individual males to sire as many offspring as they can.

A male cetacean, depending upon which species he is born into, is selected by nature to further his reproductive goals either by preventing other males from having access to a female, or by displacing the sperm of other males who have already mated with a given female, or both. And what about females? Do they have their own reproductive strategies that operate independently from those of the males?

Male-Male Competition. Like knights fighting over the hand of a lady, two narwhals joust and spar, each with its formidable spiraling tusk, which on some animals is as long as nine feet. The tusks, normally found only in males, erupt from the gums when the animals are about a year old and are thought to be used to threaten and physically attack other males who are competing for the same female. After sexual maturity, males accumulate many more scars on their heads than females. More than 60 percent of thirty-nine adult male narwhals observed had broken tusks, some of which had broken off in other males. One male had the tip of another's tusk embedded in its upper jaw. Strangely, the broken tusks of a few males were found to contain the tusk tip from another male. The Inuit of Greenland believe that old male narwhals with broken tusks somehow manage to get younger males to push their tusk into the exposed pulp cavity, then, with a jerk of the head, break off the tip. Unlike the human duels fought long ago, these whales probably don't fight to the death very often, instead engaging in sparring bouts from which a winner emerges.

With such formidable weapons, escalating a conflict would be very risky indeed. If narwhal contests follow the rules of male-male competition in other mammals, the most serious fights probably occur when the stakes are high (a fertile female), both males are evenly matched, and they are getting on in years (nothing left to lose).

Many species of beaked whales, an elusive group of odontocetes, also have impressive weapons that are capable of damaging opponents in their scuffles. The males have enlarged teeth, typically a pair either at the tip of the lower jaws or angled farther inside the mouth. Sometimes referred to as "battle teeth," these weapons can and do produce nasty scars when unleashed on an opponent.

The most famous sea battles for mating supremacy must occur between humpback whales. Male humpbacks, as we saw in the previous chapter, compete for females in the warm winter breeding waters. One male establishes himself as principal escort to a female, apparently in the hopes that she will mate with him. But a humpback's life, like any other creature's, doesn't always go according to plan.

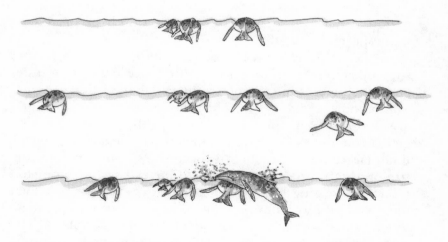

Courtship behavior of humpback whales. At top, a female and her calf are escorted by a male humpback. In the middle drawing, they are joined by other males, who swim along and compete for the female. At bottom, one of the males challenges the escort for his position near the female.

Often other males join the group, eager for a chance to mate with the female. A conflict is born and the only way to resolve it is through violence. The principal escort must retain his position nearest the female if he wants to sire her offspring and a secondary escort must displace him if he is to succeed with the female.

Humpbacks fighting for a mating opportunity will lash their tails, literally pummeling each other until one retreats. Tremendous slaps with the tail against the water (lobtailing) is a sign of anger, as is the distention of a male's throat pouch as he lunges toward a rival animal. These fearsome creatures also have been seen ramming a competitor with their very large heads.

Scientists believe that in species where the males compete in physical confrontations, females are more likely to mate with only one male during the season, thus ensuring the victor's paternity.

Sperm Competition. While some cetaceans put on quite a show in their mating games, other species have a more subtle approach, which to a casual observer might seem almost cooperative.

These whales appear not to rely on the physical domination of competitors, but to compete purely by producing more sperm.

The species that use sperm competition as a mating strategy generally are endowed with abnormally large testes and long penises in relation to their body size. Right whales, whose bodies range between forty-five and fifty feet in length, are the owners of the largest testes in the world, which together sometimes weigh up to one ton. This sexual organ is six times larger than one would expect to find on a creature the size of a right whale. In contrast to the right whale's one-ton testicles, an eighty-foot blue whale's testes weigh no more than one hundred fifty pounds. All the rorquals, in fact, have small testes, as does the pygmy right whale and the humpback. The eight-foot penis of the right whale has been known to probe research boats as well as females. The other member of the right whale family, the bowhead whale, is also well endowed.

The only other baleen whale with unusually large sex organs is the grey whale.

Theoretically, a male with large testes will produce more sperm than one whose sexual organs are smaller, and in such copious amounts that, in theory, they will replace the sperm of a less well-endowed competitor. A longer penis serves to carry that sperm closer to the female's ovum.

In species that use this form of competition, the females mate with more than one male. The males, often several gathered around a female, usually are not highly aggressive toward one another. In some observations, one male has been seen waiting for his turn while another male mates with the female.

Sperm competition may have reached a zenith in right whales, but males may still compete physically in certain situations. Right whales sport "callosities" like a moustache and sideburns of thickened skin which are home to myriad marine invertebrates, including sharp-edged barnacles. Callosities are larger in males than females and some researchers suspect that callosities function like brass knuckles in skirmishes over females. During friendly interactions, right whales appear to avoid rubbing their callosities against each other, but males courting the same female have been seen deliberately scraping their callosities against other males. Even so, interactions between male right whales are reported to be much less violent than those between male humpbacks.

Many of the smaller odontocetes also have relatively large testes, which suggests that sperm competition is impor-

During courtship, males often display to the female. One such display is the S-posture seen here.

tant. Bottlenose dolphins have large testes in relation to their body size, but they also fight for females.

Bottlenose dolphins, it turns out, can produce prodigous ejaculate with highly concentrated sperm, but only during the mating season. The rest of the year sperm production drops off markedly, suggesting that the production of sperm is energetically expensive, so dolphins don't waste it during times when sex is mostly social. In many dolphin and whale species the actual size of the testes changes during the year, being largest during the breeding season.

The Female Perspective. And where do females fit into this mating game? Are they simply objects to be won, sexual trophies awarded to the victor? Or do they have some control over their fate?

At a very basic level, females determine what mating strategies are open to males. If females are found in small groups and breed asynchronously at different times of the year, a strong male may be able to defend the group from other males and mate polygynously. Or it may be more profitable for a male to roam from group to group, seeking receptive females and defending those he finds. If females gather in large aggregations and mate synchronously, males will not be able to monopolize many females and the best male strategy may be to mate with many females without defending any.

Female behavior often receives less attention because it is less obvious and harder for a researcher to quantify. Forty-ton male humpback whales fighting over a female do not do it subtly. They threaten, hit, and slam into each other in highly visible and audible displays of aggression. What is the female mating strategy? We don't know. But it may be that females, who receive no help with parental care from males, prefer to mate with males who have the best genetic makeup, one that would confer health and strength upon their sons and daughters. One way a female might tell if a male was such a specimen would be his size and vigor. So he sings well, but can he fight? She could assess males' fighting ability by playing the role of instigator. If a female wanted to mate with the first possible male and then get away with little fanfare, she probably could. On the other hand, if she wants to ensure that she mates only with powerful males, she can cruise around and make sure all the locals know she is available. She can be reasonably assured that any male able to defend her for a period of time is a good male. Thus, an important female strategy might simply involve choosing where she goes, which could be a rather subtle behavior compared to the splash and crash of male-male combat.

In the humpback scenario, male and female strategies are in synch. Males are polygynous and the largest, most vigorous males will be successful because they can defeat other males and are preferred by females. But in other cases, the polygynous strategies of males might be in direct conflict with female interests. This seems to be the case among bottlenose dolphins in Shark Bay.

On one hand, the male alliances herd females. The success of herding as a mating strategy depends upon the ability of the males to monopolize and mate with the female when she is most likely to conceive. In many cetacean species such a strategy would probably be successful since females ovulate, breed, and conceive, in one cycle. But bottlenose females hold a trump card. They have as many as seven estrus periods during the year. This multicycling, in essence, reduces the chance of one male alliance monopolizing a female because the female mates with many males over the course of the year.

What advantage does having multiple estrus periods give the female? One likely theory is that it enables many male dolphins to claim paternity. In some primate societies where the males are not involved in parental care of the young, infants are sometimes killed by adult males. While such a practice has not been seen among bottlenose dolphins, it may be that a female's many cycles lessen the chance of infanticide because males may be less likely to threaten the young if they have mated with the mother and hence could be her infant's father. By mating with many males, the female may actually be helping to increase the chances that her infant will live to adulthood.

It was a lucky day for the scientist who got to observe the birth of this gray whale. The baby emerged head first as the mother was lying belly-up just below the surface.

Pregnancy and Birth

The age at which a female cetacean becomes capable of bearing young varies greatly. It appears that humpback females attain sexual maturity when they are between four and five years old, while a female gray is older, probably between eight and twelve years. The majority of female baleen whales mate between their fourth and tenth years.

Many of the odontocetes, on the other hand, take longer to reach sexual maturity. A sperm female will mate between the ages of seven and twelve, killer females between eight and ten, false killers may wait as long as fourteen years, and bottlenose dolphin females are around twelve years of age when they give birth for the first time.

Gestation periods range from around ten to thirteen months in the baleen whales. Many odontocetes also have gestation periods of around one year, but some, such as the sperm, pilot, and killer whales, have unusually long pregnancies, lasting up to sixteen months or more.

In the wild, a ringside seat to the nuances of cetacean pregnancy and birth is rarely granted to human observers. Perhaps because of a tendency to give birth under the cover of darkness, the actual birth is still shrouded in mystery. Researchers may watch in fascination as a female's pregnancy progresses and then one day a substantially slimmed-down mother simply reappears with a newborn calf in tow. Surprisingly, the best observations of birth in the wild come from large cetaceans such as sperm and gray whales.

Witness the arrival of a particular infant gray into the world. For more than a minute, the solitary female gray whale was vertical in the water, her head down, flukes held stiffly six feet above the surface. She lowered her flukes, then raised them again to a height of three feet, then rotated. As she lowered her flukes again to a horizontal position, the calf's snout protruded from her belly. Two other females with young calves passed within one hundred fifty feet of her but ventured no closer. The calf submerged as its mother returned to her vertical position but reappeared as the mother lay belly-up, just under the surface. Now halfway out, the newborn wobbled as the mother again sank beneath the surface. Within thirty seconds the calf popped up to the surface, separate from its mother for the first time. Thirty seconds after the calf's arrival, and ten minutes after her labors were first detected, the gray whale surfaced and took a breath.

When it comes to giving birth, what we see one female do does not necessarily predict the next. Several killer whales have been born in captivity at Sea World. One such birth seemed almost effortless, with the mother hanging at the surface as the baby emerged. Another was announced with a fast corkscrew swim by the mother, in which the baby was launched like a rocket.

A captive bottlenose dolphin birth described in 1948 provides a glimpse of the real challenges wild dolphins might face. These dolphins shared their tank with several sandbar sharks. As the infant emerged in a cloud of blood, the other dolphins formed a defensive formation around the mother and newborn, swimming below and beside them. The sharks, apparently attracted by the blood, began milling around the dolphins, but whenever one came too close for comfort, the dolphins herded it away.

Now we return to a tank at Marineland, Florida, this time to witness the unusually difficult labor of a female bottlenose dolphin and the birth of her calf, head first instead of the normal tail-first delivery.

Mrs. Jones, along with her tankmates Mona and Pudgy, had been impregnated by the same male in the month of March. While Mona's pregnancy was apparent by midsummer, Mrs. Jones, who was rather rotund anyway, didn't begin to show until the following November. It was then that observers noticed the increasing roundness of her abdomen. Shortly thereafter, her mammary glands, which are near the genital slit, began to bulge as did the area around them. By the middle of January, Mrs. Jones had begun to strain, as though she was trying to push her calf out. But it wasn't time yet. Despite her girth, the expectant mother continued to jump for fish at the feeding platform.

A few days after Mona had given birth, an event that took less than an hour, Mrs. Jones intensified her straining. She strained and paused, strained and paused, each effort dilating her genital opening. During her labor her swimming became so agitated and erratic that it was impossible for her tankmates to keep up with her. After awhile, Mrs. Jones relaxed again and she and two or three other animals formed a tight group and swam around the tank sleeping.

All night and the next day, Mrs. Jones labored. She would sometimes leap out of the water to the feeding platform, her genital slit widening with each jump. Then she would strain again and roll like a barrel.

By the third day of her labor, Mrs. Jones wouldn't even jump at the platform during feeding time. By now her straining was continuous and her companions seemed anxious, swimming under her, inspecting her genital opening. An hour later, the laboring female expelled some whitish-gray substance, thought to be amniotic fluid. Again, many of her companions swam over to examine her underbelly. Mrs. Jones barrel-rolled, her mouth wide open. At times she strained so hard that her nipples stood out. Her two-year-old daughter, Maggie, swam just ahead of her, straining in an exaggerated manner, then falling back to look at her mother's underside.

Sometime toward the end of her labor Mrs. Jones quickened her swimming pace, then glided down near the floor of the tank and whistled softly. Once she tossed an inner tube that was in the tank and then swam to some brushes to scratch herself.

More amniotic fluid gushed from her. Every ten seconds she strained, the opening widening with every effort. She napped, swam with Pudgy, and then resumed her work.

Finally, more than forty-eight hours from the onset of labor, a dark object protruded from her genital slit. Swimming up toward the surface, Mrs. Jones expelled the infant, snapped the umbilical cord, and nudged the newborn to the surface for its first breath. Amid a cacophony of whistles, the animals gathered at the birth site. Pudgy and Spray, Mona's eight-year-old daughter, seemed to maneuver the infant in circles, keeping it away from the others. A stream of blood trailing from her, Mrs. Jones, with Spray's help, ferried her newborn past the other dolphins.

Once again, this dolphin's reproductive cycle had come full circle. And now she would begin the task of raising a member of the next generation, until in three or four years' time nature would command a repeat performance.

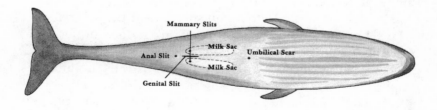

A cetacean's sexual organs are located on its underbelly, making sexual identification in some species difficult for human observers.

THE CETACEAN REPRODUCTIVE SYSTEM

Like every other part of their anatomy, cetaceans' reproductive systems have had to adapt to life in the water. Such an aquatic existence has no room for external organs that might cause turbulence in the water and slow the animal down, so a cetacean's sexual organs are housed within.

So thoroughly has nature done its work that if you were allowed the opportunity to physically examine a whale or dolphin, you would not immediately know whether you were looking at a male or female, for even the female's mammary glands are conveniently tucked away within slits on its underbelly.

Like all female mammals, cetaceans are born with two ovaries containing eggs. When the animal reaches sexual maturity, these egg cells ripen in succession, each one surrounded by a layer of nutrients that secretes a fluid in which the cell is suspended. The female's hormones bring her into estrus, at which time an egg is released from the ovary and into the fallopian tube. Down it travels, propelled by the tube's hairlike lining.

It passes into a bicornuate uterus in which the horns join to form a short body, which, in most species, ends with the cervix projecting into the top of the vagina. The cetacean vagina, much like that of a hippopotamus, has a number of folds, which are thought to retain sperm near the cervix.

The female's mammary glands are hidden under a pad of blubber outside the abdominal wall. The glands are elongated ovals that lie on either side of the vulva. The animal's nipples are retracted within smaller clefts at the side.

The male cetacean's testes can be found in pockets against the body wall, somewhat behind the kidneys. The penis, a thick organ of fibrous tissue, is under the blubber, outside the animal's abdominal muscles, with its pointed tip inside the genital slit on the underbelly, near the navel. The penis is long, extending more than ten feet when erect in some whales. When it retreats back inside the body, the abdominal muscles pull it into an S-shaped curve.

7

Bringing Up Baby

If we could witness a new life as it unfolds inside the womb of a blue whale, we would see a fertilized egg cell smaller than the head of a pin develop over the course of eleven months into a creature that weighs two tons when it struggles to escape the warm sanctuary of its mother's body.

The new whale, suddenly a separate physical entity, rises to the surface for the first of countless breaths that it will need throughout its lifetime.

And, if a whale or dolphin survives the perils of youth, a long life that will be. Fin whales may live up to ninety years, minke whales forty to fifty years, sperm whales up to seventy years, male killer whales fifty years, while the female of that species may live eighty years or longer, and the bottlenose dolphin's life probably lasts between forty and fifty years. At the other end of the spectrum, the franciscana lives only fifteen to twenty years, while the harbor porpoise doesn't live past fifteen years.

Although the numbers favor a long life for most cetacean species, many obstacles stand in the way of a whale or dolphin and its attainment of old age.

Our world's oceans and rivers are fraught with dangers. Predators lurk. Pollutants contaminate once-pristine waters. Diseases—pneumonia is a common one—gain their deadly footholds and squeeze the life out of their victims.

As with any animal species, it is the young who are at the greatest risk of death. In Shark Bay we have learned not to become too attached to infants under the age of two years.

There is little doubt that infancy for dolphins and whales is an especially precarious time and the individual who has the greatest influence over whether an infant survives is its mother. Youth and inexperience weigh heavily against the successful rearing of an infant. Inexperienced young mothers in Shark Bay have an especially tough time with their first attempts at reproduction.

Within the cetacean world there are no ties as close as those between mother and infant (remember, fathers do not play a role in caring for the young). After the newborn infant has filled its lungs with oxygen, a dolphin mother uses her tail and rostrum (beak) to guide the calf to a traveling position beside and forward of her dorsal fin. The majority of humpback whale calves seen swimming in the West Indies and Hawaii also swim above their mothers.

A cetacean calf quickly learns just how to position itself against its mother's side, enabling it to ride along on the waves generated by her movement without expanding much of its own limited energy. All the newborn need do to maintain this position is pump its flukes off and on. This hitchhiking position is comparable to the ape infant's method of clinging to its mother's belly to maintain contact. Gradually, bottlenose dolphin newborns switch from riding high along their mother's

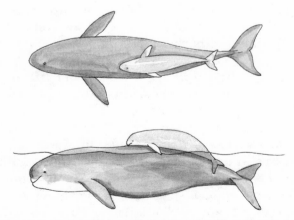

A baby Chinese finless porpoise hitches a ride from its mother. The mother's back has a roughened area whose wartlike bumps help the infant maintain its position as she dives and swims.

side to the "infant" position below and slightly to the side of her mammary area.

Belugas, or white whales, carry newborns on their backs. In the Saint Lawrence estuary in Canada, observers have seen groups with three infants riding piggyback on their mothers. Another odontocete that carries young on its back, the finless porpoise of Asia, has taken matters a step further. Its back has an area of skin covered with wartlike growths, which, scientists speculate, helps keep the youngster from slipping off.

The Infant's First Meal

A few hours after birth, when the placenta has been expelled from the mother, the infant has its first taste of milk. The calf, with its stomach empty, eagerly searches the body of its mother shortly after birth, sometimes even before the placenta has been shed. The mother then positions herself so that her belly is tilted toward the calf. The nipple, usually retracted within the mammary slit, protrudes. The young cetacean, like any infant, needs no further instruction. It grasps the nipple in the tip of its jaws and the mother's mammary muscles—probably in response to the sucking stimulus—shoot a stream of milk conveniently into the infant's mouth through a tube formed by its tongue and the nipple. All the calf need bother itself with is maintaining its position and swallowing.

Nursing behavior was observed in a mother and newborn bottlenose dolphin at the Mystic Marinelife Aquarium in Mystic, Connecticut. Prior to nursing, Turnip, the infant, would move into the infant position beneath Gabrielle, her mother, with her head just below the adult's mammary glands, as if she were orienting herself. The pair then slowed down their swimming, Turnip often closing her eyes—the same behavior normally seen when the young dolphin was resting. Sometimes Gabrielle rolled on her side to position herself for nursing, but usually it was Turnip who turned on her side before grasping her mother's nipple. When she had finished nursing, she resumed her infant position below her mother.

Unlike many infants, cetacean young cannot nurse for long periods because they are underwater and must surface for periodic breaths. So each nursing bout is brief. Southern right whale calves' nursing bouts become longer as the calf grows and is able to stay submerged for a longer period of time. In the early weeks, a calf will nurse for barely ninety seconds before surfacing for a breath, while yearling calves will nurse an average of 4.5 minutes before their need to breathe summons them to the surface. One particularly ardent yearling in waters off the coast of Argentina was observed in what was presumed to be nursing behavior for two eight-minute periods in a total of twenty-two minutes underwater. Bottlenose dolphins spend even less time nursing; five- or six-second bouts are typical, although in the early months the young can be found at their mother's breasts ten to twenty times every hour.

Nursing can be interrupted by either the mother or her calf. In a study of right whales off the coast of Argentina, researchers found that of one calf's sixty-nine nursing bouts, fourteen were obviously stopped by the mother. Sometimes she accelerated her swimming speed, which caused the calf to surface and take its traveling position next to her. At other times she abruptly left her nursing position at the surface to dive underwater, a move that catapulted the submerged infant to the surface. Once she simply turned away. Other mothers who apparently had had enough nursing for the moment rolled onto their backs to rid themselves of their hungry offspring.

Nursing among these whales usually appeared to be a one-on-one event. Typically, the approach of single whales interrupted a nursing bout. At one point, however, scientists saw three mothers and their calves lying together, while two of the calves nursed, a sort of cetacean version of a La Leche League meeting.

If you thought temper tantrums were the exclusive domain of humans, you have never witnessed a still-hungry cetacean baby whose mother has pulled in her nipples. In one such case, a right whale, christened Contrary by the scientists who watched her antics, didn't take this rebuff lightly. Like young giraffes and baboons who also aren't afraid to make a fuss when their needs are denied, Contrary caused quite a scene when her mother rolled away. She began her tantrum around her mother's tail, opening and closing her mouth, rolling, draping herself across her mother like a scorned lover. Then she breathed her frustration into an explosive blow, slapping her flipper and tail a few times for good measure before ramming her mother's body. Twenty-two times she plowed into her mother's back, using her opening and closing mouth to hammer the older whale's back and stomach just as though it was pliant wood. Although Contrary was young, she seemed to have learned at least one way her species inflicts pain on others, a torture that involves rubbing the collosity on top of the jaw against the victim's back. Anyone who has gone through the terrible twos with a child knows that there comes a time, however hard it may be to admit, when adult resolve is worn as thin as a nerve and you realize that yours would be better served with a wave of the white flag. Whale mothers apparently also know when to say enough is enough. This one, having enduring twenty minutes of battering, finally rolled over and let her infant have her way.

Cetacean mothers' milk is rich in fat and calories, all a small whale or dolphin needs for its first few months. And those needs are almost beyond our comprehension in the case of blue whales, whose infants gain two hundred pounds a day.

Nursing time varies. Bottlenose dolphins may nurse for three or four years or even longer. The franciscana and harbor porpoise may nurse for around nine months. Fin, blue, and gray whales wean their young after seven months, minke whales nurse for four months, southern right whales into their second year of life. Off the mammalian chart for nursing longevity are the last offspring of old female pilot whales and sperm whales, which may suckle for ten to fifteen years!

The young of species with shorter nursing times generally subsist exclusively on milk until they are weaned. Sperm whales and many dolphins, however, go on nursing—although less frequently—long after they have added other foods to their diet.

Bottlenose dolphins by their sixth or seventh month usually have developed a taste for something more than mother's milk, although fish does not become a diet mainstay until they are into their second year of life. Even before they are interested in eating the fish, young dolphins learn capture methods by making a game out of it. Catching one's dinner requires practice and young dolphins are amazingly creative in the ways they learn.

A favorite pastime of infants in Shark Bay is chasing tiny fish less than two inches long. The fish often jump and skip across the surface as the infants pursue them belly-up. Catching fish is hard work, requiring a good measure of skill, so it should come as no surprise that young dolphins often falter in these earliest pursuits. A youngster may visually track a fish, use its nascent echolocation abilities to zero in on the prey (see Chapter 2), snap, and still come up with an empty mouth. It is tempting to applaud when finally a catch is made. In time, these skills are honed and young dolphins grow into older ones perfectly capable of hunting and capturing fish that come in a variety of shapes and sizes.

Infant dolphins don't abruptly go from nursing to a diet of large fish anymore than a baby supplements its milk with a steak and Caesar salad. Young dolphins learn to snack with tiny silvery fish that they trap at the surface. Observers watching the captive dolphin pair, Gabrielle and her infant, Turnip, saw the mother at feeding time break up fish into small pieces, leaving the remains in the water. By breaking up the fish and removing the head, the larger bones that are difficult for a young dolphin's system to digest are discarded. For her part, Turnip at first used the fish parts as playthings. But soon after her sixth month she was seen eating a good number of what just weeks before had been her toys. We don't know if mothers in the wild go to such lengths to prepare baby food. Although adults in Shark Bay often break up large fish before eating them, we have yet to see a mother prepare a meal for an infant as Gabrielle did for Turnip.

Traveling Together

The mother right whale's newborn came into the world in the shallow coastal waters at Peninsula Valdes, Argentina. In total, scientists had been able to identify more than five hundred and eight whales that frequented these peaceful waters from June to December. The humans' purpose now was to gain insight into the behavior of mothers and their infants.

What the scientists found was intriguing. The youngest calves and their mothers did the most traveling, rarely stopping except to nurse or rest. These mothers and their less-than-week-old calves spent their days on the move, maintaining constant speed and wandering a couple of miles beyond the scrutiny of the human observers. As the calves grew, each of the mothers shortened her wandering range and she and her infant often moved back and forth, traveling only a few hundred yards in one direction before turning around.

A newborn right whale follows its mother wherever she leads. This puts her in the position of being able to direct the infant's behavior—whether it be breathing, swimming, or something else—to accomplish this movement. Even by doing nothing more than move, the mother whale may be demonstrating a subtle form of parental care, in that she is preventing the calf from staying still. Such passivity might prove detrimental to its well-being. Scientists thus far can only speculate about the purpose of this continuous movement for newborns and its gradual decrease as they become older and larger. It may be that the newborn right whale lacks buoyancy and is literally incapable of remaining still in the water without sinking. The young calf's body has a higher proportion of muscle to fat than the adult body, a factor that no doubt reduces its ability to float. It is possible that not only does the calf's body composition need to mature but the ability to remain buoyant in water may be a learned skill, a behavior literally taught at the mother's fins.

Another theory as to the reason behind this constant movement is that the newborns need exercise in breathing and swimming. The very necessary act of raising the blowholes above water to breathe is a monumental task for a recently born right whale. To breathe, the newborn must jerk its head up to ensure that it inhales air, not water. As the animal matures, so does its ability to come to the surface for breaths, and some scientists suspect that this may be accomplished by this early continuous exercise. Although similar tests have not been conducted on right whales, we do know that gray whale newborns' muscles contain almost no myoglobin, a substance like hemoglobin that aids in breathing and the ability to hold one's breath. It may be that exercise actually builds up the muscles' supply of this iron-rich protein.

The final hypothesis is that mothers and their calves are on the move as a defense against killer whales, which will even attack adult right whales. By constantly swimming, the young calves quickly gain strength. The fact that they swim in shallow water may help to prevent the killer whales from detecting their position and also reduce the chances that they will be attacked from below.

In the early weeks and months most mother cetaceans and their calves are rarely apart. In species such as the sperm whale that feed throughout the year, mothers leave their infants under the protection of a trusted associate before searching the ocean's depths for food. Food is scarce on the breeding grounds of many migrating baleen species such as humpback and right whales, so they are lucky to find any food during the early newborn period and many do without altogether.

One cetacean species whose mother-calf pairs stay together a long time are bottlenose dolphins. On average, a bottlenose mother and her youngster remain in close proximity for three to six years, although there have been reports of some youngsters staying with their mothers for much longer. Generally, though, the relationship remains strong until just before the birth of the mother's next calf. Tongue-fin, a Shark Bay female, still hadn't produced another calf by the time her daughter, Lick, turned seven. Although nearly as large as her mother, Lick was still traveling in the baby position under Tongue-fin and was even observed trying to nurse.

This does not mean that the bottlenose dolphin clings to its mother. On the contrary, young dolphins are independent souls with an apparent need to put some space between themselves and the yoke of parental authority. Within its first few months, a bottlenose dolphin calf will frequently leave its mother, often going more than a half-mile away to explore. Such wandering is probably dangerous and some infants wander about more than others. Perhaps they learn enough about their world while wandering to make the risk worth taking.

Protecting the Young

Infancy is the most vulnerable time in a cetacean's life, a period when an animal can easily fall prey to everything from starvation to the fearsome bite of a hungry shark. Luckily, most mother cetaceans are extremely protective of their young.

Mother dolphins form strong attachments to their young. Letting go of a dead infant may be difficult and mothers have been seen carrying a baby after it has died.

Among many species, individuals find safety in the social group; females and their calves often travel in nursery schools away from the possible threat of males. Sperm whale mothers and their calves live with other females and associate with mature males only at breeding time. Off Sarasota, bottlenose dolphin mothers with similar-aged infants tend to swim together and sometimes form nursery schools where infants can romp under the watchful eye of several mothers.

Females that are independent but not yet old enough to be mothers themselves often show considerable interest in infants. The benefit is twofold: a young female can learn about motherhood and the infant's mother is probably happy to have an extra pair of eyes watching out for sharks.

A glassy calm day in Shark Bay presented a scene that spoke volumes about dolphin life. Munch was swimming with her brand new infant, Slurp, who was flanked on her other side by the five-year-old female Holly, who rarely associated with Munch. About one hundred fifty feet behind them was a similar trio, Psupodee, her new calf, and another Holly-sized juvenile. And one hundred fifty feet to the side of both groups, swimming in their direction, was a five-foot tiger shark. While not much of a threat to the mothers, the shark was not good news for the infants.

If having an extra pair of eyes (and sonar beam) around is advantageous, why don't bottlenose dolphin females travel in groups of fifty or more? If sharks were their only concern they probably would. But animal group size reflects a compromise between the costs and benefits of group living. The same individual who helps by keeping an eye out for predators is also beating you to that fish you just detected. Bottlenose dolphins don't swim in large groups because they can't afford to—there wouldn't be enough fish to go around.

The life-style of baleen whales is less gregarious than that of many odontocetes and this is reflected in their more solitary approach to infant care. Most mothers and infants are seen alone or sometimes in the proximity of other mother-infant pairs. Humpback females appear to isolate themselves prior to birth and for some time afterward, although male escorts often join pairs when the infants are older and are travel-ing with their mothers on the breeding grounds.

Despite precautions, sharks, killer whales, or irksome males may threaten the young, and then it is up to a mother or her school to defend the calf. A humpback mother has been seen protecting her young by positioning herself be-tween the calf and the potential threat and hoisting the young calf onto her flipper, then lifting it partially out of the water. A defense method often seen among whales and dolphins that travel in groups is to isolate the young in the safest place. Sperm whales when threatened by killer whales will form a tight circle, heads facing outward, and with the calves in the center. And killer whale pods encountering a boat or other threatening object will close ranks around their calves.

Squid, when threatened, release a cloud of ink into the water that hides them from predators. The enigmatic and rarely observed dwarf sperm whale may have a similar defen-sive weapon. A dwarf sperm whale mother and calf were accidentally encircled by a tuna net that had surrounded a school of dolphins. Whenever one of the dolphins in the net approached the calf, its mother released a reddish cloud, probably feces, that covered three hundred square feet. Mother and calf appeared to hide in the center of the opaque cloud.

Their large relative, the sperm whale, would have trou-ble hiding behind anything short of an ocean liner, yet sperms also release feces when disturbed, possibly to confuse an at-tacker. We recall a television documentary in which divers approached a group of sperm whale mothers and calves under-water. As narrator Walter Cronkite offered a touching commentary on the bond between man and whales, the camera revealed a different story: irritated sperm whales launching clouds of feces in the water before high-tailing it out of there.

In the early weeks of a bottlenose dolphin's life, moth-ers are constantly on guard. Observers aboard a boat off Sarasota saw firsthand a cautious dolphin mother at work. When the infant, who was only a few days old, popped its head out of the water, the mother moved into position between her youngster and the craft. After awhile, when it appeared the boat was not a threat, she took a feeding break, retreating to a nearby cove to forage. The curious infant moved closer, coming within inches of the hydrophones that hung from the bow. The researchers heard a faint whistle. Within seconds the mother's whistle, loud, clear, and distinctly her own, sounded. In a flash she surfaced next to her calf and used her rostrum to gently guide it away from the boat.

The bottlenose dolphin's signature whistle may be one way in which mothers and their young maintain contact even when they are physically separated. Dolphin infants are capable of whistling from the day they are born. And after the birth, a mother dolphin whistles frequently for several days. Every dolphin's whistle has unique features, a so-called signature that enables others to identify the whistler. Presumably, the mother's almost nonstop whistling is a form of acoustical imprinting on her infant so that it will be able to differentiate her whistle from all others. By the time the calf reaches its first birthday, it, too, has developed a distinctive whistle.

As is the case in so many areas of behavior, much of what we have learned about parental care has been gleaned from observations of captive bottlenose dolphins. At Marineland, Florida, several mothers who had recently given birth were observed to take special care not to allow their infants to come into close contact with other animals. When one approached, the mother usually directed the infant to her opposite side and quickly swam away. When the infants were about two weeks old, they began to be more daring, moving from the traditional baby position alongside the mother, and instead encircling her tail, splashing about her head, and darting a foot or two away from parental authority. Always cautious, the mothers would tolerate just so much independence. This threshold of indulgence appeared to be about ten feet. When an infant dared venture beyond that point, its parent quickly retrieved it.

Even at feeding time, mothers appeared to place the welfare of their offspring above the need to fill their own stomachs. The captive mother dolphin swam within a few feet of the feeding platform with her newborn, leaving it to swim in a circle while she alone approached the platform, where she quickly snatched up one fish and then swam back to the swimming infant. Oftentimes that one trip had to suffice; the rest of the time she was frantically trying to keep her infant out of harm's way as the rest of the dolphins made a mad dash toward the platform.

The calves thrived and their mothers constantly policed their whereabouts, allowing them some—but not much—slack. Most animals that approached an infant were rebuffed; either the mother quickly spirited the calf away or she slapped the intruder with her flukes. One who appeared to be readily accepted by all the mothers as a trusted babysitter was a young female named Spray.

As it turned out, Spray, who bore her first calf when she was seven years old, should have stuck to babysitting. Unlike the other mothers who lavished care upon their infants, Spray didn't appear to take much interest in her newborn daughter. Initially, it seemed that everything was normal. The infant nuzzled her mother's side and began to nurse a few hours after birth. But within a few days it was apparent that something was amiss. Unlike most dolphin infants whose necks lose their scrawny look and whose stomachs become rounded within a few days of frequent nursing, Spray's infant failed to gain weight. Moreover, Spray was not protective like the other mothers. She frequently left the calf alone while she spent several minutes at the feeding platform.

When the infant swam away, Spray took her time about retrieving her. Soon, the baby female was venturing out on her own, swimming among the other animals. It was only when she had strayed beyond twenty feet that Spray would go after her. When this happened, Spray was apt to turn over on her back, position the infant on her chest, and rise to the surface until the calf was out of the water, a tactic used by other mothers to keep their young ones in line.

One day, Spray left the infant alone while she went off to feed, not bothering to check on her. Later, the infant attempted to nurse but Spray wouldn't slow down long enough to allow her to suckle. The next day the mother let the baby nurse almost continuously, but still allowed her to swim alone for several ten-minute periods.

The haphazard care continued. One day the calf swam directly under the feeding platform and was hit by several other dolphins as they rained down upon the water after catching their dinner in midair. Once she innocently came between a courting males and the object of his attention, both of whom made it clear they did not appreciate the intrusion. Another time the calf strayed and entered a group of dolphins. Instead of bringing her back, Spray let her make her own way out, a dangerous maneuver for a thirty-pound infant.

The next day, fifteen days after her birth, the calf was found dead. An autopsy revealed that she was undernourished and had a fractured left mandible, possibly as the result of her rough encounters with some of the tank's other inhabitants. Ironically, when employees found the dead calf, Spray was, for once, the attentive mother, pushing her baby's body ahead of her through the water.

Play: Practicing for the Future

Most young mammals love to play and cetaceans are no exception. Of course, few things in this world are free and some young cetaceans preoccupied with their games must pay the price of increased vulnerability to predators. Atlantic spotted dolphins are most vulnerable between the ages of three and five years old, the time when they are feeling quite independent and are apt to take their sport far away from the watchful eyes of older dolphins. Perhaps as a result, many of them wear scars from shark bites.

Despite the risks, it would probably be more costly for the young cetaceans to forgo their fun, for it is during playtime that youngsters experiment with new behaviors. Skills are practiced and in time perfected, relationships with peers are solidified, and one's place becomes etched in the social hierarchy. In essence, cetaceans learn, through their play, what they need to know to survive in their environment. Scientists who have had the pleasure of watching them at play are constantly amazed by the creativity these animals invest in their fun.

In the early days of oceanaria, bottlenose dolphins often shared their tanks with a variety of fish and other marine life and tormenting these animated toys was always a favorite dolphin pastime. Turtles were good for pushing across the tank, a pelican floating on the surface could be surprised from below and its feathers plucked for toys, and fish and eels could be chased and towed around. Male bottlenose dolphins are notorious for their sexual play. In 1956, researchers noted that the two male bottlenose dolphins at the Marineland of the Pacific would attempt to mate with anything and everything animate, including skates, rays, turtles, sharks, and moray eels. During public shows, it proved somewhat embarrassing when Frankie and Floyd would ignore the show routine and try to mate with a struggling moray eel.

In Shark Bay, dolphins occasionally bop a seagull or cormorant into the air. Apparently, it is also good fun to nip and harass pufferfish to make them puff up. Seaweed is another favorite toy, which can be tossed and passed around, or balanced on flippers and flukes. Once two dolphins leaped into the air, both holding onto an object that, in the photograph, looks like a fisherman's burlap sack. The dolphin rendition of a tug-of-war?

Play is also used to increase strength and coordination. Right whale calves have been seen as they learn to breach (leap out of the water) and in the beginning may practice this vigorous exercise as much as eighty times in one hour. Right whale infants also will roll upside down and slap the water with their flippers. The first behavior may be a prelude to courtship among adult right whales, the second a defense against killer whales. Through play, the youngsters practice the actions that they will need to perform as adults.

The practical value of bowhead whales playing with logs is less obvious. From their bird's-eye view in a small twin-engined airplane, a scientific team watched bowhead whales cavorting in the frigid Beaufort Sea off the north coast of Alaska. One whale spent an hour and a half pushing, nudging, and lifting a thirty-foot log. Rolling belly-up under the log, it would clasp the log with both flippers or try to push it under water with its chin.

While dolphin mothers are often seen playing with their young, right whale mothers use playtime to catch a rest. Scientists speculate that this may be a way of saving energy, since the mothers are fasting during their four-month or longer stay on the nursery grounds, yet must expend an enormous amount of energy producing milk. An interesting finding is that bowhead calves, and probably right whale calves as well, suspend their play when they reach the feeding grounds, which may be the result of the mother's desperate need to find and consume huge quantities of food during the short summer feeding season. After infancy, young right whales apparently do not indulge in much play again until after they have left their mothers and joined other juveniles.

A playful right whale calf plays its games around its mother, the center of its universe, sometimes actually frolicking on her back while she tries to rest at the surface. The weary mothers often try to discourage the youngsters from such antics, possibly because such energy-burning activity makes them even hungrier. Sometimes a mother will simply start moving to stop her infant's games. Mothers have also been seen subduing their young by rolling over, bringing the calves onto their stomachs, and holding them between their flippers. Diving also is a surefire way to interrupt play.

A large part of cetacean play involves tactile stimulation. As we saw in the previous chapter, much of dolphin sexual behavior is played out in a social rather than reproductive context, in both friendly and aggressive interactions. Such behavior starts in infancy and takes many forms. In Shark Bay, the infant Urchin would mount his mother or the young adult male Shave. The adult male Wave would lie on his side as if inviting young Cookie to mount him. Three-year-old Cookie was fond of mounting his big sister Puck or other females, often in tandem with his buddy Rabble. On one occasion, after Rabble and Cookie had spent several minutes pursuing and mounting Puck in playful imitation of adult male behavior, Rabble began traveling under Puck in the infant position and even tried to nurse from her. Evidently, Rabble wanted to be an infant again.

Cutting the Cord

Despite the close ties between mother and calf, there comes a time when the calf must go its own way. For the mother separation may be necessary because she has a new calf on the way that require the full force of her maternal instincts. Or, as in right whales, the mother may be so drained that she needs a year or so to recover before she begins another pregnancy. The need to close the chapter on this all-consuming relationship isn't one-sided, however. Like humans, cetacean young reach a point when they want to make their own way in the world.

Typically, young cetaceans and their mothers are unusually close while the infant is nursing. Once the young whale has had first taste of krill or fish, it begins to stray farther and farther from its mother; hence, the weaning that will ultimately sever the ties between the two.

For many odontocete species, these ties are not broken readily. Many species of toothed whales and dolphins live in highly stable societies where it appears that matrilineal lines associate with one another for generations. Killer whales of both sexes live with their mother as long as she lives. Even after female sperm whales are weaned, they may stay with their mother's group. And although young bottlenose dolphins become independent from their mothers when they are a few years old, they may continue to "stay in touch" with her for many more years.

Little is known about how most cetacean species actually separate from their mothers. Among bottlenose dolphins near Sarasota, however, Randy Wells and his team of researchers have witnessed several partings over the years. Daughters tend to take their leave more gradually, according to Wells's studies. They may leave for awhile to join roving groups of other young dolphins and then suddenly reappear for a visit. Sons, on the other hand, form strong alliances with one or two other males, from whom they become inseparable, and their visits home are sporadic. Still, if anything is likely to

A bottlenose dolphin usually gives birth to her infant tail first. This species' young may be dependent upon their mothers for several years.

bring a mother a visit from her independent son, it will be the birth of a new calf, an event that seems to call for a family reunion.

The weaning conflict between Holey-fin and her three-and-a-half-year-old daughter, Holly, was painfully obvious to those of us watching them interact in Shark Bay. Following her mother up and down the beach by the Monkey Mia campground, Holly whistled incessantly. Her whining and whistling was irritating even to her human observers, so we can imagine how it sounded to Holey-fin.

Separation between mothers and young—whether it be a clean break or a partial severing—is an inevitable part of life in every animal species, including our own. In a sense, the occasion calls for celebration because it means that the parent has successfully produced a new life, nurtured it, and sent it off on its own, capable of fending for itself and beginning the cycle anew.

Sometimes, sadly, the separation comes much too soon and in tragic circumstances. When a mother dolphin's infant dies, letting go can be painful, as witnesses who watched Saida Beth could easily see. The bottlenose dolphin, a member of the Sarasota community, had given birth to her first calf, which died within twenty-four hours. When the research team spotted Saida, she was with ten other dolphins, including her own mother. As the rest of the group swam north, Saida and Melba, her mother, stayed put. Saida lifted her dead son to the surface, whistling, dropping him, and then repeating the process while Melba fed nearby. For ninety minutes, the mother continued her ritual. It was only when two teenaged males swam into the area and chased Saida that she dropped her infant and took off.

After that, she made no further attempts to find the small body.

8

Intelligence

Within the high, somewhat regal, forehead of many species of dolphin sits one of the largest brains (in relationship to body size) found in any nonhuman animal. Some species of dolphins, in fact, have relatively larger brains than any of the apes, the animals evolutionarily linked most closely to man and often thought to be the most intelligent of all in the animal kingdom.

This is not to suggest that every cetacean cranium is host to an enormous brain. Despite the public perception that they are especially intelligent animals, the baleen whales have relatively small brains. The brain of a fifteen-foot pilot whale, for example, is just as large as that of a massive forty-five-foot bowhead whale. Nor is every dolphin species in possession of an exceptionally large information-processing system. The river dolphins have relatively small brains; the elusive and endangered baiji of China has a brain only one-half to one-third

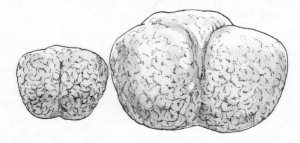

All dolphins are not intellectually equal. China's baiji is the same size as the bottlenose dolphin, yet its brain is only one-third to one-half as large.

as large as a bottlenose dolphin of similar body size, a difference almost equal to that between humans and the great apes.

What are the factors that separate the animal world's mental giants from those who are less well endowed? As of yet, no one has hit upon an all-encompassing definition of animal intelligence. But certainly one dimension of high intelligence is the ability to process information, to respond to it in strategic fashion, and to adapt that information to one's advantage in new situations.

As with most of the work today being done with cetaceans, studies that attempt to unveil dolphins' intellectual capabilities are still in their infancy. Nevertheless, many long-time observers of these animals don't need stringently controlled studies to tell them what their eyes can see: that dolphins are especially clever, highly social animals that, at times, are seen doing amazing things.

Consider some of these observations from dolphin trainers:

At Hawaii's Sea Life Park two female roughtoothed dolphins showed their trainers that they were indeed capable of learning by observation. One of the dolphins, upon hearing certain sounds, had been trained to perform specific behaviors, one of which was to jump through a hoop held high above the water. The animal had been taught to wear a blindfold, but had never performed wearing one. The second dolphin, on the other hand, wore her blindfold both when swimming around barriers and when retrieving rings on her rostrum.

The animals had watched each other perform in the past but had never been trained to duplicate the act. That changed one day when the trainers accidentally switched their performers. The result? The show went on as usual, and the audience didn't have a clue that anything was amiss. Each dolphin performed the other's part as though it was second nature. So flawless were their performances that the trainers didn't even learn of their mistake until later.

In another example of imitation, a male bottlenose dolphin named Daan watched a diver clean algae from the glass underwater viewing port in his tank. After several observations, Daan picked up a seagull feather and began to scrape the glass, making sounds and blowing bubbles almost identical to those that emanated from the diver's air-valve apparatus.

Can dolphins delay their response to a stimulus, or once the moment passes, is it gone from memory? One swimmer found that the dolphin—like the elephant, if folklore is to be believed—doesn't forget. One day as the trainer was leaving the tank, he accidentally kicked a dolphin. The morning after, when the trainer reentered the water, that dolphin was there to wreak its revenge with a blow of equal intensity.

A similar example of dolphins disciplining trainers involved a female roughtoothed dolphin who frequently solicited stroking from her trainer. When, during one of these sessions, the trainer stroked her one-month-old infant, the mother whacked the trainer with her tail, after which she offered herself up for more stroking. Roughtoothed dolphins have a reputation for being extremely bold and not taking any guff. One actually pulled a hypodermic syringe from a tankmate during medical treatment and then went for the veterinarian!

The bonds between dolphins can be remarkably strong. During the 1950s, methods of capturing dolphins for display were often brutal. A female common dolphin injured during capture was having trouble swimming when placed in a tank. A male who was captured a few days later and placed in her tank immediately sought her company. As she struggled to swim, he would swim under her and nudge her to the surface. She soon was swimming normally and the pair became inseparable. Unfortunately, the female's wounds became infected and she died two months later. The male circled her body, whistling constantly. He continued to circle the tank and whistle, refusing food, until he, too, died three days later.

Cetaceans are capable of cooperative behavior when the end result is mutually beneficial. Two young cetaceans, a false killer whale and a Pacific bottlenose dolphin, were kept in adjoining tanks at Sea Life Park. This housing arrangement, however, was unsuitable; the two preferred to room together. So when no one was around (apparently the animals knew they were doing something wrong), the dolphin, by far the more agile of the two, would jump over the partition that separated the tanks and join the whale. The trainers, who wanted to keep the animals separate, erected a larger barricade, one that was too wide to jump over. Even this did not deter the determined pair. The strong whale was able to move the barricade just enough for the dolphin to jump into its tank.

Creative tool use? Frankie and Floyd, the two male bottlenose dolphins we met in the last chapter who enjoyed mating with moray eels, were trying to get an eel out of its hiding place in a rock crevice. When they failed to dislodge the eel, one of them killed a scorpion fish, carried it over to the crevice, and poked the moray with the sharp poisonous spines on the fish's dorsal fin. That rather ingenious innovation worked, the eel emerged from the crevice, and the dolphins caught it.

In a similar example of creativity, a year-old male used bits of squid or fish as a tool to tease a red grouper. He would place the squid on the floor of the tank about a foot and a half from the grouper's rock home, then back away. When the grouper emerged to take the bait, the dolphin rushed in and grabbed it before the grouper could.

Dolphin Learning

Studying something as nebulous as intelligence is difficult under the best of circumstances. Try to measure cognitive abilities on an animal and the task becomes that much more complicated, the results even more subject to suspicion. A weakness, however small, in the experiment itself or in the researcher's ability to get the animal to respond can lead to false conclusions. And even when animals perform well, could they do better? Are we pushing them to the outer limits of their capabilities?

That depends on our ability to ask the animal the right question in the right way. We would like to say to a rat, dolphin, chimpanzee, or parrot, "Show us your best stuff." In reality, asking that question requires extensive training in which the animal is rewarded for responding to certain stimuli or commands with specific behaviors. Once the animal responds to commands in a predictable fashion, we can see how it reacts to novel stimuli or tasks. Can it solve a challenging new problem based on its previous training? It is also important that the commands and stimuli we choose for training are best suited for the perceptual abilities of the animal. It wouldn't make sense to use visual stimuli to study cognition in a nearly blind river dolphin

Visual Studies. A dolphin and a human looking at the same object may see things differently. Thus, in measuring dolphin visual cognition, it is important that we ask dolphins to respond to features that are relevant to *them*, not necessarily the ones important to *us*. The early experiments to determine bottlenose dolphins' ability to visually discriminate among different stimuli did not realize this. Long known for their acoustical prowess, dolphins were thought to be less gifted visually and early experiments seemed to confirm this notion.

In one experiment a Pacific whitesided dolphin had a problem discriminating between a blank white card and a card that contained two black lines. The dolphin's performance improved somewhat when the task was simplified by substituting a solid black card in place of the lined one.

A few years later, experimenters began reporting more encouraging dolphin performances on visual tasks. One research team tested a bottlenose dolphin's ability to discriminate discriminate the relative distances of in-air targets. From a stationary viewing bar, the dolphin was shown the targets and was taught to choose the nearer of the two by pushing one of two switches. The dolphin choose correctly in more than 90 percent of the trials.

Dolphins also did well in matching-to-sample experiments. Three-dimensional objects held by human trainers were presented at delays ranging from zero to eighty seconds. The animal's task was to look at the shapes and match the one designated as the "sample" stimulus with one of the others. Initially, with two-dimensional objects, dolphins had trouble generalizing the match-to-sample rule from one set of objects to another. That changed in later experiments, though, when three-dimensional objects were used or two-dimensional white objects were presented against a uniform black background

Another important visual study was perfomed at Louis Herman's Kewalo Basin Marine Mammal Laboratory in Hawaii. A bottlenose dolphin was presented with visual stimuli on a video screen. The dolphin, which had been trained to use a form of sign language, watched the small video monitor through an underwater viewing window as a trainer signed a command by moving her hands in a particular way. The dolphin responded correctly. Given that the dolphin responded correctly to a tiny video representation of a person, could it respond to an even more abstract signal? Through a series of steps, the image was reduced to the point where two white balls moving against a black background represented the movement of the person's hands. Incredibly, the dolphin still understood the commands. Researchers concluded that it was not the dolphin's vision that had improved but the experiments. The early studies did not take into account the way a dolphin's eyes work.

If a dolphin or any cetacean is to survive in the wild, it must be able to quickly recognize and categorize two- and three-dimensional forms and their movement. The cetacean eye is especially adapted for discriminating objects against the dark backdrop of their underwater world. What is that dark shadow looming up from below, how far away is it, and how fast is it moving? In the initial studies, researchers did not clearly differentiate between the relevant figure and the background. When presentation methods were designed to provide greater contrast, by presenting the figure against a uniform background, by changing how far away the figures were from the dolphin, or by moving them against a stationary background, the dolphins' performance markedly improved.

Training a Dolphin to Do Something New. A remarkable early breakthough in dolphin cognition studies came in 1965 when Karen Pryor, a dolphin trainer turned researcher, succeeded in training dolphins to perform novel behaviors, that is, behaviors that they had not been trained previously to perform. The subject of Pryor's training experiment was a female roughtoothed dolphin named Hou.

The experiment was frustrating for Hou because the protocol required that she not be rewarded for the same behavior that had earned her a fish in previous training sessions. Her pattern became routine. If she wasn't rewarded for her first behavior, Hou would run through her repertoire of previously rewarded behaviors, then fall into a rigid pattern of "porpoising," turning upside down, and circling. Then, one morning before the fifteenth session, the trainers noticed that Hou was unusually active.

She tail-slapped, and because that was unusual, the trainer rewarded it even before the session began. That session was like the others, with Hou going through her routine of previously rewarded behaviors, followed by the circling and porpoising. The one change was the addition of a tail slap when she reentered the water. That tail slap was rewarded and more followed. Before the session ended, Hou was doing nothing but tail slaps. Something must have clicked. Session sixteen began ten minutes later, and when the trainer reappeared, Hou became very excited. A fountain of novel behaviors came pouring out—twisting leaps, somersaulting in mid-air, swimming in figure eights. No more dejected circling; Hou was a changed animal.

Almost every session saw Hou perform a new behavior—sinking head downwards, jumping upside down, spitting water at the trainer. Eventually, the trainers were even able to control Hou's enthusiasm by rewarding only one new behavior per session. Hou had understood the concept, "Do something new." Although Pryor's achievement made a splash, it would be twenty-five years before researchers would use the ability of dolphins to perform novel behavior on command in controlled studies of dolphin intelligence.

Imitation: Mimicking Movement. One way in which individuals learn is by imitation, and dolphins have been frequently spotted imitating the behaviors, movements, and sounds of all types of creatures.

Haig, a captive bottlenose, frequently adopted the postures of her swimming mate of the moment. When that companion happened to be a skate, a member of the ray family of fish, Haig began to swim like a fish. The skate, with Haig following, swam in a straight line, made contact with the circular wall of the tank, and used one wing to push off from the wall, changing its direction. Haig, using her flipper, followed suit. Lying flat on the bottom beside a sleeping turtle, Haig would rise to the surface with the turtle for air. Unfortunately for the turtle, Haig later decided that it was fun to take the turtle back down before it made it to the surface, so that the turtle, and many successors, drowned. One dolphin that shared a pool with a seal soon was seen patterning its swimming style after its poolmate. In normal circumstances, the dolphin uses its flippers to steer and its flukes to propel it through the water. But after only a few months spent with the seal, the dolphin, like the seal but with a certain clumsiness, was using its flippers for propulsion, its flukes suddenly excess baggage in the water.

Another captive, a calf named Dolly, frequently tried to gain the attention of observers watching from the underwater viewing chamber by presenting them with feathers, stones, fish skins, and any other object she managed to get hold of. One day, as Dolly peered through the viewing window, an observer emitted a thick cloud of cigarette smoke. Dolly bolted off, found her mother, and after a moment swam back to squirt her reply: a mouthful of milk aimed at the glass through which the observer watched, astonished.

Dolphins have shown an ability to imitate tool use. In an earlier example, Daan, after watching a diver remove algae from a window in the tank, used a seagull feather, fish, sea slugs, stones, and paper to duplicate the diver's window cleaning. Several other dolphins in the same tank were unusually interested in the workings of a hollow steel scraper attached to a suction hose that a diver used to vacuum seaweed and other debris off the bottom of the tank. One night, the diver left the equipment in the tank. When humans looked in the next morning, Haig was pushing the hose with her flippers, with her rostrum resting on the scraper. Using a rocking motion, she moved it back and forth. A cloud rose from the tank's bottom, and Haig took a break from her work to eat some of the dislodged seaweed. Even after the suction apparatus had been removed from the tank, Haig was seen using a broken tile to scrape seaweed off the tank floor.

While there are many anecdotal examples of dolphin imitation, only recently have researchers tackled this area. Scientists at the Kewalo Basin Marine Mammal Laboratory in Hawaii worked with two dolphins to study imitation. One dolphin would be given the command to perform a behavior. The second dolphin, which could watch the other dolphin perform but could not see the command it was given, was asked to do what the other dolphin did—and did so.

Kewalo Basin dolphins Phoenix and Akeakamai were taught to create novel behavior and to perform behaviors synchronously. Phoenix and Akeakamai were then given both commands, meaning "Do something creative and do it together, simultaneously." Receiving the two commands, the dolphins circled underwater for some length of time before they began to swim synchronously and then leaped straight up into the air and, amazingly, simultaneously spit out jets of water.

Imitation: Mimicking Sounds. Although many birds learn their vocalizations, most mammals' sounds are genetically programmed and are not influenced by what they hear while they are growing up. While vocal learning is obviously important in our own species, it is surprisingly absent in our closest relatives, the great apes. Chimpanzees, however, may be capable of a limited amount of vocal learning, because individuals from different chimpanzee populations make the same calls in slightly different ways.

The converging songs of the humpback whales and the dialects of the killer whales both suggest that vocal learning is important in some cetaceans. Another marine mammal, the harbor seal, has shown a remarkable ability to learn new sounds. Hoover, a harbor seal at the New England Aquarium, learned to mimic human speech, even with a recognizable New England accent! Dolphins also have demonstrated exceptional skill at mimicking sounds.

At the Naval Oceans System Center in San Diego, workers around the beluga bay pen kept hearing a muffled conversation. Thinking that some people were around the corner chatting, a worker went to investigate and soon realized that the source of the chatter was a beluga whale.

We are able to tune in to a conversation, even in a crowd-ed room, because we have internal "filters" that enable us to ignore irrelevant noise. Sometimes these filters turn off and we suddenly become aware of the incoherent babble in the room around us. That is what the beluga sounded like, lots of people talking but nobody saying anything.

What sounded like human chatter, may, in fact, be part of the beluga's natural repertoire. In 1949, scientists made the first underwater recordings of a group of belugas conversing in the Saint Lawrence estuary. One sound was reminiscent of children shouting in the distance.

Animal psychologist Douglas Richards taught dolphins to imitate computer-generated sounds that were not within the animal's inherent repertoire. The sounds the dolphins were asked to mimic were like whistles and in the same frequency range as dolphin whistles. One of the dolphins not only imitated any new sound, but spontaneously imitated changes in the loudness of the sound.

In another study, when experimenters commanded a dolphin to imitate a sound, they would also play the model sound and hold up an object the animal had been taught to associate with the sound. The dolphin, for example, might be shown a pipe at the same time it heard a computer generated "whurrp." After the dolphin was accustomed to the exercise, the researcher might hold up the pipe but omit the sound, requiring the dolphin to reach into its memory and produce the sound that went with the object. Which, with practice, the animal was able to do.

Dolphins can deftly mimic artificial sounds but do they mimic each other? We don't know. Studying the underwater sounds of a group of dolphins was once no better than guesswork because it was impossible to know which animal in the group was doing the "talking." Ethologist Peter Tyack of the Woods Hole Oceanographic Institute overcame that obstacle when he developed devices that enable the observer to know the source of the whistle. A tool called a vocal light is attached to a dolphin's head or back with a suction cup. Then, every time the animal produces a sound, the vocalight lights up. The vocalights are made in several colors, a definite advantage when there are several dolphins in the pool together. Underwater hydrophones record the whistles and a poolside observer indicates which color vocalight is illuminated.

Vocalights were first used on a pair of captive bottlenose dolphins at a marine park on Cape Cod. As we've discussed, every dolphin has its own signature whistle, a sort of vocal fingerprint that identifies it. Some researchers have found that most of a dolphin's whistling repertoire is made up of its signature whistle. In the case of the Cape Cod dolphins, however, observers found that in addition to producing its signature whistle, each dolphin was adept at mimicking that of its tankmate. In fact, almost 20 percent of each dolphin's whistling was an imitation of the other's signature whistle.

Tyack suspects that when a dolphin imitates another's signature whistle, it is, in a sense, calling out the other's name. If one dolphin can imitate another's whistles as a way of calling its name, the animal also must be capable of making the same associations between each member of its group and their signature whistles. Tyack's team is now looking at dolphins' exact behavior, both when they emit their own signature whistles and when they mimic those of others. By studying how other dolphins respond when a dolphin whistles, they hope to test this hypothesis.

Can Dolphins Understand an Artificial Language?

Dr. John Dolittle, the fictitious defender of animal rights, spoke to the animals with ease, kindling the imagination of countless young and even not so young readers. Unfortunately, conversations between humans and intelligent animals in the real world are a far cry from the intellectual discourses that the good doctor and his animal devotees entertained us with. No, scientists and dolphins, chimpanzees, and other intelligent animals do not sit around, like Dolittle and his nonhuman friends, discussing the state of world affairs. But throughout the world, researchers and their animal subjects are navigating their way through the relatively uncharted waters of artificial language. Can intelligent animal species be taught to comprehend an artificial language, to understand that different word sequences mean different things? Is a word in an artificial language really used by animals in the same way we use words, to represent actions, objects, and concepts? You be the judge.

In the 1970s, a chimp and a gorilla sparked a bitter debate among behavioral scientists when it was disclosed that they had been taught sign language. One side argued that the acquisition of this "speech" reflected the animals' ability to think in symbols and communicate those thoughts. Skeptics scoffed. The results, they said, were due to nothing more impressive than rote conditioning. In the end, the doubters prevailed and a large body of work was dismissed as irrelevant.

But the gloom and doom were relatively short-lived. Stubborn researchers swallowed the bitter pill of rejection, dug in their heels, and concentrated on designing experiments that would hold up under the toughest scrutiny. The controversy continues, but today no one is laughing, least of all the scientific world.

One researcher who has contributed a large body of evidence on dolphin language comprehension is Louis Herman, the founder and director of Hawaii's Kewalo Basin Marine Mammal Laboratory, whose two captive bottlenose dolphins, Akeakamai (Ake) and Phoenix we met earlier in this chapter.

Herman used the pair to study language comprehension capabilities. Phoenix was taught a languagelike system in which objects and actions (for example, a Frisbee and "fetch") were represented by whistlelike computer-generated sounds. Ake was taught a sign language similar to the American Sign Language used by deaf people, which was communicated by the arm and hand gestures of a human trainer. Each "language" had a vocabulary of between thirty-five and forty gestural or sound "words" and a set of rules that determined how the words should be ordered to form "sentences." Some words represented objects in the dolphins' captive world, such as *gate, person, ball,* and *hoop.* Other words referred to actions—*toss, fetch, over;* object location—*surface, bottom;* or direction—*right, left.* The dolphin vocabulary also included words like *yes, no, question,* and *fish,* the reward for a good performance. In total, more than two thousand sentences could be constructed from this small vocabulary, each one with a specific meaning.

In communicating Ake's sign language, the trainer made gestures, each one representing a specific object, position modifier, and action that the dolphin had been taught. A signed command might be *person surfboard fetch,* commanding the dolphin to take a surfboard to a person. If, however, the word order was different—say, *surfboard person fetch*—the correct response would be for the dolphin to take the person to the surfboard. Sometimes the commands were longer, such as *water right basket fetch,* meaning that Ake should take the basket that was to her right (not the one to her left) to the stream of water that entered the pool from a hose.

In another phase of the study, the dolphins were trained to answer simple questions with either a *yes* or *no* response. The signer might gesture *hoop question,* asking the dolphin whether the hoop was present in the tank. The dolphin then was required to press either a paddle that indicated *yes* or one that meant *no.*

Herman's dolphins learned their new languages well. During a three-year period, both averaged more than 75 percent correct responses.

What is even more impressive than their ability to learn and respond correctly to the artificial language was the dolphins' reaction to novel variations of their vocabulary. Researchers mixed up word order, in some cases rendering the sentence nonsensical, to determine whether the dolphin had enough understanding of the vocabulary to alter its response accordingly. So good was the dolphins' understanding of these unfamiliar sentences that they often had to go out of their way to create a situation where following the command was possible. One day, for example, Phoenix for the first time was commanded to *bottom hoop through.* The hoop was lying flat on the bottom of the tank and this dolphin knew that even the most agile can't swim through a flat hoop. So she dived to the bottom of the tank and, using her rostrum, raised one edge of the hoop until it was vertical, and then swam through it. The dolphins had frequently been asked to toss various objects— Frisbees, balls, or other things floating in the tank—but never *water toss.* Yet when given that command, both attempted to toss the stream of water flowing into the pool by moving their heads through the water in much the same manner they used to toss a Frisbee.

Herman contends that his dolphins have clearly shown themselves to have a conceptual understanding of the words they've been taught and the rules governing word order. While most scientists agree that the dolphins' feats demonstrate impressive cognitive skills, they still debate whether those cognitive skills truly reflect linguistic ability.

At any rate, we haven't heard the last from either side.

DOLPHIN TOOLS

The fisherman spoke about a dolphin he saw regularly which sported a "funny growth" on its nose.

Our interest was sparked, but it was our first year of research at Shark Bay and we didn't even have our own boat. When we were able to borrow a small dinghy for a couple of days, we went searching for the dolphin the fisherman spoke of, but found nothing unusual.

A couple of years later, two members of the research team decided to have another look. Motoring out into the channel on a glassy calm day they saw it—a dolphin foraging with a strange-looking golden-brown growth on its snout. They watched the elusive dolphin for a while, trying to get a better look at the growth, when suddenly the dolphin surfaced without it! And then the next time the dolphin had it again. Once they got closer, they saw that the dolphin's funny nose was not the product of some disfiguring disease but was instead a cone-shaped sponge that hugged its beak like a glove over fingers. Sponges are filter-feeding invertebrates resembling plants, which are found on the ocean floor, and apparently the dolphin was using them deliberately. We subsequently identified several sponge wearers, all of them female.

The sponge wearers, it turned out, spend most of their time in a large channel in the Shark Bay area. Unlike most dolphins, which are highly social animals, these females are loners who spend most of their energy foraging with a sponge. Not necessarily always the same sponge, though; they sometimes trade in a worn-out one for a new model. Some sponges are small, barely covering the tip of the animal's snout, while others are huge, ungainly affairs that hang all over the wearer's head.

The sponge carriers clearly use the sponges to forage, but exactly how, we don't know. During the few times they come to the surface without a sponge, we may see them eating a fish or rapidly surfacing as though in hot pursuit of one. We suspect the sponge is used as a tool to protect the wearer's beak from rough encounters with rocks, sand, or the spines of poisonous fish as she probes at the bottom of the sea for food.

Sponge carriers apparently learn the trade from their mothers; we've seen infants wearing tiny sponges. Whatever they are doing with the sponge, the payoff does not seem very great as they spend an inordinate amount of the day foraging, leaving little time for a social life.

Dolphin Intelligence at Work in the Wild

In doling out the characteristics of a species, nature, like any penny-pinching accountant, carefully balances the benefits against the costs.

One trait that is particularly expensive, metabolically speaking, is a big brain. Twenty percent of the oxygen humans breathe goes to nourish their large brains. So from the stand-point of natural selection, it makes sense for only those creatures that truly need greater information-processing abilities to pay such a high price.

The question then becomes Why have dolphins evolved such large brains in relationship to their body size?

One idea is that the dolphins' remarkable echolocation capabilites have powered the evolution of the large brain. Much of their brain does seem devoted to rapid sound processing. But this hypothesis fails to explain why other species of echolocating dolphins and bats have much smaller brains, unless the larger brained dolphins are processing echolocation information in ways that are vastly more sophisticated than those of the small brained dolphins.

Another idea is that the dolphin brain enhances the animals' foraging abilities. Like the ape, which must remember where the best fruit trees are located and what time of year they ripen, the dolphin may also have a mental map of where and when this or that kind of fish can be found. Certainly, the dolphin's energy-rich diet of fish and squid may have smoothed the road to the evolution of a large brain more effectively than the simpler fare that is the mainstay for other animals.

Dolphins are social animals and it is the complexity of their social relationships that may deserve the most credit for promoting the evolution of a larger brain. It would be remarkable indeed if humans and dolphins developed large brains for the same reason. In both cases an external force created the necessary tension between cooperation and conflict that would favor more sophisticated social skills and hence a larger brain. The primary threat to humans was probably other groups of humans; dolphins may have been similarly threatened by other groups or alliances of dolphins. Some have suggested that the driving force behind dolphin intelligence was the threat from sharks, an especially dangerous predator to dolphin mothers and their calves.

It is certainly true that bottlenose dolphins have extremely complex social relationships. Consider the Shark Bay male alliances discussed earlier, in which each male forms long-term bonds with one or two other males for the purpose of herding females. Each of these pairs or trios has one or two other such alliances with whom they travel. The bonds between alliances are also based on access to females. Two alliances will attack another alliance to take their female or will jointly defend their own females from such attacks.

Males are not always bosom buddies, however. In some of the male trios, there seems to be considerable conflict; two of the males will be closely bonded and swim together for a while, even pushing or chasing the other male away. At different times, each of the males may be subjected to such temporary ostracism by the other two.

The same kind of odd-man-out behavior applies to alliances. At Shark Bay we've seen buddy alliances turn against each other when a third pair or group muscled in. The outsiders began spending time with each alliance, but rarely when both alliances were together. The newcomers even instigated an attack by one alliance against the other on an occasion when all three were together.

Nor is an individual's position guaranteed within an alliance. Before Real Notch and Hi befriended Chop, Bottomhook, and Lambda, they were very tight with Patches.

But when the new threesome joined the others, everybody ganged up on poor Patches. During one encounter, both alliances lined up head-to-head against Patches. The last male to join the lineup actually swam from behind Patches to take his place beside the others. Then they all attacked Patches, chasing and biting him. Shortly after that observation was made, Patches disappeared from the area and was never seen again.

If all of this strikes you as Machiavellian, you have the right impression. There is only one other species we know of that forms such complex male alliances. That species is *Homo sapiens*, as we know all too well—family against family, village against village, nation against nation.

9

Learning from Our Mistakes

If there was ever an animal in crisis, it is the baiji, the blue-gray river dolphin which makes its home in an ever-shrinking area of China's Yangtze River.

Documents dating more than sixteen hundred years ago make mention of this small dolphin with its tooth-lined snout and short, muscular tail. It is impossible to speculate how many baiji once inhabited the river, swimming strongly but slowly, foraging where tributaries join the Yangtze, sometimes working up a cloud of mud as they hunted at the river bottom. Today, however, we have a good idea of this species' population and the news is indeed grim.

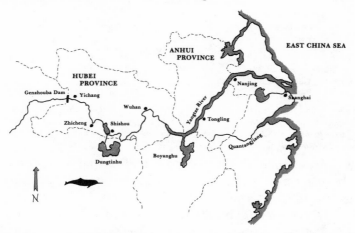

This map shows the distribution of China's baiji, a river dolphin whose numbers have shrunk to around 200 individuals, making this the most endangered of all cetacean species.

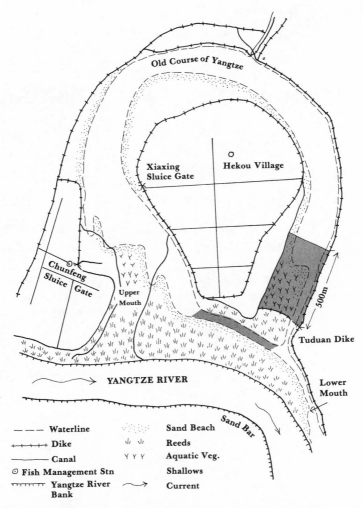

In an effort to halt the destruction of the endangered baiji river dolphin, the Chinese government has designated several protected areas. Scientists hope to establish breeding groups in reserves that are adjacent to (but isolated from) the Yangtze. Only time will tell whether this action will ultimately save this dolphin from extinction.

An estimated two hundred baiji are all that remain, a number that makes this small dolphin the rarest and most endangered of all cetaceans.

How is a species driven to the brink of extinction? Some cetacean species' numbers have dwindled dangerously due to widespread slaughter. But the weapon that has struck what ultimately may be the fatal blow to the baiji is not the deadly harpoon but progress, a word that implies positive changes—that is, unless you are an animal.

At one time, some baiji were deliberately killed for their skin, meat, and fat. But these were isolated catches, never organized like commercial whaling operations elsewhere. Since 1949, the Chinese government has considered the baiji a "protected" animal and has made clear that anyone who intentionally kills the dolphin will be severely punished. Unfortunately, most of the baiji killed are victims of accidents.

Living in the most important waterway in the most populated country in the world is not for the faint of heart. Boat traffic is reminiscent of a freeway at rush hour. Fishermen and their nets of death have rendered the Yangtze a minefield for anything unlucky enough to live there. The shore frequently—and literally—explodes as new ground is broken for yet another commercial establishment. Dynamite, used in construction and sometimes illegally for fishing, kills baiji; in one construction blast, six dolphins' lives were claimed.

These days the greatest threat to the dolphins—by some accounts responsible for half the deaths—are the bottom longlines that fishermen set to snag bottom-feeding fish. Dolphins become snagged in these so-called rolling hooks when they go near a fish that has been caught in the sharp barbless teeth. While the government has now banned rolling hooks, that hasn't stopped some fishermen from casting these destructive devices.

Collisions with boat propellers also have claimed a fair share of baiji, as many as 32 percent of accidental known deaths. And over the next decade an anticipated doubling of river traffic is almost bound to increase these numbers.

Finally, the destruction of habitat has a detrimental effect on the continuation of the species. Dams and other water barriers have changed both the distribution and supply of fish. The baijis' food supply has been further diminished by overfishing, widespread pollution, and the draining of lakes to increase the amount of farmland in China's countryside.

The Chinese government is waging an education campaign designed to make people, especially fishermen, more aware of this endangered creature and its need for protection. While the number of accidental deaths may be waning slightly, the fishermen appear reluctant to abandon the traditional methods of their trade for more dolphin-friendly methods.

Seminatural reserves are being developed in areas where the dolphins can be protected. A captive breeding program would take place, with the goal of maintaining the numbers and genetic diversity of the *baiji*. Eventually, some of the animals would be set loose in the wild.

It is too soon to know if any of these solutions will rescue the baiji in time. Killing the dolphins was easy. Conserving them is a more challenging proposition.

A History of Death

Long ago, years before man discovered that the body of a whale could be used in the production of so many useful things or that nets could be used to catch fish, the earth's waters abounded with cetacean life. Large numbers of the majestic blue whale fed on swarms of krill close to the Antarctic pack ice. The diminutive vaquita prospered in the Gulf of California. The rather solitary Ganges river dolphins traveled upstream yearly as the water level rose, entering smaller streams where the young may have remained for their first year of life. Four stocks of bowhead whales, among the most vocal of the baleens, lived their lives among the ice. And northern right whales flourished in the North Pacific.

Today, these dolphins, porpoises, and whales, as well as some others, are either endangered or teetering on the brink.

Determining the population of a species is an important, although uncertain, task. By surveying a population of whales or dolphins, we get a sense of whether the species is endangered or, at the other end of the spectrum, thriving.

In the days of active whaling, a number of methods were used to assess the status of a population, most of which have now been proven unreliable. The catch was often used as an indicator of whether or not a species was abundant in particular waters. Pregnancy rates and the age of maturity were ascertained by examining the reproductive organs of dead animals. Individuals were sometimes marked to estimate population size and to determine from which stock they were derived. In many cases where it was clear that the current population level was much lower than in the past, the initial population size was calculated based on the number of whales killed.

Today, there is a movement toward more reliable population surveys. Researchers are now attempting to directly assess whale populations, many of which have never been counted.

What they have found is that some populations have been seriously depleted—perhaps irreparably—by humans. Here are some of the ways in which we have killed dolphins and whales.

Ships of Destruction. This was a frequent scenario until the end of the 1980s: The factory ship sat in the waters near Africa's Cape of Good Hope. The size of an aircraft carrier, the ship and its crew of seven hundred were a testament to progress. Each factory ship traveled with its own fleet: the catcher boats' job was to find the whale and kill it, while the tow boats were responsible for hauling the bodies back to the mother ship. Gone were the days when small ships shot their instruments of death, watched them hit their mark, and then carried the fruits of their labors back to port to be processed. Now a whale could be killed, chopped, boiled, and baked without ever having to touch down on land.

The whalers were hunting blue whales. Lookouts in the catcher boats scanned the sea for feathery spray, the mark of a whale that had exhaled. When the lookout spotted evidence of a blow, the boat revved up its engine in hot pursuit. The captain, a crack shot, manned a swiveling gun in the prow of the boat. As he closed in on the whale, he mentally calculated the distance—one hundred yards, eighty, seventy-five— at fifty he pulled the trigger. A harpoon plunged toward the whale and struck deep. The head of the harpoon contained four claws, to which a grenade was attached, along with a trailing rope. When the hit came, the whale dived to escape it, providing the catalyst that exploded the harpoon's head, opening up the claws, whose greedy fingers pierced the whale's vital organs. Once these were in place, any motion, however slight, only served to do more damage.

Had the harpoon torn through the whale's heart, death would have been quick. But quick hits were the exception. More often the whale fought, diving deep. Then the crew might use winches to hoist the animal up, so that a second harpoon could be launched. Fighting, lashing, blood streaming, vomit spewing, the whale would tear through the water, sometimes dragging the boat behind it. Death might be a long time in coming. Studies showed that it took minke whales almost four minutes to die once the harpoon found its mark, fin whales more than six minutes, and sperm whales as long as fifteen minutes.

When the harpoon had finally done its job, the whale's body turned over, belly-up, the result of the distribution of air and oil. A hunter pierced the body with a lance and pumped compressed air into it to keep the whale afloat. Then workers loped off all but the stubs of the animal's flukes, cut a notch in what was left of the tail to identify the boat that was responsible for the trophy, and drove a flag into the belly to signal the tow boats. Then the catcher boat was off in search of another victim.

Tow boats could carry as many as seven dead blue whales behind them. The carcasses they found, upturned and bereft of flukes, bore little resemblance to the formerly magnificent creatures. The compressed air had forced the female whales' nipples from their slits and sometimes a male's penis hung pitifully.

When the whales were brought to the factory ship, an enormous crashing, clanging claw known as a grab was fitted onto the tail stump. The whale was then pulled through the air to the flensing platform where workers cut through its skin and blubber. Hooks were inserted into the skin, then winches yanked away strips of blubber as deftly as a paring knife peels a potato.

Then it was time for the saw, whose teeth ate through the head, severed the vertebrae, crunched bone.

Almost every part of the whale found its way into the appropriate boiling or baking vats. Within thirty minutes after it had entered the factory ship, nothing even remotely resembling a whale remained.

Commercial whaling struck a blow from which much of the baleen world has yet to recover. Whalers reduced the population of northern right whales to a few hundred in the North Atlantic, probably even less in the North Pacific. At the beginning of our century, a quarter of a million blue whales swam the waters of the Southern Hemisphere; now there are only a few hundred blue whales left there. Fin, sei, and humpback whale populations were also decimated.

Compared to their not-so-distant ancestors, today's whales are lucky. Since 1986, commercial whaling has been banned, except for the purpose of so-called scientific research.

It was a victory all too long in coming. The International Whaling Commission (IWC) was established in 1946, but was frequently criticized as a "whaler's club," whose primary concern was with stabilizing the world market for whale products, not with the conservation of whales. In the 1970s, however, whales gained some political clout when a growing number of humans began speaking out against their treatment. There were two separate issues: first, conservation, to protect species from extinction, and second, animal rights, to halt the inhumane ways in which these animals were killed, or the killing itself.

The first battle in the war against the widespread slaughter of whales came in 1974 when the IWC voted to regulate whaling according to the principles of sustainable utilization. Under this system, the IWC attempted to manage each whale population so that it could not dip below a certain level from which it might never recover. This move was somewhat successful in protecting especially depleted species such as fin and sei whales and some populations of sperm whales.

Gradually, thanks to growing public support, the noose was tightened around the commercial whaling industry's neck.

Catch quotas were reduced for some species and the IWC moved to control the number of bottlenose and other beaked whales, pilot, and killer whales that could be taken, species whose slaughter had never before been restricted. By 1980, more than three-quarters of the catch permitted to commercial whalers was comprised of minke whales—a species that still had abundant numbers, with 14 percent of the catch made up of sperm whales.

The IWC called a moratorium on commercial whaling in 1982, to become effective in 1986. All whaling nations had complied with the moratorium by 1989. The moratorium was not permanent, however, and was subject to review beginning in 1990. Since that time, Iceland, Norway, and Japan have all clamored for the resumption of commercial whaling on species such as minke whales, which have large, viable stocks.

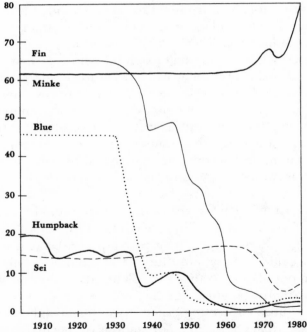

With the exception of minke whales, the populations of the baleen whales were devastated by commercial whaling in this century.

Dissatisfied with the IWC's negative response to its request, Norway announced plans to resume whaling on its own and Iceland left the IWC to start a new organization. The IWC is in danger of losing its ability to regulate whaling.

From a conservation perspective, some people worry that if the IWC crumbles, commercial whaling will be difficult to regulate, especially if African and other nations not previously involved in large-scale whaling begin to take it up. Minke whale populations appear healthy and could withstand limited whaling, but the long-term viability of other species is still very much in doubt because of relatively new dangers such as marine pollution and the loss of food resources. We don't know why, for example, over the past few years, a number of sperm whales have washed up on beaches in northern Europe. If a factor such as pollution is causing whale deaths, then a resumption of whaling based on models of a healthy population could have disastrous consequences.

The argument from the animal rights perspective is that whales should not be killed, regardless of their numbers. Whales, some argue, have an intrinsic value that sets them apart from other commercially taken animals such as cows and chickens. Supporters point to their large brains and intelligence as factors that should weigh against their commercial exploitation—although, as we have seen, not all cetaceans have particularly large brains. The thought of killing a creature so large and regal also offends many people. Some believe that, given our miserable track record of taking care of things on land, we should leave the great mammals of the oceans alone. But try telling that to a coastal culture that depends on the sea for its living.

Subsistence Whaling. On a cluster of islands halfway between Scotland and Iceland, an annual event is anticipated with much the same relish that in most places might greet a national holiday. Here on the Faroe Islands, though, you won't find fireworks marking this momentous day. What you will find are entire families, often right down to the smallest child, lining the shore ready to sever the spinal cords of the long-finned pilot whales that some of the village men drive to shore.

For centuries the Faroe Islanders have preyed upon the pilot whales that often visit their coasts during the summer. When a herd is sighted, some of the best sailors jump into their small boats and attempt to encircle it, banging and slapping their oars against the water to turn the whales toward shore. Given the fact that pilot whales are one of the most socially cohesive species and are likely to follow one another, regardless of the consequences, this is not as difficult as it sounds. After the pilots are driven onto the shore, they are killed with a large knife called a gaff. The whales, or *grindhval,* as they are called in the Faroe Islands, are then butchered and their meat divided among the population.

Subsistence whaling by native populations is not banned under the IWC moratorium on commercial whaling, although in some cases the commission has set quotas on the number of whales that can be taken.

Throughout the world, whales continue to be hunted by native populations, often by the same methods used by their ancestors. In the Philippines, natives hunt Bryde's whales by jumping from small boats onto the whale and plunging heavy fourteen- to eighteen-inch hooks into its back. After the whale has exhausted itself attempting to escape the hook, it is killed with a cut behind the head. Until recently, residents of the Azores and Madeira, island groups belonging to Portugal, hunted sperm whales with hand harpoons. Madeira has now declared its waters a marine mammal sanctuary. On the islands of Lembata and Solor in Indonesia, natives use long bamboo poles topped with a razor-sharp blade to kill about fifty sperm, Bryde's, and minke whales each year. And Alaskan Eskimos kill about two dozen bowhead whales each year, while Canadian and Alaskan natives take a couple of hundred belugas as well.

Proponents of subsistence whaling argue that it is not only necessary from a material standpoint, but that whaling occupies an important place in these native cultures. The opposing side points to the inhumane ways in which the whales

are killed and argues that the culture argument is weak because native hunters often use nontraditional technology such
as motor boats during their hunts.

Small Cetacean Fisheries. In some parts of the world
the waters still run red with the blood of small cetaceans killed
for their meat. An estimated one hundred thousand dolphins,
porpoises, and small whales meet this fate each year. Unlike
the large whales, small cetaceans are not protected by the IWC
moratorium. In fact, in some countries the ban on the big
whales has only served to make dolphins and smaller whales
more attractive to hunters.

As of 1988, Japan had increased its take of Dall's porpoises to forty thousand a year, a number that has since been
dropped back to eighteen thousand. Hunters in the Arctic
may have seriously compromised white whale and narwhal
populations, and fisheries off the coast of Sri Lanka may pose
a threat to several species in that part of the world. Thus far,
however, the best the IWC has done is to affirm its resolve to
collect information on small cetacean fisheries and to determine the status of the individual species' populations.

Japan is a major exploiter of dolphins and some small
whales. Visit a local market on Japan's Izu Peninsula, forty
miles southwest of Tokyo, and you will find the remains of
countless striped dolphins, now nothing more than dark
bricks of flesh enveloped by blubber. After a dolphin school is
spotted, village fishing boats form an arc behind the animals.
Metal pipes with bottoms flared like trombones hang over the
sides of the boats. To maneuver the school into the harbor,
fishermen bang on the pipes with hammers. When the dolphins have been successfully driven into the harbor, a net
closes off their escape.

For many years, the dolphin catch was more than plentiful, so much so that nine villages on the Izu Peninsula
maintained dolphin fleets. Only a decade ago, a drive was likely
to yield a thousand dolphins at a time. Now the only fleet left is
at Futu and the fishermen have plenty of free time. One
drive—the first in two years—resulted in a catch of only thirty
animals. There are few dolphins left in these waters to kill.

Death by Net. They've been called curtains of death and they are a dolphin's worst nightmare come true. Although the 1980s saw the end, at least temporarily, to the commercial slaughter of the baleen and sperm whales, the decade gave birth to a new death instrument, the drift net. As of 1990, the U.S. Marine Mammal Commission estimated that twenty-five thousand miles of nets—enough to encircle our planet—had invaded our seas.

Like invisible fences, the nets hang throughout the water, entrapping and killing anything that is unlucky enough to make contact with these invisible fiber walls. Scores of cetaceans, fur seals, and seabirds, as well as fish, meet their end when they become trapped in the nets. For reasons that are not yet understood, the dolphins' echolocation abilities do not prevent them from making their way into the nets. And once they are in, they drown.

It is impossible to know how many cetaceans have been killed in these nets, but the numbers have to be incredibly high. In one study, more than forty-one million animals representing more than one hundred species died in drift nets so that fishermen could harvest one hundred six million neon flying squid. Many of the nets have torn free during storms and drifted farther out to sea—ghost nets, impervious to rot, continuing to vanquish an assortment of marine life.

The devastation wrought by these nets has been so great that the United Nations General Assembly called for a halt of all large-scale drift net fishing by mid-1992. Even though no new nets are being cast, the effect will no doubt be felt for generations.

Racing the baiji toward extinction is the vaquita in the Gulf of California. Around 1929, fishermen pursuing the prized totoba switched from fishing with spears to gill nets, which have entrapped vaquita. It has been difficult to assess the current population levels of the vaquita, but there are thought to be only a few hundred left. Ironically, the totoba themselves are now endangered and fishing for them is illegal. Yet fishermen continue to illegally take these fish, along with thirty to forty vaquita every year.

The incidental take of dolphins is not always by fishermen trying to make a living. Around the South Island of New Zealand, weekend recreational gill netters helped deplete the Hector's dolphins, whose total population of only three to four thousand resides solely around the South Island. Even though the fishermen weren't economically dependent upon gill nets, the opposition to relinquishing their use was strong. Subsequently, New Zealand established a marine mammal sanctuary in the area where the dolphins were most heavily concentrated.

Other dolphins whose numbers have been driven dangerously low as a result of nets include harbor porpoises in the eastern and western North Atlantic, and bottlenose and humpbacked dolphins along the eastern coast of South Africa.

If you have ever doubted the power of one person to make a positive impact on the world, consider the case of Samuel LaBudde. In 1987, LaBudde joined a Panamanian tuna boat as its cook. Armed with a video camera, LaBudde appeared to be taking casual pictures of the ship and its crew. What he was really taping was the widespread destruction of dolphins—fifteen years after the Marine Mammal Protection Act had ordered fishermen selling tuna to the United States to approach "zero mortality" for dolphins. Despite such "protection," one hundred fifty thousand dolphins were killed that year by fishermen pursing tuna.

Purse-seine fishing had been used by the tuna industry since 1959. Tuna vessels comb the ocean for dolphins because the fish are often found swimming beneath the larger creatures. After the school is spotted, the fishermen encircle both dolphins and tuna with a mile-long seine net, closed off at the bottom like a purse. In the early years more than a quarter of a million dolphins were killed in these nets annually. Gradually, however, American tuna fishermen found a way to reduce the number of dolphins killed—a method known as "backdown," which allows the net to dip below the surface, enabling the dolphins, but not the fish, to escape. Even so, the dolphin slaughter was still substantial, as LaBudde's tapes showed, and the tapes rallied the world, resulting in the drive

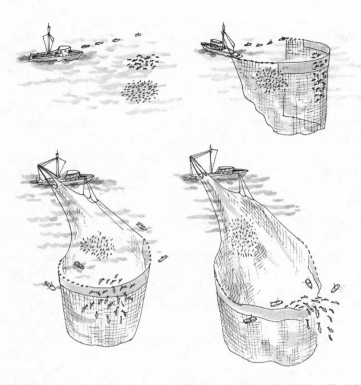

The purse-seine method for capturing tuna that are swimming with dolphins. The dolphins, along with the tuna, are trapped in the net, then part of the net is lowered in hopes that the dolphins will escape. This "backdown" method of releasing dolphins has helped to reduce the number of deaths; unfortunately, many dolphins still die in the nets because they either are unable to get out or aren't given sufficient time to do so. Survivors may be recaptured repeatedly and we don't know how this may affect their ability to feed or reproduce.

for "dolphin safe" tuna. Today, most nations ban imports of tuna caught by the encirclement of dolphins and the number of dolphin deaths attributable to that method is down to twenty thousand a year.

Destroying the Cetaceans' World. The main foe threatening the continuation of some of the most vulnerable cetacean species is the destruction of habitat. The animals who are most affected are those who live in rivers or coastal areas.

We've seen what development along the Yangtze has done to the baiji, but this small dolphin species is by no means a lone victim. Other river species are being devastated by the damming of rivers, which can split already small populations into even smaller groups, too small to remain viable. Hydroelectric development on the river systems of western India has virtually wiped out the Indus susu from that area. Today, only about five hundred of them are left, and these are all in Pakistan. Damming and other coastal development in South America has had a negative effect on the boto, especially those in the Amazon basin. Coastal mangrove swamps rich in fish are being destroyed, and with them the food source for many dolphins.

Pollution. The muddy brown Galveston ship channel is not the sort of waterway where one would voluntarily go for a swim. Huge freighters unload oil platforms for repair and some of the oil spills into the bay in greasy black pools. Nevertheless, it isn't unusual to see trawlers scraping the bot-

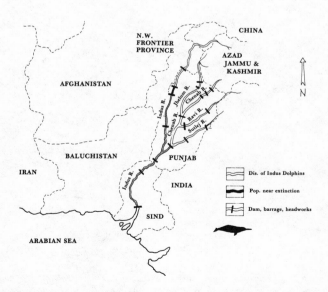

Distribution of the Indus River dolphin. This endangered dolphin used to be found in India but today its range is limited to two provinces of Pakistan.

tom of the channel for grass shrimp. And following the boats, bottlenose dolphins are sometimes in plain view, snapping up the shrimp and fish that the boats stir up.

In modern times oceans and rivers have become dumping grounds for the waste products of our increasingly industrialized society. Oil spills are no longer big news. Pesticides, polychlorinated biphenyls (PCBs), and heavy metals are dumped, blown by the wind, or transmitted by air particles into the sea, where they enter the food chain. A predator eats prey contaminated with the chemical. Later, that predator is eaten by a larger animal, and so the chemical becomes even more concentrated. By the time the cetaceans and seabirds, animals at the top of the food chain, eat the pollutant-carrying prey, the chemical is more highly concentrated and, as such, much more dangerous.

What is it like to live in such a polluted environment? And what physical effect does eating food that lives in such a world have on cetaceans?

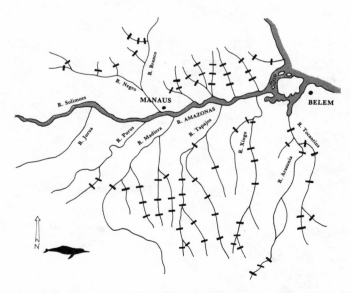

A major problem facing many of the world's river dolphins is a dwindling habitat. This map shows how the construction of dams on the Amazon River has radically reduced the waters in which these creatures are free to roam.

Autopsies have found pesticides and heavy metals in the blubber, muscle, liver, and brain of many species. Some parts of the world—the Baltic Sea, the western Mediterranean, the California coast, the Gulf of Mexico, and the coasts of Japan—are fouled beyond belief; even the Arctic and Antarctic, the earth's last frontiers, have not been able to escape some pollution.

It is impossible to say just how many cetaceans die as a result of eating polluted food. Most deaths due to pollution probably aren't recognized as such unless several individuals die together, as happened to some fin whales in the Mediterranean which were poisoned by heavy metals from industrial waste dumped into the water. What we do know is that when a whale or dolphin eats food containing pollutants, the chemical finds its way into the animal's blubber. There it stays, apparently causing no real harm, until the animal's body comes under stress. Perhaps the fish are in scant supply, or maybe the animal is a nursing mother. Whatever the reason, when an animal has need of its food store, the floodgates open and its body is suddenly bombarded with poisons. When that happens, death may be quick.

Or slow. In 1982, scientists began examining dead belugas who had lived in the Gulf of Saint Lawrence, and what they found was horrifying. These whales were swimming toxic waste dumps, contaminated with more than two dozen organic and inorganic substances including levels of PCBs, DDT, and mirex that were among the highest ever recorded in marine mammals. Chemical concentrations in stillborn calves revealed that females passed their contaminants to the fetus through the placenta. In fact, so much of the poison had been transferred by nursing mothers to their young that females actually had lower toxin loads than males.

The researchers examined forty dead animals and found a multitude of ailments: malignant tumors, a herpes-like skin disease, perforated gastric ulcers, and a host of other maladies. Although the commercial whaling of these animals was halted as long ago as the 1950s, there are still fewer than five hundred belugas in the Gulf of Saint Lawrence. Will these belugas survive? That depends on whether the flow of toxic compounds into the Saint Lawrence and the Great Lakes basin can be reduced significantly.

The Gray Whale—A Small Glimmer of Optimism

If there is one success story, proof that man's protection *can* make a difference, it is the recovery of the gray whale.

Prior to the days of commercial whaling as many as forty thousand grays bore their calves off the coast of Baja California and then made their way to the summer feeding grounds in the Bering Sea. It isn't known to what levels this eastern North Pacific stock of grays was depleted by whaling, but they were so endangered that legislation was passed in 1937 to protect them from the harpoons of the commercial whaler. Today, there are more than twenty-one thousand of this stock of gray whales and the population is estimated to have increased 3.2 percent each year during the past twenty years.

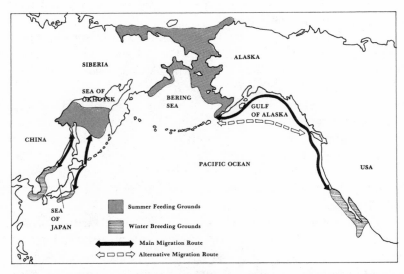

The migration patterns of the world's two populations of gray whales. The North American population has enjoyed a strong recovery from the days of commercial whaling and now supports a booming whale-watching industry. The Asian population, however, has not recovered significantly.

Thanks to their protected status, these whales may once again approach their original numbers. The International Whaling Commission now allows up to 179 of this stock of grays to be harvested each year by local communities, a number that does not appear to have adversely affected the population's growth.

Alas, the gray whale's success has not been a total one. Long ago, gray whales swam the cold waters of the North Atlantic. Now this stock is extinct—possibly the victims of commercial whaling. No one knows for certain. Another stock of gray whales that has not readily bounced back from exploitation is the one that makes its home in the western North Pacific. An estimated one to two hundred gray whales currently migrate between the waters off the Korean peninsula and those of the Sea of Okhotsk. Before the days of commercial whaling, as many as ten thousand of these bottom-feeding whales may have lived in this area. Despite governmental protection, this stock thus far has not shown signs of recovering.

Conserving What Is Left

Within the pages of this book we have attempted to take you on a journey into a world where only a few humans can travel. If we have accomplished only one thing by drawing back the curtain on this seldom-seen world, let it be your new-found appreciation and respect for the creatures we call cetaceans.

As far back as records take us, humans have been fascinated by the mammals that moved to the sea. Yet we've done everything we can to destroy them. Still, they live on, in populations often battered beyond belief, but nevertheless a continued presence.

In recent years, those of us who care about the fate of dolphins and whales have seen enormous hurdles crossed. People from all walks of life have rallied to the cetacean cause, helping to rid our waters of large-scale death factories and the maze of nets that make swimming through the ocean as perilous as traveling the wrong way on a busy city street. Captive breeding programs are now under way to try to enhance the chances that many of the especially vulnerable species will be alive to witness the next millennium. In some cases, reserves are being planned where activities harmful to the protected cetaceans would be prohibited. Moreover, scientists throughout the world are every day uncovering new information about whales' and dolphins' feeding and breeding habits, their life cycle, and social structure, all of which may prove invaluable in our quest to improve the quality of their existence. These are all steps in the right direction, and those who have worked so hard to see them enacted should be commended.

But it is not time to rest yet, nor to pat ourselves on the back, confident that the future of the world's whales and dolphins is assured. Solving the problems of the past may prove relatively simple when compared to what we're up against both now and in the future. Stopping a harpoon is certainly less complicated than halting the myriad types of pollutants that flood into the ocean continuously. Thousands of dolphins each year meet their end in nets, and small cetacean fisheries, unregulated, for the most part, also claim vast numbers.

No, it will not be easy. But throughout history, humans driven by nothing more than iron will and a desire to do what is right have often accomplished what was thought to be impossible.

Given their role in the food chain, the well-being of cetacean populations is a good barometer of the health of the ecosystems in which they live. Likewise, our ability to safely see all of the world's species of whales and dolphins into the next century and beyond may foretell our own ecological future on this planet.

Glossary

Altruism: Helping behavior in which an individual performs personally costly behavior for the welfare of another.

Baleen: A series of horny plates made of fingernail-like material that grow down from the sides of some whales' upper jaws. The baleen strains huge amounts of water containing plankton and other minute food particles. The mysticete whales, also called baleen whales, feed in this manner.

Bow-riding: Cetaceans' habit of riding pressure waves created by the bow of a boat or sometimes even by a larger cetacean.

Breaching: Action in which a whale or dolphin leaps out of the water.

Cetacea: The taxonomic order to which whales and dolphins belong.

Cetacean: A whale, dolphin, or porpoise.

Cetology: The branch of zoology that deals with whales and dolphins.

Delphinidae: A taxonomic family that includes many of the dolphins.

Drift nets: Invisible gill nets used to trap fish but that also trap and drown countless numbers of cetaceans.

Flukes: The two lobes of a cetacean's tail.

Lobtailing: The raising of the flukes above the water and slapping them down against the surface.

Migration: The two-way movement of some species between their breeding and feeding grounds.

Monogamy: Mating system in which one male and one female mate for one season, several seasons, or even for life. There is no evidence that any whale or dolphin species is monogamous.

Mysticeti: Taxonomic suborder to which the large baleen whales belong.

Odontoceti: Taxonomic suborder to which the toothed whales and dolphins belong.

Polygamy: The mating of one individual with more than one individual of the opposite sex.

Polygyny: A form of polygamy in which one male mates with more than one female.

Promiscuity: A system in which both sexes breed with several members of the opposite sex.

Purse-seine nets: Nets used to trap tuna, which also have been responsible for the deaths of hundreds of thousands of dolphins.

Rorquals (Balaenopteridae): A family of mysticete whales that includes humpback, minke, fin, and blue whales.

Rostrum: A whale's or dolphin's beak.

Spy-hopping: The cetacean's habit of rising vertically out of the water head first, often with just the eyes above the surface, sometimes with the entire head, and slowly rotating, scanning a 360-degree field.

INDEX

NOTE: Italicized page numbers refer
to picture captions.

A

Aeriel feats, 5. *See also* Breaching;
Leaping; Lobtailing
Affection, 43. *See also* Touch
Age, 41, 42, 149-50, 203.
See also type of whale or dolphin
Altruism, 106, 129-35
Amundin, Mats, 80
Anchovies, 69-70, 111
Anger/aggression, 33-34, 43, 91, 113-
14, 143, 149, 197-98. *See also* Males:
relationships among
Animal rights, 205, 207
Aristotle, 13
Artificial languages, 192-94
Artiodactyles, 19

B

Babysitters. *See* Caretaker females
Baiji river dolphins, 15, 81, 181-82, 199-
202, *199, 200*
Baleen whales
characteristics of, 9, 14-15, 17
and commercial whaling, 205, *206*
communication of, 77, 79, 80, 88-91,
112
and cooperation, 132
and defense, 109
diet of, 15, 17, 50-51, *52*, 59
examples of, 14-15
feeding methods of, 50-53
and foraging/hunting for food, 57-58,
59, 67, 111, 168
gender differentiation among, 14, 42
groupings/social lives of, 17, 105, 106,
107-8, 109, 111, 112
hearing of, 27
intelligence of, 181
magnetic sense of, 34
male relationships among, 153
migration of, 57-58, 139
mother-calf relationships of, 168, 170
odontocetes compared with, 14
parasites of, 116

physiology of, 27, 50-53
reproduction/mating of, 57-58, 112,
139-40, 148, 153, 156
size of, 14, 42
and smell, 28-29
sperm whales relationship to, 17
as a suborder of Cetacea, 14
toothed ancestors of, 17
and touch, 33
traveling characteristics of, 17
See also specific type
Ballance, Lisa, 69
Barnacles, 115-16, 153
Bats, 27, 196
Beaked whales
and anger/aggression, 55
"battle teeth" of, 151
communication of, 81
conservation of, 206
diet of, 54
feeding methods of, 54-55
gender differentiation among, 42,
54-55
as odontocetes, 15
physiology of, 54
reproduction/mating of, 151
species of, 16
Beluga whales
age of, 41
and the bends, 46
and color, 41
and commercial whaling, 208
communication of, 18, 76, 77, 79, 91,
92, 190
diet of, 54, 55
feeding methods of, 54, *54*
and foraging/hunting for food, 58,
176
geographic location of, 18, *76*
groupings/social lives of, 110-11
intelligence of, 190
migration of, 110-11
and mother-calf relationships, 163
narwhals as relatives of, *76*
as odontocetes, 15
physiology of, 54, *54*
and pollution, 215-16
and small cetacean fisheries, 209
stress sensitivity of, 30

and taste/smell, 30
and touch, 32
and vision, 41
Bends, 46-47
Biopsy darting, 146
Birds, 112, 115, 146-47
"Bite and spit" method of attack, 118
Blowholes, 21, *22*, 33, 42, 89-90
Blubber, 19-20, 21, 74, 116, 215
Blue whales
    as baleen whales, 15
    commercial slaughter of, 203-5
    communication of, 88
    decline in number of, 202, 205
    diet of, 53, 58
    as food, 58
    and foraging/hunting for food, 58
    male relationships among, 152
    mother-calf relationships of, 165
    pygmy, 51
    reproduction/mating of, 152, 161
    size of, 14, 15
Body language, 43
Boto river dolphins
    feeding methods of, 53
    geographic location of, 18
    groupings/social lives of, 108
    habitat destruction of, *213*
    navigation of, 44
    physiology of, 36, 53
    and sleep, 45
    and touch, 32-33
    uniqueness of, 15
    and vision, 36, 44
Bottlenose dolphins
    age of, 42
    and altruism/cooperation, 64-66, 128-
    29, 132, 134-35, 184
    anger/aggression of, 43, 113, 114,
    125, 197, 198
    brain of, 18
    calves of, 49, 113, 155, 175, 178-79
    characteristics of, 18-19
    communication of, 79, 82, 84-85, 87-
    88, 91, 97, 98-100, 114, 125, 172, 191
    conservation of, 206
    and defense, 39-40, 170, 171-74
    diet of, 24, 50, 62-64, 68, 69
    and drift net fishing, 211

and echolocation, 24-27, 79
escorting of, 124-25
and false killer whales, 184
female relationships among, 49, 114,
127-29, 157, 177-78
and foraging/hunting for food, 39,
49, 55-56, 58, 61, 62-64, 68, 71, 72, 82,
172-73
"free rides" of, 30-31
gender differentiation among, 42
gender relationships among, 114-15,
125, 128, 155, 177- 78, 197
geographic location of, 18
groupings/social lives of, 31-32, 108-9,
112-13, 114-15, 120,123-29, 170,
197-98
herding of, 114, 124-27, 132, 141, 155,
197
intelligence of, 181-82, 184, 185, 186,
188, 191, 192-94, 197-98
life span of, 161
male relationships among, 18-19, 113,
114, 123-27, 132, 141, 154, 155, 177-
78, 197-98
male-calf relationships of, 155
migrations of, 55-56
mother-calf relationships among, 49,
82, 84-85, 128, 162-63, 164, 165, 166,
168-69, 170, 171-74, 177-79, *178*
physiology of, 24-27, 36, 37
pilot whales' associations with, 62-63
and pollution, 214
and predators, 74
predators of, 117, 118
reproduction/mating of, 87, 113, 125-
26, 127, 128, 139, 140, 141, 142-45,
142, 146, 148, 149, 154, 155, 156, 157-
59, *178*, 184
size of, 42
and sleep, 45
social sex of, 113, 114, 175, 176-77
status of, 128
strandings of, 72, 104, 134-35
and taste/smell, 29
and touch, 30-31, 112-13, 134-35
and vision, 36, 37, 39-40, 42, 43
Bowhead whales
    as baleen whales, 15
    calves of, 175-76

and commercial whaling, 208
communication of, 75-77, 88, 90-91, 92
decline in number of, 202, 208
and defense, 109
diet of, 67
feeding methods of, 51
and foraging/hunting for food, 58, 67, 106, 107, 176
geographic location of, *76*
groupings/social lives of, 106, 107, 109
intelligence of, 181
male relationships among, 152
migration of, 75
reproduction/mating of, 148, 152
Brain, 14, 28, 34, 45, 196-98.
See also Intelligence; *type of whale or dolphin*
Breaching, 4-5, 42, 44, 61, 175
Breeding, 217-18.
See also Mating; Reproduction; *type of whale or dolphin*
Brownlee, Shannon, 67-68
Bryde's whales, 51, 53, 72-74, *73*, 139, 208
Bubbles, 43, 66, 67, 80, 91
Bull sharks, 117

C
"Callosities," 153, 165
Calves
anger/aggression of, 164-65
break from mother of, 177-79
breathing of, 168
death of, 161-62, *169*, 174, 178-79
diet of, 163-67
and foraging/hunting for food, 166
and infanticide, 155
play of, 174-77
protection of, 169-74
schools of, 170
traveling of, 167-69
See also Males: calf relationships with; Mother-calf relationships
Captive breeding programs, 217-18
Caretaker females, 3, 4, 110, 132, 168,
170, 173
Carousel method, 69
Catch quotas, 206
Cetacea
evolution of, 19-20, 21
reproductive system of, 160
variety among, 14
See also specific suborder or family
Charging, 113
Chemoreception, 29-30, 91
Chimpanzees, 119, 189
Clark, Christopher, 76, 89, 90
Clicking, 6, 7, 9, 10, 11, 85-88.
See also Echolocation; *type of whale or dolphin*
Clumping, 69
Color, 40-41, 44, 70
Commerson's dolphins, 33, 70
Communication
and anger/aggression, 91
and blowholes, 89-90
and body language, 43
and bubbles, 80, 91
and chemoreceptive senses, 91
and defense, 172
and foraging/hunting for food, 39, 81-82, 85, 87-88, 94
and gender differences, 84, 85
as genetic or learned, 97
and groupings/social lives, 79, 85-86, 89, 112, 114
and individuality, 83-84
and intelligence, 189-91
leaping as, 39
and the lek system, 94
and memory, 93-94
and migration, 75
and mimicking, 98-99, 189-91
and mother-calf relationships, 82, 83-85, 89, 97, 172
and natural language, 98-100
nonverbal, 91
and physiology, 79-81
and pulsed sounds, 78-79, 82, 85-88
and reproduction/mating, 87, 89, 94, 97, 112, 140-41, 144
and smell, 78
and stress, 82, 87, 91
and touch, 33-34, 78, 91

and vision, 78, 91
See also Clicking; Echolocation;
Whistles; type of whale or dolphin
Conservation, 205, 217-18
Cookie-cutter sharks, 117
Cooperation
and altruism, 106, 129-35
between dolphins and fishermen,
64-66
and foraging/hunting for food, 64-66,
111, 121
and predators, 135
among various species, 184
See also Caretaker females; type of whale
or dolphin
Copulation, 144-45
Corkeron, Peter, 62-63
Courtship, 114, 140-45.
See also Mating; type of whale or dolphin
Cousteau, Jacques, 77
Crassicauda, 116
Creativity, and intelligence, 184
Cronkite, Walter, 171
Cuvier's beaked whales, 16, 34

D
Dall's porpoises, 34, 40, 41, 209
Dawson, Steve, 86-87
Defense
and communication, 172
and female relationships, 118
and foraging/hunting for food, 170
and gender relations, 111
and groupings/social lives, 105-6, 109-
11, 115-18
and male-calf relationships, 110-11
and mother-calf relationships, 110,
168, 169-74
and vision, 39-40
See also Caretaker females; Predators;
type of whale or dolphin
Diatoms, 116
Diet. See type of whale or dolphin
DNA, 17, 109, 146, 147
Dolphins
age of, 41
altruism/cooperation of, 64-66, 129,

131, 132-34
anger/aggression of, 114
and artificial languages, 192-94
calves of, 166, 178-79
characteristics of, 14
communication of, 5-6, 33-34, 77-91,
95-100, 190-91
and defense, 39, 110, 170
diet of, 53-54, 54, 196
and drift net fishing, 210, 211-12, 212
echolocation of, 27, 33-34, 67-68, 210
evolution of, 181
examples of, 15
and false killer whales, 132-33, 184
feeding methods of, 53-54
female relationships of, 120, 170
and foraging/hunting for food, 29-30,
38-39, 49, 55-56, 58, 59, 60, 60, 61, 63,
67-70, 71-72, 111, 166, 195-96
gender relationships among, 183
and grooming, 33
groupings/social lives of, 17, 31-32,
106, 110-11, 120, 183, 197
individuality of, 56, 83-84
intelligence of, 181-83, 184-91, 192-94,
196-98
and killer whales, 132
locating other, 29
magnetic sense of, 34
male relationships of, 120
migrations of, 55-56
mother-calf relationships among, 31,
165-66, 169, 177
navigation of, 44-45
as odontocetes, 15
orientation of, 30
pelagic, 38, 108
physiology of, 24-27, 36, 54
predators of, 53, 117-18
reproduction/mating of, 30, 131, 140,
143-45, 148
respiratory system of, 22
size of, 12, 41
sleep of, 45
and small cetacean fisheries, 209
and social sex, 113, 114, 154
as sponge wearers, 195-96
on the surface, 38-39
swimming position among, 31-32

and taste/smell, 28-30
"tools" of, 195-98
and touch, 32, 33-34, 143-45
and vision, 36, 38-39, 44-45
See also type of dolphin
Drift net fishing, 210-12, î212ï
Dusky dolphins, 39, 69, 110, 111, 120, 148
Dwarf sperm whales, 15, 171

E
Echelon formation, 31
Echolocation
    as communication, 78, 79, 81-82, 85, 87-88
    and foraging/hunting for food, 24-27, 38, 60, 67-68, 85, 87-88
    and intelligence, 196
    limitations of, 38
    and physiology, 24-27, *25*
    purposes of, 27-28
    and the stun theory, 67-68
    and vision, *37*
El Niño, 56
Elephants, 120
Endangered species
    and animal rights, 205, 207
    baiji river dolphins as, 199-202, *199, 200*
    and commercial fishing, 203-7, 210-12
    and conservation, 205, 217-18
    and determining specie population, 202-3
    and drift net fishing, 210-12
    and food, 207
    and habitat destruction, 212-16
    optimism about, 216-17
    and pollution, 207, 212-16
    and small cetacean fisheries, 209
Evolution
    of Cetacea, 19-20, 21
    of dolphins, 181

F
Factory ships, 203-7
False killer whales

and altruism/cooperation, 132-33, 184
    diet of, 16, 53
    and dolphins, 132-33, 184
    groupings/social lives of, 103, 104-5, 119
    physiology of, 36-37
    reproduction/mating of, 156
    strandings of, 103-5
    and vision, 36-67
Faroe Islands, 207-9
Females
    caretaker, 3, 4, 110, 132, 168, 170, 173
    as core of societies, 118
    and foraging/hunting for food, 119
    relationships among, 118, 119, 170
    status of, 114-15, 123
    See also Mother-calf relationships; *type of whale or dolphin*
Fin whales
    commercial slaughter of, 204, 205
    communication of, 79
    diet of, 53, 55, 67
    feeding methods of, 51
    and foraging/hunting for food, 67
    as friends of mankind, 13-14
    groupings/social lives of, 107
    life span of, 161
    mother-calf relationships of, 165
    parasites of, 116
    and pollution, 215
    reproduction/mating of, *138*
    vision of, 43
Finless porpoises, 120, *162*, 163
Fins, 42
Flatflukes, 116
Flippers, 33, 41, 42
Flukes, 21, 33, 41, 42, 71, 74, 157
Folklore, about whales and dolphins, 13-14
Food
    and echolocation, 24-27
    and endangered species, 207
    and hearing, 23-28
    See also Foraging/hunting for food; *type of whale or dolphin*
Foraging/hunting for food
    and associations between species, 62
    and breaching, 61

and calves, 166
and the carousel method, 69
and clumping, 69
and color, 70
and communication, 9, 39, 81-82, 85,
87-88, 94
and cooperation, 64-66, 111, 121
and defense, 170
and echolocation, 24-27, 38, 60, 67-68,
85, 87-88
and females, 118, 119
and flukes, 71
and groupings/social lives, 58-59, 105-
6, 107, 109, 111, 119
and hunting techniques, 58-64, 66-72
and intelligence, 196
and leaping, 61
and lunge feeding, 71
and migrations, 55-58
and mother-calf relationships, 168,
176
and the ocean's topography, 59-60
and reproduction/mating, 57-58
and scouting, 61
and strandings, 104
and taste/smell, 29-30
and vision, 38-39, 60, 71
See also type of whale or dolphin
Ford, John K. B., 95-98
Franciscana, 161, 165

G
Gender
and aeriel feats, 5
and behavior, 42
and communication, 84, 85
and mother-calf relationships, 177-78
and physiology, *159*
and size, 42
See also Females; Gender relations;
Males; *type of whale or dolphin*
Gender relations, 111, 114-15, 118-19,
149-50.
See also Mating; Reproduction; *type of
whale or dolphin*

Genetics, 154. *See also* DNA
Gestation periods, 156
Gingerich, Philip, 20
Gray whales
age of, 41
as baleen whales, 15
barnacles on, 52, 115
characteristics of, 18
and color, 41
and commercial whaling, 216, 217
communication of, 79, 80, 88, 91
and defense, 40, 109
diet of, *50*, 52-53
as an endangered specie, 216-17
feeding methods of, 51-53
and foraging/hunting for food, 57
geographic location of, 18
groupings/social lives of, 107, 109
male relationships among, 114, 153
migration of, 15, 57, 107, 216, ï216ï
mother-calf relationships of, 165, 168
navigation of, 44
predators of, 74
reproduction/mating of, 57, 139, 141,
147, 148, 153, *156*, 157
size of, 15
spy-hopping of, 40
and vision, 40, 41, 44
Great white sharks, 117
Grooming, 33
Groupings
advantages/disadvantages of, 109-12,
170
and communication, 112
and defense, 109-11
definition of, 107
and foraging/hunting for food, 58-59,
61, 106, 107, 109, 111, 119
and gender relations, 118-19
and migration, 107
and mother-calf relationships, 110
purpose of, 17
and reproduction/mating, 107, 109,
112
size of, 106-9, 170
spacing among members in, 44

unisex, 110-11
and vision, 44
See also Social lives; *type of whale or dolphin*

H

Habitat destruction, 212-16, *213, 214*
Harbor porpoises, 45, 87, 120, 140, 161, 165, 211
Hearing, 20, 23-28.
  See also Clicking; Echolocation; *type of whale or dolphin*
Hector's dolphins, 14, 15, 81, 86-87, 211
Herman, Louis, 192-94î
Historia Animalium (Aristotle), 13
Humpback whales
  age of, 41, 42
  anger/aggression of, 33, 43, 114, 122
  as baleen whales, 15
  barnacles of, 115, 116
  blowholes of, 43
  breaching of, 42, 44
  bubbles of, 43, 66, 67, 141
  characteristics of, 18
  and color, 41, 44
  commercial slaughter of, 205
  communication of, 78, 79, 80, 89, 92-94, 97, 114, 121-23, 190
  cooperation of, 121
  and defense, 11, 170-71
  diet of, 53, 66
  as escorts, *47*, 122-23, 151-52, *151*, 170-71
  feeding methods of, 51
  female relationships of, 120-21, 123
  flukes of, 41
  and foraging/hunting for food, 66-67, 94, 111, 120-21, 168
  gender differences among, 92, 156
  gender relations among, 154
  geographic location of, 18
  groupings/social lives of, 44, 107-8, 111, 112, 120-23

  identification among, 41
  intelligence of, 190
  lobtailing of, 66-67
  magnetic sense of, 34
  male relationships among, 114, 120-23, 151-52, *151*, 152, 154, 155
  migration of, 92, 121
  mother-calf relationships of, 162, 168, 170-71
  navigation of, 45
  as polygynous, 155
  reproduction/mating of, 43, 92, 94, 112, 120, 121-23, 139, 140, 141, 151-52, *151*, 154, 155, 156
  S-posture of, 43, î47î
  sexual maturity of, 156
  status among, 123
  and touch, 33
  and vision, 41, 42, 43, 44, 45
Humpbacked dolphins, 211
Hunting techniques, 58-64, 66-72

I

Imitation/mimicking, 98-99, 182-83, 188-91
Individuality, 40-42, 83-84. *See also* Signature whistles
Indus river dolphins. *See* Boto river dolphins
Infanticide, 155
Intelligence
  and altruism/cooperation, 184
  and anger/aggression, 197-98
  and artificial languages, 192-94
  and brain, 181, 196-98
  and communication, 189-91
  and creativity, 184
  definition of, 182
  and echolocation, 196
  and foraging for food, 196
  and imitation/mimicking, 182-83, 188-91
  and learning, 182-83, 184-91
  and memory, 183

and sign language, 186
and social lives, 197
and training to do something new,
187-88
and vision, 185-87
See also type of whale or dolphin
International Whaling Commission
(IWC), 9, 205-7, 208, 209, 217

J
Janik, Vincent, 85
Jaw-claps, 87
Johnson, Christine, 33

K
Killer whales
age of, 41
anger/aggression of, 113, 114
calves of, 113, 132
and color, 41, 44, 70
communication of, 81, 82, 91, 95-98,
190
conservation of, 206
cooperation among, 70, 132
defense of, 171
defenses against, 109
diet of, 16, 53, 55, 58, 59, 70-71, 72-74,
73, 149
as dolphins, 15
and dolphins, 132
and foraging/hunting for food, 39,
58, 59, 61, 69, 70-74, *73*
groupings/social lives of, 17, 44, 95-
96, 105, 112, 118, 119
individuality of, 41, 149
intelligence of, 190
life span of, 161
male relationships among, 114, 118,
119
and male-calf relationships, 132
mother-calf relationships among, 17,
97, 171, 177

as odontocetes, 15
as predators, 9-11, 40, 168, 171
pygmy, 16, 39, 53
reproduction/mating of, 97, 112, 119,
139, 148, 149, 156, 157
size of, 41
and strandings, 104
and touch, 32
transient, 55, 59, 97-98, 149
and vision, 39, 41, 44
See also False killer whales
Kinship, and altruism, 130, 132

L
LaBudde, Samuel, 211
Language
artificial, 192-94
body, 43
natural, 98-100
sign, 186
See also Communication
Leaping, 39, 42, 43, 44, 61, 111, 144
Learning, and intelligence, 182-83,
184-91
Lek system, 94
Lobtailing, 5, 66-67, 152
Lopez, Juan Carlos, 132
Lung nematodes, 116
Lunge feeding, 71

M
Magnetite, 34
Males
calves' relationships with, 110-11, 132,
155
and groupings, 118-19
and mother-calf relationships, 118-19
relationships among, 106, 150-52
sexual activities among, 114
and sperm competition, 152-54
See also type of whale or dolphin
Mammals, characteristics of, 14

Mann, Janet, 84
Marine Mammal Protection Act, 211
Mating
  and anger/aggression, 143, 149
  and communication, 7, 87, 112
  female interest in, 145
  and gender relations, 149-50
  and groupings/social lives, 106, 107, 109, 112
  and S-position, 143
  systems of, 145-50
  and vision, 43
  See also Courting; Reproduction; *type of whale or dolphin*
Mechanoreception, 31-34
Melon-headed whales, 103
Memory, 93-94, 183
Mesonychids, 19
Migration
  of birds, 112
  and communication, 75
  and foraging/hunting for food, 55-58
  and groupings, 107
  and reproduction, 139
  See also type of whale or dolphin
Mimicking, 98-99, 182-83, 188-91
Minke whales
  as baleen whales, 15
  and color, 41
  and commercial whaling, 204, 207, 208
  communication of, 79
  conservation of, 206
  feeding methods of, 51
  and foraging/hunting for food, 71
  identification among, 41
  life span of, 161
  predators of, 74
  size of, 15
  and vision, 41
Mohl, Bertl, 80
Monogamy, 145, 146-47
Moratorium on commercial fishing/whaling, 206-7, 208, 209
Moray eels, 184
Mother-calf relationships

  and caretaker females, 3, 4, 110, 132, 168, 170, 173
  closeness of the, 162
  and communication, 82, 83-85, 89, 97, 172
  and death of calves, 161-62, *169*, 174, 178-79
  and defense, 110, 118, 168, 169-74
  and fission-fusion societies, 120
  and foraging/hunting for food, 168, 176
  and gender of calf, 177-78
  and groupings/social lives, 105, 110
  and males, 118-19
  and nursing calves, 163-67
  as primary in societies, 118
  and traveling, 162-63, 167-69
  See also type of whale or dolphin
Mysticetes. *See* Baleen whales

N
Narwhals
  age of, 41
  anger/aggression of, 33
  beluga whales as relatives of, *76*
  and color, 41
  feeding methods of, 54
  gender differentiation among, 42
  groupings/social lives of, 110-11
  male relationships among, 150-51
  as odontocetes, 15
  physiology of, 54
  reproduction/mating of, 148, *149*, 150-51
  and small cetacean fisheries, 209
  and touch, 33
  tusks of, 42, 150-51
  and vision, 41
Natural selection, 150, 196
Navigation, 44-45
Nets, death by, 210-12, î212î
Newcomer, Michael, 72-74
Nicklin, Flip, 133
Norris, Ken, 23-25, 26
Northern right whales, 15

O

Odontocetes
  baleen whales compared with, 14
  brain of, 14, 28
  communication of, 78, 81-88
  diet of, 16, 53
  and echolocation, 6, 38
  examples of, 15-16
  feeding methods of, 53-55
  and foraging/hunting for food, 67-70
  groupings/social lives of, 17, 105,
    108-9
  mother-calf relationships among, 177
  physiology of, 53-55
  reproduction/mating of, 140, 156
  size of, 14
  and smell, 28
  strandings of, 103
  as a suborder of Cetacea, 14
  See also type of whale or dolphin
Orientation, 30, 44-45

P

Parasites, 115-18
Parenting. *See* Males: calf relationships
  with; Mother-calf relationships
Pelagic dolphins, 38, 108
Pennella, 116
Perception. *See* Hearing; Smell; Taste;
  Touch; Vision
Perez-Cortez, Hector, 72-74
Physiology
  and communication, 79-81
  and echolocation, 24-27, *25*
  and reproduction, 137, 153-55, *159,*
    160
  and smell, 28-30
  and taste, 28-30
  and vision, 35-45
  See also type of whale or dolphin
Pilot whales
  and altruism/cooperation, 131, 132,
    134
  and the bends, 46

bottlenose dolphins' associations with,
  62-63
and commercial whaling, 207-9
communication of, 82
conservation of, 206
diet of, 54
feeding methods of, 54
and foraging/hunting for food, 61,
  62-63
groupings/social lives of, 17, 105, 118,
  119
intelligence of, 181
male relationships of, 118, 119
mother-calf relationships of, 165
physiology of, 54
reproduction/mating of, 119, 156
strandings of, 103, 119
and touch, 32
Pink river dolphins. *See* Boto river
  dolphins
Platanista dolphins. *See* Susu river
  dolphin
Play, 174-77
Pneumonia, 116
Pollution, 207, 212-16
Polyandry, 145, 147
Polygyny, 145, 147-48
Popov, Vladimir, 26
Porpoises, 15, *16*, 53, 55, 81, 209.
  See also type of porpoise
Porter, James, 132-33, 134
Predators, 10, 11, 115-18, 135.
  See also Defense; Killer whales; Sharks
Promiscuity, 145, 148, 149
Pryor, Karen, 187
Purse-seine fishing, 211, *212*
Pygmy blue whales, 51
Pygmy killer whales, 16, 39, 53
Pygmy right whales, 15, 51, 152
Pygmy sperm whales, 15, 103

R

Ramming, 114, 152
Rearing of offspring. *See* Calves; Males:

calves' relationships with: Mother-calf relationships
Reciprocal altruism, 130, 132-35
Remoras, 117
Reproduction
  and altruism, 131
  and captive breeding programs, 217-18
  and communication, 89, 94, 97, 112
  and copulation, 144-45
  and courtship patterns, 140-45
  cycles for, 138, *138*
  and determining specie population, 203
  and female age, 139, 156
  female perspective of, 154-55
  and flukes, 157
  and foraging/hunting for food, 57-58
  and genetics, 154
  and gestation periods, 156
  and groupings/social lives, 109, 112
  and indicators of readiness, 140-41
  and mating systems, 145-50
  and migration, 139
  and physiology, 137, 153-55, î159ï, 160
  and pregnancy/birth, 156-59, î156ï
  and sexual politics, 150-55
  and sperm competition, 152-54
  and survival, 13
  and taste/smell, 30
  See also Mating; *type of whale or dolphin*
Respiratory system, 21, *22*, 46-47, 168
Richards, Andrew, 39-40
Richards, Douglas, 190
Right whales
  anger/aggression of, 164-65
  as baleen whales, 15
  barnacles of, 115
  "callosities" of, 153, 165
  calves of, 175, 177
  characteristics of, 15, 19
  commercial slaughter of, 205
  and defense, 109
  diet of, 67
  feeding methods of, 51
  and foraging/hunting for food, 67,

168
  geographic location of, 19
  groupings/social lives of, 107, 109
  male relationships among, 152, 153
  mother-calf relationships among, 164-65, 167-68, 176, 177
  northern, 15
  pygmy, 15, 51, 152
  reproduction/mating of, 141, 152, 153
  See also Southern right whales
Risso's dolphins, 41
River dolphins
  altruism of, *133*
  communication of, 81
  decline in number of, 199-202, *199, 200*, 212-13, *213, 214*
  and defense, 110
  examples of, 15
  groupings/social lives of, 110
  habitat destruction of, 212-13, *213, 214*
  intelligence of, 181-82
  and mating systems, 146
  as odontocetes, 15
  See also Baiji river dolphins; Boto river dolphins; Susu river dolphins
Rorquals, 15, 51, 152
Roughtoothed dolphins, 182-83, 187

S
S-shaped posture, 43, *47*, 143
Samuels, Amy, 114-15
Sayigh, Laela, 84
Scouting for food, 61
Sei whales, 51, 53, 205
Sensory system, 21, 23. *See also* Hearing; Smell; Taste; Touch; Vision
Sexual dimorphism, 148
Sexual politics, 150-55
Sexual relations, 32-33, 34.
  See also Mating; Reproduction; Social sex
Sharks

as food, 53, 62, 63-64
as predators, 9-11, 117-18
as scavengers, 10
See also type of shark
Sign language, 186, 192
Signature whistles, 83-85, 99, 172, 191
Silber, Greg, 72-74
Size
  of brain, 14, 181, 196
  and gender differentiation, 42
  of groupings, 106-9, 170
  See also type of whale or dolphin
Slapping, 67. *See also* Tail slapping
Sleep, 45
Smell, 20, 23, 28-30, 78
Smolker, Rachel, 84
Social lives
  advantages/disadvantages of, 106
  and altruism/cooperation, 106, 129-35
  and communication, 85-86, 89, 114
  and defense, 105-6, 115-18
  and fission-fusion societies, 120
  and foraging/hunting for food, 105-6
  and gender relations, 114-15
  and group size, 106-9
  and intelligence, 197
  and mother-calf relationships, 105
  and reproduction/mating, 106
  and status, 114-15
  and strandings, 103-5
  and touch, 32-33, 34, 112-13
  See also Groupings
Social sex, 113, î113î, 114, 138, 154, 175, 176-77
Socially enforced altruism, 130-32
Sound. *See* Communication
Southern right whales
  as baleen whales, 15
  blowholes of, 89-90
  and color, 41
  communication of, 89, 91
  identification among, 41
  and mother-calf relationships, 89, 164, 165
  reproduction/mating of, 89, 139, 148
  and vision, 41

Sperm whales
  and anger/aggression, 55
  baleen whales relationship to, 17
  barnacles of, 115
  and the bends, 46
  and commercial whaling, 204, 205, 206, 208
  communication of, 5-6, 9, 10, 11, 78, 80, 81, 82, 85-86
  cooperation among, 3, 4, 129, 132
  defense mechanisms of, 10-11, 110, 170, 171
  diet of, 3-4, 6-7, 8-9, 54
  DNA of, 109
  dwarf, 15, 171
  as an endangered species, 2, 204, 205, 206, 208
  feeding methods of, 54-55
  female relationships among, 3, 4, 110, 119, 168
  and foraging/hunting for food, 8-9, 38
  gender differentiation among, 2-3, 42, 54-55
  gender relations among, 3
  groupings/social lives of, 3, 110, 119
  hearing of, 5
  life span of, 161
  male relationships among, 8, 119
  mobility of, 4-5
  mother-calf relationships among, 3, 6-7, 110, 165-66, 168, 170, 171, 177
  as odontocetes, 15
  parasites of, 116
  physiology of, 1-3, 54
  predators of, 9-11
  pygmy, 15, 103
  reproduction/mating of, 1, 3, 7-8, 119, 140, 148, 156, 157
  sexual maturity of, 2-3
  size of, 1-2, 8, 42
  strandings of, 103
  teeth of, 7
  utility of, 2
  and vision, 38
Spinner dolphins, 33, 42, 61, 62-63, 68, 82, 117, 148

Spotted dolphins, 41, 61, 62-63, 83, 110, 174
Spy-hopping, 39, 40, 44, 69
Squid, 3-4, 171
Status, 41, 114-15, 123
Strandings/beachings, 34, 71-72, 103-5, 119, 134-35
Strap-toothed beaked whales, 16, 42
Stress, 30, 82, 87, 91, 134-35
Striped dolphins, 29, 131, 209
Stun theory, 67-68
Subsistence whaling, 207-9
Supin, Alexander, 26
Sustainable utilization, 205
Susu river dolphins, 15, 35, *35*, *37*, 53, *54*, 60, 213

T
Tail slapping, 33, 91, 113, 114
Tapeworms, 116
Tasman beaked whales, 16
Taste, 23, 28-30
Teeth, 33, 42.
    See also Odontocetes; Toothed whales; *type of toothed whale*
Tiger sharks, 117
Toothed whales, 6, 27, 32, 79, 177.
    See also Odontocetes; *type of whale*
Toothless whales, 11.
    See also Baleen whales; *type of whale*
Touch, 23, 30-34, 78, 91, 112-14, 134-35, 143-45, 176-77
Tuna fishing, 211, *212*
Tyack, Peter, 123, 191

U
Unisex groupings, 110-11
U.S. Marine Mammal Commission, 210

V
Vaquita, *16*, 210
Vibrissae, 32-33
Vision, 20, 21, 23, 35-45, *37*, 43, 60, 71, 78, 91, 185-87

W
Wang Ding, 81
Watkins, Bill, 6
Wave riding, 30-31
Weinrich, Mason, 121
Wells, Randy, 56, 124, 177
Whale lice, 116
Whales
    "bad," 13-14
    characteristics of, 14
    coexistence among species of, 9
    commercial slaughter of, 203-7, *206*, 208
    communication of, 78-91
    comparative sizes of, *12*
    decline in number of, 202-7
    DNA of, 17
    feet of, 20
    life span of, 161-62
    magnetic sense of, 34-35
    and subsistence whaling, 207-9
    See also type of whale
Whistles, 78, 79, 80, 81-85, 172
Whistling. *See also* Signature whistles
White whales. *See* Beluga whales
White-tipped sharks, 10
Whitesided dolphins, 185
Williams, Terrie, 30-31
Woods Hole Oceanographic Institute, 6
Würsig, Bernd, 39, 69, 111

ABOUT THE MUSEUM

One of the world's great treasures, the 125-year-old American Museum of Natural History has been referred to as a library of life on the planet. It is the world's largest privately operated science museum and attracts some 3 million visitors annually drawn from all over the world.

Among its incomparable collections are more than 36 million artifacts and specimens, which include more dinosaurs, birds, spiders, mammals, fossils, and whale skeletons than any other museum. Equally important, though less well known to the general public, the Museum's work in scientific research involves more than 200 scientists and researchers. The American Museum of Natural History plays a significant role as a gatherer, evaluator, and disseminator of information on ecological systems, to scientists and the lay public alike.

ABOUT THE AUTHORS

Richard C. Connor earned his Ph.D. at the University of Michigan. He has been a postdoctoral fellow at Harvard University and the Woods Hole Oceanographic Institute. His work at Shark Bay extends back to 1982. At present, he is associated with the Museum of Zoology at the University of Michigan.

Dawn Micklethwaite Peterson, a former award-winning newspaper reporter, is a freelance writer and editor. In addition to this book, she worked on the first book in the series, *The Lives of Birds,* and has been involved in the writing and editing of several healthcare books. She lives in Maplewood, New Jersey, with her husband and their three daughters.